MATT KRAMER'S

Making Sense
OF
Italian Wine

DISCOVERING ITALY'S GREATEST WINES AND BEST VALUES

RUNNING PRESS
PHILADELPHIA · LONDON

9 8 7 6 5 4 3 2 1
Digit on the right indicates the number of this printing

Library of Congress Control Number: 2006928035

ISBN-13: 978-0-7624-2230-2
ISBN-10: 0-7624-2230-0

Cover design by Maria Taffera Lewis
Interior Design by Rosemary Tottoroto
Edited by Jennifer Kasius
Cover photographs provided by Cephas Picture Library:
(left and right) ©Dario Fusaro and (center) ©Mick Rock
Typography: Bembo

This book may be ordered by mail from the publisher.
Please include $2.50 for postage and handling.
But try your bookstore first!

Running Press Book Publishers
125 South Twenty-Second Street
Philadelphia, Pennsylvania 19103-4399

Visit us on the web!
www.runningpress.com

For Karen, my Italy — and more.

Contents

Preface

I am much happier thinking of Italy as a place that forces a
sense of engagement—that does not let us stand aloof, however
admiringly, but whose spirit is so intoxicating that we feel compelled
to join in, to connect, to feel we have to be a part of it.
— PAUL GOLDBERGER, ARCHITECTURE CRITIC (1997)

Anyone who sets out to write a book about Italian wines had better have clear in his mind both the purpose of the book and its intended reader. This is because Italian wine, like quantum physics, is such a vast subject that even the most assured, experienced tasters are left scratching their heads over some new madness. No nation so relentlessly, even profligately, issues so many wines. No winegrowers anywhere are so willing—insistent, even—on throwing over the old order as Italians. Yet no sooner do they do so than a revisionist reaction sets in. It's as close to a permanent wine revolution as can be imagined.

So allow me to explain about *Making Sense of Italian Wine* and how it came to be. Like millions of wine lovers worldwide, I am enthralled by Italian wines—by their uniqueness, variety, originality, and profusion. I've written about them for decades in my newspaper and magazine wine columns. I've lived in Italy, wrote a cookbook on Piedmontese cuisine, and traveled the country extensively for many years.

That said, I feel free to admit that I don't know anywhere near as much as those wine writers who have devoted themselves exclusively to Italian wines for decades, such as the great American authority on Italian wines Burton Anderson or the great Italian wine authority Luigi Veronelli. They are like census takers on a planet of shapeshifters, so fluid and transformative is Italian wine. I doff my *cappello* to them and others like them.

7

For my part, over the past thirty years I've written books on wine in general, on Burgundy, California wine, Piedmontese cuisine, and more than two thousand wine columns in magazines and newspapers. With those columns, especially, I'm in the "recommendation trenches" every week. So I'm constantly foraging for the best picks for my readers. A disproportionate number of those are Italian wines. (My editors have occasionally complained about this. I ignore them. Italian wines are too numerous and such good values that I'm certain my readers feel the same way I do.)

I mention this by way of pointing out that I love Italian wines. That I taste them constantly. That I live with them—which is to say, *drink* them—daily. And that I've had the privilege, thanks to extensive travel and occasionally living in Italy, to attempt to understand them in their contexts, from Sicily to Südtirol. I believe that I know a little something about this rich subject.

This book is not intended for wine lovers who are already deeply knowledgeable about Italian wines. You are increasingly numerous and I am impressed with, and respectful of, what you've achieved. I know firsthand what it takes to acquire such knowledge, especially if you have a real day job (unlike a fulltime wine scribe such as myself). *Complimenti*, as the Italians like to say.

Instead, this book is for relative newcomers to Italian wines. It's for everyone who has enjoyed a bottle recommended to them in an Italian restaurant and would like a little guidance about how to go about having another such delicious experience.

What I've had in mind while writing this book is the idea of accompanying you as we gaze at the selections on the shelf in a good wine shop. What is this wine? What's the grape variety? How do you pronounce it? Who are the good producers? Should I buy it?

Consequently, the perspective of *Making Sense of Italian Wine* is not that of Italy's official wine maps, legal regulations, and wine district boundaries. Instead, it's from the perspective of how an American actually sees Italian wines, which is to say from the sight lines of the shelves of a wine shop.

So you won't see any discussion of Italy's near-Talmudic wine legislation. Who, after all, walks into a wine store, picks up a bottle, and says, "Is this wine a DOCG?" (*Denominazione di origine controllata garantita.*) No one.

The buzzing complications of Italy's DOCs and DOCGs, with all their legalistic minutiae, are not for the Italian wine beginner or even the average Italian wine lover. In fact, you won't see the acronyms DOC or DOCG or IGT (*indicazione geografica tipica*) much used in this book. There's no need.

What you will find is one man's opinion about some of the more worthwhile Italian wines that you might find in a good wine store. The wines highlighted are far from an exhaustive compilation. To do that would result in an off-putting tome (to the casual wine book reader, anyway) that could sprain your wrist holding it. I wanted something more manageable and less intimidating.

So if you're deeply knowing about Italian wines and you flip through this book only to discover that I write about, say, the red wines of the Rosso Cònero district and not about the admirable reds of next-door Rosso Piceno or Lacrima di Morro d'Alba, forgive me. If you didn't want *your* readers' eyes to glaze over from information overload from Italy's almost fractal wine localism and complication, which would *you* choose?

So I made my (selective) choices, like wishing on one star while gazing at an entire, dazzling galaxy. You may wonder why *that* star, but the desire for manageable selectivity informs the choice. After all, for we Italian wine enthusiasts, there are always yet more wonderful, more delightfully new or esoteric wines to recommend. To paraphrase the late Senator Everett Dirksen: A billion Italian bottles here, a billion wines there, and pretty soon you're talking about a really huge book. I didn't want that.

What I hope you'll find is useful information, a reasonably informed set of recommendations and, above all, a sense that landing on a great, even thrilling, Italian wine and understanding it the first time out is actually easy—and certainly within one's literal grasp.

That's the intention and purpose of this book. If I've achieved it, I will be content that I've added a small gloss to the shining wonderment of Italian wine today.

Introduction

Italian wines are the world's most wonderful, maddening, frustrating bottles you can buy. Italy abounds in grapes, not just in vast numbers of vineyards but also as the world's greatest repository of grape varieties. No sooner do you hear about, say, Trebbiano, than you quickly learn of a dozen localized strains or clones of that grape. Growers of each tell you that theirs is the true Trebbiano. The others, they assert, are imposters or, at minimum, lesser versions.

And so it goes. Eventually, if you follow Italian wines long and closely enough you become aware of what might be called the Great Italian Wine Paradox: The more you know about Italian wines, the less you know.

Like a Dobos torte, Italy is too rich to ever be simple. You've got to take it on, layer by delicious layer, accepting the fact that the only way out is, paradoxically, to dive in. That is what *Making Sense of Italian Wine* is all about. It is one man's attempt not so much to make Italian wine simple as to make it comprehendible.

Most books about Italian wines proceed, understandably, from a geographical perspective. You get a chapter on Piedmont, another on Tuscany, a third on Campania, and so on all the way from the Alps in the north to Sicily in the south.

The problem with this approach is twofold: The writer feels obligated to at least mention every obscure wine or district in a region, even if the reader isn't likely to ever see the wine, let alone actually want it.

The second problem is that it presumes a map in the reader's mind. I call this the "Gravellona Toce syndrome." Allow me to explain. Italian road signs never say north, south, east, or west. Instead, they substitute the names of, typically, the towns or cities at the most extreme ends of the highway.

Many years ago, my wife and I were moving at a blistering pace on one of the high-speed *autostrade* in the Piedmont region of northwest Italy. At the time we didn't know much about the area, so all of the names were new to us. Anyway, we were coming up fast upon the intersection with the autostrada we were seeking (Autostrada 26). The sign read: "Genova/Gravellona Toce." Genova we knew; it's the famous port city on the Mediterranean. But Gravellona Toce?

I was driving at a hundred miles an hour, the fork in the road was fast approaching, and I was declaring in an ever more exasperated voice to my wife, who was frantically flipping through the Italian road atlas, "Where the hell is Gravellona Toce? Is it north or south? East or west?"

Equally exasperated, she replied, "I have no idea. I can't find it anywhere!" We decided to go, literally, with what we knew. We took the turn for Genova, which we knew was south.

Eventually we did locate Gravellona Toce. It's a small town in the north of Piedmont. Why did it get such big-time billing? Because that's where Autostrada 26 abruptly ends.

All of which is a long-winded way of explaining why *Making Sense of Italian Wine*, unlike nearly every other book about Italian wine that I've seen, does *not* view Italian wines geographically.

Does geography matter? Of course it does. But do you have a map of Italy in your head? Do you go into a wine shop saying, "I'd like a nice wine from Lazio, please?" (Lazio is the region surrounding Rome. It's also known as Latium.)

In the same way that almost none of us knows where Gravellona Toce is, so too are we collectively in the dark about Italy's many provinces, regions, and innumerable wine districts. These places matter, to be sure, but not to the average American buyer of Italian wines.

It is this American buyer of Italian wine—someone enthusiastic about Italy and its wines, but not necessarily a diehard wine buff or the winner of a quiz show about Italian geography—for whom *Making Sense of Italian Wine* is intended.

My desire is straightforward and relatively simple: I want you to know about some of Italy's greatest wines. I want you to understand, without feeling like you're pursuing an advanced degree, what makes these wines so wonderful. And not least, I want you to land on what I, anyway, believe are some of the best producers of the wine under consideration.

Consequently, the perspective of this book is that of the wine shop. We look at the shelves and we see a blur of names, some of them (we come to learn) are place names such as Barolo, Barbaresco, and Chianti, while others refer to grape varieties such as Barbera or Falanghina.

So instead of methodically, dutifully tracking Italian wines from their places of origin, *Making Sense of Italian Wine* highlights some of Italy's wine hits, the ones you're likely to spy in a wine shop that you should know about and buy.

Inevitably, much will be missing. Italy has thousands of wine districts and tens of thousands of producers. Many are commendable or at least tasty. But they're also mostly of local interest. If you're in the area, you drink them, with pleasure.

The wines I've chosen represent a good slice of Italy's best. They can turn your head and change your mind. They are Italian messages in a bottle—in a language we can all understand—that tell us why Italy today is the most exciting, dynamic, and flat-out wonderful place on the planet for fine wine.

ABOUT ALL THOSE CONTROLLED APPELLATIONS

As mentioned previously, Italy has an elaborate system of controlled appellations. Although they certainly mean something to the producers—and even more so to Italy's sizable wine bureaucracy—the multiplicity of these designations is dizzying and ultimately of little real guidance to everyday wine buyers.

Nevertheless, it's revealing to get a sense of the scale of it all, which is the sole intent of displaying the following statistics, which came from *Istituto Economia Nazionale di Agraria 2004*. With that in mind, consider the following:

In descending order of prestige, Italian wines are classified as:

DOCG (*denominazione di origine controllata garantita*) — controlled and guaranteed designation of origin

DOC (*denominazione di origine controllata*) — controlled designation of origin

IGT (*indicazione geografica tipica*) — indication of geographical origin. There are approximately 330 Italian wines classified in this pyramid. At the bottom of the quality pyramid is the catchall category called *vino da tavola* (table wine) or VdT.

Italian government estimates for 2003 show that 13.8 million hectoliters (365 million gallons) of DOC and DOCG wines were produced in Italy, which is about 33 percent of the Italy's total wine production.

When IGT wines are included, the classification system embraces 60 percent of Italy's total wine production.

Northern Italy produces the most DOC and DOCG wines: 7.9 million hectoliters (209 million gallons), or 57 percent of Italy's entire DOC-designated production.

DOCG, DOC, AND IGT WINES BY REGION
(from north to south)

Piedmont—8 DOCGs and 45 DOCs
Valle d'Aosta—1 DOC
Lombardy—3 DOCGs, 15 DOCs, and 13 IGTs
Trentino-Alto Adige—7 DOCs and 4 IGTs
Veneto—3 DOCGs, 20 DOCs, and 10 IGTs
Friuli-Venezia Giulia—1 DOCG, 9 DOCs, and 3 IGTs
Liguria—7 DOCs and 1 IGT
Emilia-Romagna —1 DOCG, 20 DOCs, and 10 IGTs
Tuscany—6 DOCGs, 34 DOCs, and 5 IGTs
Umbria—2 DOCGs, 11 DOCs, and 6 IGTs
Marche—12 DOCs and 1 IGT
Lazio—26 DOCs and 5 IGTs
Abruzzo—1 DOCG, 3 DOCs, and 9 IGTs
Molise—3 DOCs and 2 IGTs

Campania—3 DOCGs, 17 DOCs, and 8 IGTs

Apulia—25 DOCs and 6 IGTs

Basilicata—2 DOCs and 2 IGTs

Calabria—12 DOCs and 13 IGTs

Sicily—20 DOCs and 7 IGTs

Sardinia—1 DOCG, 19 DOCs, and 15 IGTs

Total for all of Italy: 28 DOCGs, 302 DOCs, and 115 IGTs (*as of June 2004*)

Worth noting: These totals change annually as some areas get upgraded to DOCG while existing DOCs are annulled and replaced by larger, more flexible new IGTs

Also: The national totals for DOC and IGT wines are lower than the sum of the regional totals because some of the wines are interregional.

FREQUENTLY SEEN WINE LABEL WORDS

ABBAZIA (ah-bah-*zee*-ah): abbey

AZIENDA AGRICOLA (ah-zee-*yen*-dah ah-*gree*-koh-lah): a wine estate; suggests a property that has both a winery and an attached vineyard

BRIC/BRICCO (breek/breek-oh): Piedmontese dialect term for the top or crest of a hill

CANTINA/CANTINE (cahn-tee-nah/cahn-tee-neh): winery/wineries

CA'/CASA/CASCINA (kah/kah-zah/kah-*shee*-nah): all words for "house" or "farm house"

CAMPO (kahm-poh): field or plain, e.g. Campo Rotaliano

CASTEL/CASTELLO/CASTIGLIONE (kah-*stel*/kas-*el*-low/kah-*steeg*-l'yoh-neh): all references to castle

COLLE/COLLI/COLLINE (*koh*-leh/*koh*-lee/koh-*lee*-neh): hill/hills/range of hills

CONSORZIO (kohn-*sorts*-yo): consortium; commonly used term for winegrowers' trade groups, e.g. the Asti Spumante Consorzio

CONTE/CONTI/CONTESSA (*kohn*-teh/*kohn*-tee/kohn-*teh*-sah): aristocratic title: count, counts, countess

COSTA (koh-stah): coast or coastline

FATTORIA (fah-tore-*ree*-ah): farm or farmhouse

FORNO/FORNI/FORNACE/FORNACI (*fore*-noh/*fore*-nee/fore-*nah*-cheh/fore-*nah*-chee): oven/ovens/furnace/furnaces; used as a town or village name, also for a vineyard, as references to a warm location

IL/I (eel/ee): masculine article for "the," singular and plural

LA/LE (lah/leh): feminine article for "the," singular and plural

MASSERIA (mah-seh-*ree*-ah): farm

MARCHESE/MARCHESA/MARCHESI (mahr-*keh*-she/mahr-*keh*-sah/mahr-*keh*-zee): aristocratic title: marquess (male)/marquise (female)/marquesses (plural, referring to the hereditary line)

MONTE (mohn-the): mountain or hill

PALAZZO/PALAZZOLO (pah-*lahtz*-zoh/pah-lahz-*zoh*-low): palace or mansion/smaller palace

PIAN/PIANO (pee-*yahn*/pee-*yahn*-oh): a plain, flat spot or meadow, especially on a hillside

PIETRA (pee-*eh*-trah): stone or rock

PIEVE (pee-*eh*-veh): parish church; most commonly seen in Tuscany

PODERE/PODERI (poe-*deh*-reh/poe-*deh*-ree): farm/farms

POGGIO (poh-joe): a small hill or hillock

PONTE (pohn-teh): bridge

PRATO (prah-toe): a meadow or field; variations include *prà* or the prefix "prad"

PRINCIPE/PRINCIPESSA (preen-*chee*-peh/preen-chee-*peh*-sah): royal titles: prince/princess

PRODUTTORI (proh-doo-*tore*-ree): producers, e.g., Produttori del Barbaresco

ROCCA/ROCCHE (roe-kah/roe-keh): rock/rocks

RONCO/RONCHI (rawn-koh/rawn-kee): a word commonly seen in Friuli in northeastern Italy; originally *ronco* meant hilltop, but now refers to a terraced vineyard; *ronchi* is the plural

ROSSO/ROSSA (roh-so/roh-sah): red (masculine/feminine)

SAN/SANT'/SANTA/SANTO (sa'hn/sa'hnt/sa'hn-ta/sa'hn-toe): saint

SERRA (seh'r-rah): literally "greenhouse"; typically used in a vineyard name, e.g. Barolo "La Serra," suggesting an exceptionally good exposure, such as a suntrap

Società cooperativa/cooperativa sociale (soh-*chee*-eh-*tah* koh-awp-eh-rah-*tee*-vah/koh-awp-eh-rah-*tee*-vah soh-*cha'hl*-eh): synonymous terms for winegrowers' cooperatives

Sorì (soo-*ree*): Piedmontese dialect term for an (ideal) south-facing slope

Tenuta/tenute (ten-*oo*-tah/ten-*oo*-the): an estate or farm

Terme (tair-meh): a thermal spring, e.g., Acqui Terme in northwest Italy

Terra/terre (teh'r-rah/teh'r-reh): soil or land; *terre* is plural, e.g., terre di pietra (rocky soils)

Torre/torri (tore-reh/tore-ree): tower/towers

Val/valle (vahl/vahl-leh): valley/valleys

Vecchio/vecchie (veh-k'yo/veh-k'yee-eh): old (singular/plural), e.g. vigne vecchie (old vines)

Vigna/vigne (veen-yah/veen-yeh): vine/vines

Villa (veel-lah): a good-size house or residence; not as grand as a palazzo

Vinicola (veen-*ee*-koh-lah): refers to winemaking facility or winery, e.g., azienda vinicola

Viticoltori (vee-tee-kohl-*tore*-ree): grape growers; often seen as part of a winegrowers' cooperative name, e.g., Viticoltori dell'Acquese

Thinking Italy

BELLA FIGURA: THE ITALIAN LOVE OF THE BEAUTIFUL GESTURE

We live the strangeness of being momentary,
And still we are exalted by being temporary.
The grand Italy of meanwhile. It is the fact of being brief,
Being small and slight that is the source of our beauty.
—JACK GILBERT, *Refusing Heaven* (2005)

B*ella figura*, the beautiful form, gesture, style, is the phrase that sweeps into a neat pile all those small, elegant and—to Italian eyes—oh-so-meaningful details that make, as the poet Jack Gilbert puts it, "the grand Italy of meanwhile."

For Italians, *bella figura* is a motivational force, something that impels them—no matter how poor or rich, uneducated or overeducated—to aspire to transcend the mundane and quotidian. And they'll spend a lot of money doing it, too, from such unnoticed-except-by-Italians details such as replacing your jacket or shirt buttons with something more distinctive to presenting extravagant gifts to friends or business colleagues.

Just why *bella figura* is so significant, even fundamental, to Italian life is actually not that difficult to fathom. Although largely unseen by outsiders, there's a deep vein of resignation and cynicism in daily Italian life. It's nothing new. It's been going on for centuries, even millennia. Ordinary, everyday Italians have suffered occupiers from Spain, England, France, Austro-Hungary, and, most recently in the mid-twentieth century, Germany. And they've been oppressed by their own kind as well: the church; innumerable aristocrats and nobles; organized crime cadres such as the Mafia (Sicily), the Camorra (Naples), and the 'Ndragheta

(Calabria); and not least, ordinary owners of inordinately vast landhold-ings—plantations, really—everywhere from north to south.

You've got to extract pleasure and, above all, dignity, somehow. The small gesture, something personal, individual, distinctive, even idiosyn-cratic, is the ticket. Such a *bella figura*, however small or modest, demonstrates to those in your world not only that you exist, but also that you exist as a thinking being, as someone who may be oppressed but is still vital, aware, and capable of the kind of flourish and thought that only an unbroken spirit can summon. It is a personal triumph that, no matter how small, is consequential all the same.

Of course, to outsiders, especially tightly wrapped sorts from north-ern Europe, where a prim modesty and an almost ostentatious under-statement is the essence of good taste, the embroidery and apparent extravagance (financial or stylistic) of *bella figura* seems excessive. In their eyes it comes off as insecurity and ostentation rather than a wink-ing, even witty, defiance of the drabness of daily life.

The idea that today's Italians, especially in the wealthy north, could feel so oppressed and, yes, depressed, may strike the casual visitor as implausible. Yet anyone who has lived there soon discovers that Italian life, even at its headiest and most luxury-laden, is still a confined and confining world. Campanilismo hems you in. (See page 26.) Family obligations are like one of those clever knots that become more restraining the more you struggle to free yourself from them. "What can I do?" is the universal shrug when Italians, especially the young, get together to (happily) commiserate about the limitations of their lives.

This is mostly unseen by tourists because no group is better at put-ting on a happy face than Italians. The finest contemporary analyst of the Italian mind, Luigi Barzini, in his landmark book *The Italians* (1964) puts his finger on this better than anyone else:

> Dull and insignificant moments in life must be made decorous
> and agreeable with suitable decorations and rituals. Ugly things
> must be hidden, unpleasant and tragic facts swept under the carpet
> whenever possible. Everything must be made to sparkle, a simple

meal, an ordinary transaction, a dreary speech, a cowardly capitulation must be embellished and ennobled with euphemisms, adornments and pathos. These practices were not (as many think) developed by a people who find life rewarding and exhilarating, but by a pessimistic, realistic, resigned and frightened people.

Hence *bella figura*. What Italians will do not merely to create a *bella figura* but also to avoid its dark twin, the dreaded *brutta figura*, strikes outsiders as sometimes preposterous. A person who can barely afford his monthly car payment will insist on paying for the entire table at a restaurant, never mind that everybody present knows he really can't afford it. It would be a *brutta figura* to have others think that you are a down-at-the-heels sponger.

And the *bella figura* way of paying, by the way, is to discreetly leave the table and settle up the bill out of sight of your companions. Restaurant bills in better Italian restaurants are never presented at the table. The host—or whoever makes the earliest preemptive strike at the bill—always pays well away from the dining room.

Everything in Italian life that is otherwise economically unjustifiable or inexplicable is usually explained—often correctly—by *bella figura*. For example, years ago, the famous Piedmontese winegrower Angelo Gaja decided that he wanted to have the longest cork in the world for his wines. Today, long corks are commonplace. But in the early 1980s, they were unknown.

Gaja insists that his demand for a long cork was a way of ensuring the highest quality, as Sardinian and Portuguese cork manufacturers were notoriously lax about quality control. An ultra-long cork requires exceptional raw material in the form of exceptionally thick cork bark from very old trees, like Rolls-Royce specifying unscratched leather seats made from the hides of steers pastured in paddocks without barbed-wire fences. It's a backdoor way of ensuring unique quality that mere specifications couldn't achieve.

Anyway, when Gaja first introduced his ultra-long cork (it was sixty-three millimeters, or nearly two and one-half inches long) in

1982, he was ecstatic. *This* was *bella figura*! But there was a problem.

"I was very proud," recalls Gaja. "I went to a customer in Milan who was then selling between 60 and 100 cases of Barbaresco a year. A very important customer. I told him, 'Look, the Barbaresco has a special long cork. Be careful.' He said, 'No problem, no problem.' A week later, he called me and said 'This is a disaster.' 'What's happened?' I said. He told me, 'The waiters don't like opening the bottle.'

"The problem was that the corkscrews used by the waiters in Italy, given to them as gifts by big wine companies, were too short," says Gaja. "It was impossible, or nearly so, for them to pull out the cork. Customers get a little bit nervous, you know, watching a waiter struggling with a wine bottle," he adds with a laugh.

Gaja had introduced a cork so long that no one with a conventional corkscrew could easily extract it. Now, everyone who wanted to drink Gaja wine had to have a special corkscrew. Fortunately, such a corkscrew already had been invented by a Texan who was marketing it under the brand name Screwpull.

"As it happens, I was just back from the States," says Gaja. "And when I was in New York I had bought about 100 Screwpulls. So I gave 30 or 40 to that restaurant and the rest to my agents with instructions to show them around. I had no choice, my dear. I had to import Screwpulls to Italy!" he says, radiantly happy. Yet more *bella figura*.

A close friend of Gaja's, the late Giacomo Bologna, was a roly-poly Piedmontese winegrower who was a great favorite among his colleagues for his generosity and wit. He delighted in Gaja's new long corks and immediately used them to tweak the already-tetchy jealousies of Gaja's fascinated competitors.

Once, at the annual Vinitaly trade show in Verona, where every Italian winegrower can be found, Bologna was telling an enthralled audience of fellow producers about Gaja's new long, longer, longest corks. Like a talented older boy telling scary stories around a campfire to impressionable younger boys, Bologna described how impressive it was to see these Gaja bottles opened.

"You know this Gaja is smart," he proclaimed, like a carny barker setting up the rubes to be fleeced. "You know how much that cork costs? One thousand *lire*! " The audience members shook their heads in amazement. Gaja was *matto*, *pazzo*, crazy. At that time, a cork cost two hundred *lire*, tops.

"Sure, Gaja is crazy," confirmed Bologna. "But Gaja is not crazy. He spends one thousand *lire* for a cork, yes. But he saves one centiliter of Sorì Tildin [an ultra-expensive Barbaresco wine produced by Gaja] with the longer cork. And you already know how much he gets for that wine. This is not so dumb. He always has money in his pocket!"

In the penny-counting mentality of this rapt audience of Italian wine-growers, many of whom were one generation away, if that, from being *contadini* or peasant farmers, they could see that, in so expensive a wine, all those one centiliters (one-third ounce) could add up. In fact, Gaja's wines, like everyone else's, contain the legally required 750 milliliters or 25.3 ounces. But Italians, especially Italian farmers, are sure that the smart ones, the rich sorts such as Gaja, are forever *furbo*—admirably crafty.

Bologna was not finished with them. "And there's another reason," he exclaimed. "You know why else?" All the men said no, they couldn't think of another reason why someone would spend five times more than he had to on a cork.

"Maybe *bella figura*," offered one, rather timidly. Everyone nodded in agreement. But of course! That made sense. Really, it was the only conceivable explanation. Everyone agreed that this must be the reason.

"No!" cried Bologna. "The other reason is that with these corks he obliges all the restaurants in Italy to use the Screwpull. Which he imports and sells to them!" It was so obvious, so deliciously *furbo*, they wondered how they could have missed it. Gaja is smart, they said in awe and envy.

Anyone viewing Italian wine in the past few decades cannot help but be struck by the forcefulness of the *bella figura* imperative on infusing Italian wines. The most superficial aspect, literally, is packaging. No wines anywhere in the world offer more beautiful, innovative, original wine labels and even bottles than Italy. Seemingly nothing hasn't been tried, such as Cappannelle in Chianti creating, back in the '80s, an expensive custom-made bottle with a recessed oval indentation into which was fitted an oval label in sterling silver or even gold. (Most bottles just had paper labels, however.)

More recently, Cascina Castle't in Piedmont came up with a charming label depicting a 1950s-vintage color photograph of four little girls in smart dresses sitting or standing on an old Vespa. What has that to do with the Barbera in the bottle? Nothing. But who cares? It's a charming *bella figura*.

The examples are endless. Hundreds, even thousands of Italian wines today are packaged with a flair, originality, and insouciance that is more than Italy's oft-cited (and real) design sense. It's rooted in *bella figura*. In a world populated with seemingly as many wine producers as there are Italians, you must do something to make your individual (and individualistic) presence known.

Then there's the wine itself. Although the ubiquitous presence of small (225 liters or sixty gallons) oak barrels, typically from France but also from Slovenia, Hungary, and elsewhere, was probably inevitable, there can be no question that for many small producers their use is a sign of modernity and *bella figura*. You've *got* to have some. Otherwise, a visiting colleague or foreign wine writer might see you as hidebound. And that would be a *brutta figura*—except for those traditionalist producers who, in a kind of jujitsu move, make the absence of small oak barrels their *bella figura*, like French royalists proving their fealty by declaring modern democracy illegitimate.

Then there's pricing. Although it would seem to childlike rationalists such as Americans that of course you want more money if you can get it, pricing of Italian wines is not so simple. Naturally, the market ultimately establishes a wine's price over the long term. But an improbable number of Italian wines, especially in the rip-roaring 1990s, demanded astronomically high prices, especially for newly created *fantasia* wines, where the producer is making a personal statement about his or her style, nontraditional grape preferences, or political opinions about outmoded or oppressive wine laws. Or all three.

A high price—$50, $75, $150—for a label nobody had ever seen before sent a message: We have confidence. We are making a statement. We are equal to the best, i.e., most expensive, wines from France or California. Certainly greed and vanity play a role. But *bella figura* is part of the mix, in the same way that driving a certain car (an American SUV, British Jaguar, or Land Rover) makes a statement about your cosmopolitanism. In Italy today, you're nobody if you don't have your high-priced *fantasia* wine. So everyone has one.

It would be a mistake to take *bella figura* at its seemingly superficial word, as it were. Sure, there's a lot about *bella figura* that is indeed superficial, shallow, and overly concerned about others' perceptions. It's not Hegelian philosophy, after all.

But *bella figura* is an essential ingredient that liberates Italians from the narcotic stupor of their powerful traditions and time-honored way of doing things. As the playwright Luigi Pirandello once observed, "In Europe it is the dead who make life, crushing the life of the living with history, tradition and customs. The permanence of the old hinders and checks every vital movement."

Bella figura vitalizes Italian daily life and helps justify the new—or at least the different—in a culture that, for all its seeming effervescence, wrestles almost daily with the weight of centuries, like a ship with a hull so barnacle-encrusted that it struggles to make headway. An overtly public change requires an excuse, however flimsy. *La bella figura* serves, in its seemingly superficial fashion, to restore life to the living.

CAMPANILISMO: THE ITALIAN LOVE OF LOCATION

*Ligurio: And what you said first must worry you, because
you're not used to losing sight of the campanile.
Nicia: You're wrong! When I was younger I was a great runaround.
They never made a fair at Prato that I didn't go to. And there
isn't a single village around where I haven't been.
And I'll tell you more: I've been to Pisa and Livorno, I have!*
—NICCOLÒ MACHIAVELLI, *Mandragola* (1518)

Anyone who spends even a small amount of time in Italy soon becomes aware of Italy's intense, seemingly irrational, localism. Personal and family identities are so intimately entwined with one's birthplace (which, in turn, often means your parents' birthplace and their parents' birthplace and so on for a dozen generations) that the line between you and your town is no line at all. In the Italian mind, you are your town (or neighborhood) and vice versa.

Naturally, this has a name: *campanilismo*. It refers to a reluctance to stray farther than the sound of the bell of your town's campanile or bell tower. It's a well-known concept that remains vibrant for the simple reason that campanilismo is real.

For we famously restless, footloose Americans, the idea that campanilismo is that forceful can sometimes be hard to accept. Our mental territorial map is huge. As Antonio Marinoni observed in his now-forgotten 1931 book, *Italy, Yesterday and Today*, "Too many Americans . . . swarm over the highways of the Old World with the self-reliance of people whose geographical notions are in terms of continents."

Campanilismo can be inhibiting, even stifling. But it can also strengthen a deep commitment to place, which is essential to fine wine. The world's best wines—never mind the nation or the grape variety—are always expressions of place. Italy's campanilismo, especially when harnessed to grapegrowing, translates to something far more substantial than unthinking provincialism. It results in a devotion to "unfashionable" sites and "antique" grape varieties. The locals don't care. They say proudly *"nostrano"*—it's from our place. (You see this on signs at local farmers' markets all the time: pomodori nostrano or peperone nostrano—locally grown tomatoes or peppers.)

For most folks, "think globally, act locally" is little more than a bumper sticker. For Italians, it's actually a way to enjoy their beloved campanilismo while simultaneously beating back the underbrush of provincialism. With apparently effortless flexibility, Italians have somehow managed to be susceptible to campanilismo *and* capable of a border-free, modernizing awareness.

For wine lovers, the result is Italy's unique championing of grape varieties and wines that more market-driven cultures would reject as insupportable. To Italians, however, the pull of campanilismo is far stronger than the allure of mere money.

For example, to grow Aglianico in Campania (the region around Naples) is not just convention. It's what *makes* you a Campagnolo. The variety defines you as much as it does the wine itself. What's more, if your locality happens to grow a particular strain of a grape (which is often the case given the antiquity of Italy's vineyards), campanilismo magnifies that too: Your allegiance is transferred to your place's particular, always-proclaimed-as-unique strain or clone.

Collectively, the effect of campanilismo is seen in the proliferation of Italy's controlled appellations of origin or DOCs (*denominazione di origine controllata*). Legally delimited wine districts first appeared in France starting in the 1930s, but they appeared in Italy only in the 1960s.

Originally seen as signaling places of great distinction, both nations now are glutted with increasingly meaningless appellations. Their numbers became so inflated in Italy that the government subsequently instituted a now-we-really-mean-it new category called DOCG: *denominazione d'origine controllata garantita*. The "guaranty" is a certain level of purported quality, a variation on saying this currency, unlike the old one, is actually worth something. (French wine authorities are now considering doing the same thing, by the way.)

Really, they are a manifestation—a proclamation, even—of campanilismo. And as with religion, you cannot delegitimitize peoples' devotion to their places. All wine (politics) is local. Hence all those DOCs.

This, in turn, helps explain why so many wine laws are so openly flouted in Italy. The dark side of campanilismo is its inhibiting traditionalism. Campanilismo strongly suggests (compels is too strong a word) that you do what your town and your neighbors have always done. Every Italian knows this suffocating pressure.

Yet simultaneously, campanilismo is also strengthening. After all, it's tribal. It means that no matter what (or nearly so), you will always be a member of your local tribe. This, in turn, empowers you to flout the law. After all, your neighbors—even if they disapprove—cannot deny your birthright. Short of committing a true moral outrage, a real *infamia*, you will always have a place among your own kind.

Besides, all Italians instinctively align themselves against authority anyway. This is one reason campanilismo emerged in the first place. Centuries of ever-shifting political alliances and numerous invasions from neighboring city-states or nations taught you that you were safest within the confines of your *località*.

You could see this, literally, in Vittorio De Sica's landmark neo-realist movie, *The Bicycle Thief* (1948). The protagonist, Antonio, has his bicycle stolen on his first day of work, a small but real catastrophe. (Antonio's wife pawned the family linens to retrieve the already pawned bicycle.)

Antonio finds the thief. The thief's neighbors, who very likely know that he is indeed the culprit, nevertheless close ranks, as noted by Princeton University sociology professor Bart Bonikowski:

> "De Sica illustrates the phenomenon of campanilismo in the sequence following the thief's apprehension by Antonio. As Antonio roughs up the young man, he does not realize that they are standing outside of his apartment. A crowd gathers quickly and begins to defend the thief, accusing Antonio of slander. The solidarity among

the members of the neighborhood is evident, proving that even if the thief's actions contradict widely accepted norms, the integrity and interests of the local community take precedence." [1]

For wine lovers, Italy's irresistible campanilismo results in a bewildering, delightful profusion of wines. Many of these—most even—are not mentioned in this book. They are too small, too local, too difficult to obtain on these shores. But that does not mean that these "little" wines aren't worthy. Or that your local, Italy-smitten wine merchant may not bring them in after having spent a dreamy vacation in some tiny Italian hill town. That happens all the time. So keep an eye peeled, and a palate open, for such imported souvenirs.

What campanilismo means, above all, is that Italy—far more than homogenized France—is capable of resisting the tsunami of globalism that is seemingly swamping more "sophisticated" cultures. The power of market forces is not negligible anywhere, including Italy.

For wine lovers, the result is a profusion of wines and versions and varieties of those wines—sparkling, still, rosé, sweet—that's more akin to the profligacy of a Brazilian jungle than the superficially impressive but ultimately narrow and oppressive topiary of a "refined" garden.

Italy, more than any other European nation, has persevered with its own vision, to its own satisfaction. After all, once you have your place, what else do you really need?

MEZZADRIA: HOW SHARECROPPING PROFOUNDLY AFFECTED ITALIAN WINE

"If the mezzadri and the poor of the village didn't go about the world themselves, the world had come, in the war years, to awaken them."
—CESARE PAVESI, *The Moon and the Bonfire* (1950)

Although few think about it today, one of the great turning points in Italian wine was the disappearance of the practice called *mezzadria*,

[1] "Italy In Crisis: An Analysis of Vittorio de Sica's *The Bicycle Thief*" by Bart Bonikowski (2000).

or sharecropping. It defined and degraded Italian agriculture. And it didn't even begin to end—as the great Italian novelist Cesare Pavese pointed out—until after World War II, with its effects lingering for decades after that. Anyone seeking to understand just how radical was Italy's achievment of wine greatness in the last two—at most three—decades of the twentieth century needs to recognize the powerful undertow of mezzadria.

Italian wine couldn't have changed, and never would change, until sharecropping or mezzadria was abolished. Amazingly, that didn't happen technically until the 1980s. The beginning of the end, however, was World War II.

Every Friday at the farmer's market near where I once lived in Piedmont, standing next to sometimes embarrassingly small quantities of vegetables and fruits, I met the living legacies of Italy's now-forgotten but hugely influential agricultural class, called *mezzadri* or sharecroppers. You could see them everywhere in Italy—even more so in the more impoverished South—at similar markets.

Mostly, they are old peasant farmers, collectively called *contadini*, with outsize knobby hands and weathered, sunbeaten skin. Invariably, they have not shaved for several days. Their tough, grizzled, old men's beards make their faces look like worn, furrowed lava fields through which a crop of tiny cactuses are pushing up. They speak dialect insistently. A handful still do not know Italian, which is now unusual in the North, but more common in the South, although it's fading there too. (According to Tullio De Mauro, an Italian language scholar, 13 percent of the population in the southern Italian regions of Calabria and Basilatica still cannot speak or understand Italian and rely exclusively on dialect.)

These men, their wives, and even some of their older children, once were mezzadri. They were not, however, migrants. But they were effectively excluded from owning land by the feudal system of mezzadria. The word *mezza*, meaning half, reveals clearly enough how the system worked. In exchange for their labor, they got half of the crop. They were allowed to live on, and off of, the land they tended. Sometimes a house—really a hut—was included. Sometimes they had to build them for themselves. The landowner provided seed and sprays and little else.

Mezzadria differed from region to region, but only in scale, not in practice or effect. You had an overseer, called a *fattore*, employed by the landowner. He was the go-between. Indeed, many landowners of large estates never once met their mezzadri. Distances were often great, and travel by horseback or carriage (even by car before the 1960s) was slow.

Besides, the landowners were often urban aristocrats or professionals such as doctors or lawyers. They inherited or bought land, but they themselves were almost never agricultural, any more than inheritors of ample stock portfolios are active investors. Others do it for them. The same was true for a fattore and the landowner.

Typically, the fattore would decide himself what to grow and when to plant. He would create contracts with new mezzadri. At the end of the year, the fattore would meet the owner for an accounting of the year's efforts. Sometimes the owners didn't even care about that, leaving it all to the fattore and yet another go-between such as a clerk or a local lawyer.

In Tuscany, for example, the property of the Barons Ricasoli was more than 25,000 hectares (61,775 acres). Keep in mind that even in intensively cultivated wine zones such as Barolo, Barbaresco, and parts of Friuli—where it's now all a sea of vines—the landscape looked different even into the 1960s. Today, these zones are a monoculture of grapevines. But they were once polycultures, with fields for grazing animals. The mezzadri liked to have stalls for cows and oxen, which meant valued milk and meat.

For the mezzadri, theirs was a world with no possibility of ownership of any really decent land and, of course, no incentive toward energy or ambition because there was no reward for such exercise. It was just subsistence farming.

In Piedmont, Marchese Alberto di Grésy is an aristocratic vineyard owner whose inherited property, called La Martinenga, is arguably the single best vineyard in the Barbaresco zone. For generations his land was worked by mezzadri, a practice that continued into the 1960s.

"Frankly, we wanted to continue using mezzadri." admits di Grésy. "Because it was easier for us. But in the end it became too expensive. It used to be that they got fifty percent of the harvest. And then the contracts began to change: they got sixty percent. And then it went to seventy percent. Finally, to keep them, we would have had to give them ninety percent of the crop, which was ridiculous."

For di Grésy, like others in his situation everywhere in Italy, there were only two choices: Sell the land and get out of the (low-paying) agriculture business or set out on his own, creating his own wine that he hoped would command a premium, which it now does. That was the only way to afford workers and essential improvements.

Two forces aligned to firmly usher mezzadria out of Italian life. The first was Italy's post-war industrialization. After Italy picked itself up from the devastation of the war, the cities and mid-size towns everywhere north of Rome began to industrialize. By the 1960s, Italy saw its first economic boom, and by the 1980s, its economy was the fifth largest in the world.

Decades, if not centuries, of agricultural lassitude had, by the war's end, made Italy's farms literally and figuratively untenable. For example, writing in 1901, Bolton-King in *Italy of To-Day* compared the wheat yields of various European countries. Even though a higher proportion of Italy's farmland was devoted to producing wheat than any other European nation, its average yield was just eleven and one-half bushels per acre. France, in comparison, produced almost one-third more at sixteen and one-half bushels per acre. Great Britain reported thirty bushels per acre, or more than two and one-half times that of Italy. Only Russia, itself struggling with its own agrarian feudalism, reported lower wheat yields than Italy.

With urban industrialization offering an alternative, to say nothing of a siren call, the glacial mezzadria system began to dissolve. The lawyers, doctors and other upper middle-class professionals, who owned two, three, or four farms, as well as the landed aristocracy, soon found themselves saddled with properties that, because they were so badly managed, could not support workers earning a decent wage. Certainly they could not compete with factory wages. Only the cheap labor of mezzadria kept these farms economically plausible for their owners. Even the farms owned by peasants, which were equally badly run, if not worse, also could not compete with the new factory wages. Everywhere in Italy, the countryside began to be drained of its workers, all of whom fled to the cities in search of a living, or at least a future.

The government was rightly alarmed at the prospect of deserted farms. So, in the 1950s, the government offered Italian farmers a deal: If the farmers stayed on the land and made money only from crops on land they owned or leased, they would be excused from paying any business income tax. Effectively, they paid no income tax at all because most farmers had no other sources of income.

This law proved enticing. And in the beginning it probably didn't cost the Italian government very much simply because the farms generated so little income anyway.

But when the Italian economy improved, those once negligible incomes became increasingly more substantial.

In the case of winegrowers, as long as they made wine only from grapes they grew on land they owned or leased—buying not a single grape or a drop of juice or wine from anyone else—their income was gravy. And in the 1970s and '80s, that gravy was lip-smacking.

I recall being baffled in the early 1980s when I would visit tiny Italian wineries whose owners would proudly show me their gleaming new stainless steel fermenting tanks and their $50,000 German-made sterile bottling lines. All to produce, say, 5,000 cases of wine that sold locally for maybe five bucks a bottle. It didn't pencil out. Only later did I learn about the tax exemption law.

Given the notorious inefficiencies of Italian government, to say nothing of its endemic corruption, allowing farmers to legally keep their money was probably the best use of that money that Italy could ever have hoped to achieve.

Italians, despite their preposterous image as endlessly lunching layabouts, actually are insistently industrious. It was trickle-up economics at its best. They took their money and reinvested it. They bought more land, and better machinery and sent their sons—and sometimes even their daughters—to agricultural schools. In the case of wine, the result was better-quality wines, an awareness of marketing, and, eventually, a higher return. Only in 1987 was the law rescinded.

But the income tax exemption was only one incentive. The other involved a redistribution of the ownership of the land itself. The previously landless mezzadri benefitted from yet another critical piece of 1950s legislation: a low-interest loan program for mezzadri as well as an option to buy the land they worked if the owner put it up for sale.

Without the cheap labor of the mezzadri, the professional and aristocratic landowners found their farms an insupportable burden. They had no choice but to sell, which they did in droves. The government, for its part, recognized that what the mezzadri lacked was not a willingness to work the land but access to capital with which to buy it.

If a landowner put up for sale a property worked by a mezzadro—which he was not, in any case, compelled to do—the mezzadro had first rights of refusal to buy the property. The government made available low-interest loans to the mezzadro, with the stipulation that he work this land himself for a certain number of years. It was a clever idea, serving the interests of the landowners—they had a ready buyer already on the property—and the mezzadro, whose labor could make the land economically viable.

The combination of the Italian government's inspired legislation not only broke the back of mezzadria, but it also transformed who farmed, what they farmed, and not least, how they farmed. For Italian wine, the results—slowly at first and then with breakneck speed by the 1980s—were revolutionary. Italian wine reached out to world markets on terms—and with quality—that previously only French wines could command. Without the demise of mezzadria, this simply could not have happened. There was no incentive to excel, no incentive to risk capital; indeed, there was no pride. That's all changed, forever.

Drinking Italy

HOW TO USE THIS BOOK

This section of *Making Sense of Italian Wine* adheres to a common format intended to convey as much usable information as possible without making you feel you're reading a doctoral thesis on Italian wine. The format proceeds along these lines:

Type or Name of Wine: Italy's wines typically (and often confusingly) are identified by either place name or grape name. Making matters more complicated yet, sometimes they use both.

For example, in the Piedmont region of northwest Italy you have the famous wine called Barolo. It's a place name. You also have wines labeled Dolcetto. It's a grape name. But on labels you'll typically see Dolcetto d'Alba or Dolcetto di Dogliani, where place names (Alba, Dogliani) are added to the grape name.

Like other European wine countries, Italy has legally defined geographic appellations called DOCs (*denominazione di origine controllata*). Hundreds of these exist, each defining the geographic boundaries of a particular place and stipulating—with legal force—which grape varieties may be grown there and how the wine must be made.

As elsewhere in Europe, these DOCs are literally conservative in nature, designed to preserve and codify centuries-old traditions. Not surprisingly, many producers chafe under the restrictions and have successfully (and often illegally) wriggled out from under the perceived burden to create more "modern" wines. This was often winked at by the authorities, as Italy has an equally long tradition of officially saying one thing while allowing others to go about their business. In almost every wine district in Italy, you have legalistic, and sometimes social, tensions between "traditionalists" and "modernists."

That said, regulations have loosened in many areas to bring modernist "apostates" back into the fold by making legal what was once forbidden. Italy is famously flexible, often to a fault, as the Italians themselves are frequently the first to point out. Remember, Italy has been around for five thousand years. Italians long ago learned that rigidity is unhelpful to longevity.

Region: Italy is formally divided into twenty political regions such as Lombardy or Tuscany. Every Italian has a mental map of all of the regions in the boot, and regional names are used in daily Italian life freely and frequently in the same way we refer to one state or another. The rest of us, however, are lost. "Region" gives you at least a general notion of where in Italy a wine comes from.

Grapes: Nothing defines Italian wines as much as the diversity of its grape varieties. Many Italian wines are blends of several different grapes, sometimes even blends of both red *and* white grapes. Yet other wines are strictly required to be composed of only a single variety (Sangiovese in the case of Brunello di Montalcino; Nebbiolo for Barolo and Barbaresco). "Grapes" reveals what's inside the bottle.

The Tradition: Every bottle of Italian wine tells a story. Nothing in Italy is without history, often a long and complicated one. Of course, this is what makes Italian wines so fascinating. But "tradition" is more than empty, if colorful, cultural pageantry. With wine, it's the foundation of why a wine tastes as it does. Understanding the tradition of a particular wine allows us to grasp what its local "modernists" are opposing or seeking to modify. There's *always* a dialectic in Italian life, and their wines are no exception.

How It's Changed: As previously noted, every Italian wine occupies two dimensions: its long tradition and an imagined future. Every Italian wine district has its cadre of traditionalists and futurists. The conflict is not always as bitter or implacable as it sounds. Rather, it's reflective of an ancient country and culture trying to make its way in a modern world without losing its soul in the process. No nation anywhere has navigated this more deftly than Italy. Its wines reflect this endeavor. "How It's Changed" seeks to explain the often-shifting modifications.

Noteworthy Producers (The Traditionalists/The Modernists): You can't tell the players without a scorecard. This is it. Please do keep in mind that, even within the local wine culture, terms such as "traditionalist" and "modernist" are slippery. Nowhere is Yeats' famous line, "Things fall apart; the center cannot hold," more true than in establishing who or what is "modern" in Italian wine. Italy's craving for modernity is such that the "center" always shifts, making yesterday's modernist today's traditionalist.

This section tries to pin the butterfly to the board. But it keeps fluttering away anyway. Still, the attempt is worthwhile, as these divisions *are* real, if fluid.

What Do The Locals Eat With This Wine? If Italian wines are indeed distinct from all others in the world, it's partly to do with the fact that you cannot separate Italy's extreme wine localism from its equally extreme food localism. Where much of France, for example, has sadly become homogenized in its food culture, Italy still retains a vibrant individuality. Its wines often do taste best when paired with local dishes. Many Italian reds, for example, have good acidity, the better to "cut" the richness of, say, a few slices of salami. To better understand the wine, it helps to know the food, as well as what we Americans might be more likely to pair with the wine in question.

One Man's Taste—Whose Wine Would I Buy? If we were looking at a wine list together in a restaurant, or walking the aisle of a wine shop, you might well turn to me and say, "So, whose wines would *you* buy?"

This listing is the answer.

As it declares, this is "one man's taste." I am neither a devout traditionalist nor a to-the-ramparts modernist in my Italian wine preference. What I look for are those producers who, by dint of low vineyard yields and personal rigor, make compelling, memorable wines. I try never to lose sight of the worth of local wine tradition, while at the same time recognizing the desirability of change. Call me a wine centrist, if you like.

Worth Searching For? However charming Italian wines can be, they're not *all* worth running around to locate. There are too many wines (and producers) to pretend that every Italian wine is equally compelling. Some wines really are worth their expense and trouble to locate. Other wines are worth a bit of your time and effort. Yet others are good finds—*if* you happen to see them.

Here are the (self-explanatory) categories:
Don't die without trying it.
Absolutely worth an effort.
If you happen to see it.

Similar Wines From The Same Neighborhood: Like planets with orbiting moons, many of Italy's most significant wine districts have less famous neighboring zones creating similar wines. In Tuscany, for example, you have the most important Chianti district called Chianti Classico. Less well-known are other neighboring "Chiantis" such as Chianti Colli Senesi (the hills around Siena) and Chianti Colli Fiorentini (the hills around Florence). It's good to know these wines exist, as they often can be bargains, as well as competitive in quality.

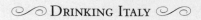

The Wines

Aglianico del Vulture

(ahl-*yahn*-ee-koh del vul-*toor*-eh)

RED

Region: Basilicata (southern Italy, south of Naples). The locals call Basilicata by a different name: Lucania, which is the ancient Roman name for the region. The name Basilicata became official only in 1932.

Grapes: 100 percent Aglianico (red) (See also Taurasi, page 233.)

The Tradition: To talk about tradition with the Aglianico grape variety is to reach back—*way* back. It's pretty much agreed that the word Aglianico is a corruption of *ellenico*, meaning Hellenic or Greek, which suggests that the grape originally came from, or was brought to Italy by, the ancient Greeks. This makes sense because it's known that Aglianico has been grown in Basilicata since the sixth or seventh century BC, or more than 2,600 years.

Aglianico is diffused throughout the Basilicata region as well as the Campania region to the north. But no one disagrees that potentially *the* most significant source of Aglianico goodness anywhere in Italy is Monte Vulture, a 4,350-foot (extinct) volcanic mountain thick with layers of ancient lava, which over time makes for rich, nutritious soil. (However, at the moment, it's the Taurasi district in Campania that has the greater prestige.)

How It's Changed: Until very recently, the tradition for Aglianico del Vulture was "anything goes." You had slightly sweet or *amabile*red wine, you had sparkling red wine, and of course, you had classical dry reds. Even within the dry reds you had some that were meant to be drunk young while yet others (called *vecchio* or *riserva*) are meant for long aging. As marketing sorts would say, Aglianico del Vulture lacked focus.

The past decade or so has brought to Aglianico del Vulture—as it has to so many places in southern Italy—a new determination to achieve. You can still find the old sweet or sparkling versions, but today Aglianico del Vulture is really all about a serious red wine that can age and transform in a cool cellar for a decade or more.

All of the usual suspects for this sort of winegrowing renaissance are in place: lower vineyard yields, modern winemaking equipment, small French oak barrels, and above all, a "think globally and act locally" awareness of world standards for fine wine.

The best Aglianico del Vulture bottlings today are superb: clean, fully dry, exhibiting a rich, earthy flavor, and clearly capable of rewarding extended cellaring. Such wines are truly memorable.

Noteworthy Producers (The Traditionalists/The Modernists): There's little sense in distinguishing the traditionalists from the modernists in Aglianico del Vulture—or, for that matter, anywhere else in southern Italy. Little about the tradition—high yields, dirty old casks, sloppy winemaking—is worth mentioning, let alone retaining. All of the following producers are modernists in the best sense: They have high ambitions, use modern equipment, and employ ever-greater rigor.

BASILISCO—A joint venture between Elena Fucci (see below) and Michele Cutolo, the small (twenty acres) estate is one of the bright new lights among the growing number of superior Aglianico del Vulture producers. Small oak barrels are used, but deftly so, creating very rich, dimensional Aglianico that achieves refinement but not at the expensive of Aglianico's robust and frank character.

BASILIUM—A new venture that holds much promise. In addition to an unusual white wine made from Aglianico called Pipoli Chiaro, there's a more conventional red wine also using the same brand name of Pipoli Rosso. The former has surprising heft for a white; the latter is a pleasing, if one-dimensional, red. A good quaffer. More resonant are I Portali and Valle del Trono. I Portali is a good, solid Aglianico del Vulture. Valle del Trono is quite unusual in that part of the grapes are dried in the sun for two to three weeks and then added to the fermentation. It's a quasi-*passito* or dried-grape Aglianico. The wine is aged in oak for more than two years. The result, not surprisingly, is a very rich, dense, blackish wine that's almost too much of a good thing. Still, it's striking stuff.

FEUDI DI SAN GREGORIO—Located farther north in Campania, this powerhouse producer knows good Aglianico when they taste it, which is why they added an Aglianico del Vulture called Efesto to their own signature Taurasi from Campania, also made from Aglianico. Not surprisingly, it's superb Aglianico del Vulture: dense, rich, earthy, yet also suave.

ELENA FUCCI—The Fucci family issues a superb, high elevation, always late-picked, single vineyard Aglianico del Vulture called Titolo, after a tower near their vineyards. Aged partly in small oak barrels, this is rich, intense, supple Aglianico of superb quality.

CANTINA DEL NOTAIO—One of the most ambitious producers in the zone is Cantina del Notaio, whose owner, Gerardo Giuratrabocchetti, is making his vineyards entirely biodynamic, an extreme form of organic cultivation. Two Aglianico del Vulture bottlings are found in America: La Firma and Il Repertoio. Both are very rich, intense, oak-inflected Aglianicos that rank among the very best of the zone. La Firma seems to be the better of the two, but it's a real (thoroughbred) horse race. Worth seeking out.

PATERNOSTER—The benchmark producer in Aglianico del Vulture, Paternoster issues two significant Aglianico del Vulture bottlings, Solomonically dividing the stylistic baby between their oak-influenced, modern-style Rotondo wine (smooth, supple, meant for early drinking) and their more traditional, sterner, intended for long-aging Don Anselmo Riserva del Fondatore bottling. The latter is unquestionably one of the best Aglianicos made anywhere in Italy, a real powerhouse of a wine. It too sees time in small oak barrels, but unlike Rotondo, it spends an additional year in large casks. This is a serious producer setting a standard for the zone.

TENUTA LA QUERCE—Another bright star in the area, the ambitious Tenuta La Querce benefits from a modern winery and superb winemaking, along with about fifty acres of well-placed vines. Three Aglianico del Vulture bottlings are issued. The Il Viola bottling is soft, rounded, and modern in the best sense, a wine that makes a very good first impression for newcomers to Aglianico del Vulture. More serious (and oaky) is Rosso di Costanza, which delivers impressive depth and concentration. Most New World—yet inarguably very fine—is the single-vineyard Vigna della Corona, which is just 3.8 acres at a high elevation. It sees a long fermentation and maceration, along with lots of new oak. Still, it can handle it. Worth watching closely.

What Do The Locals Eat With This Wine? Aglianico del Vulture is, at its best, a massive, intense, rich dry red wine with notes of cherry, blueberry, blackberry, licorice, coffee, mint, and a certain earthiness. Some modernist versions are oaky, too much so for this palate. But the scale and richness of any good Aglianico del Vulture fairly begs for comparably strong, rich food. Certainly, this is a wine meant for roasts of all kinds: beef, lamb, and goat.

Basilicata is an impoverished, intensely sunny, and rock-filled terrain. The local cuisine is correspondingly intense yet simple. Meat is rare, although lamb is most common and much loved. Hot red peppers are a signature of the region; you see them drying in long cascades everywhere. Pasta is ubiquitous, especially elongated, chewy shapes such as cavatelli and a local specialty called lugane. Basilicata's is an honest, simple cuisine of strong, straightforward flavors.

One Man's Taste—Whose Wine Would I Buy? Because Aglianico del Vulture's ambition is so new, it would be a mistake to confine oneself only to the tried and true. At this moment, my top pick would be Paternoster's top bottling called Don Anselmo Riserva del Fondatore, which is still a benchmark bottling.

But really, any of the Aglianico del Vulture wines from Basilisco,

Elena Fucci, Cantine del Notaio, Tenuta La Querce, or Feudi di San Gregorio are compelling and very much worth seeking out.

Worth Searching For? Absolutely worth an effort.

Similar Wines From The Same Neighborhood: Any wine using the name Aglianico, e.g., Aglianico del Taburno Rosso. Also, Taurasi and Falerno.

Arneis

(ahr-*nayz*) or Roero Arneis
WHITE

Region: Piedmont, specifically the Roero district (northwest Italy)

Grape: Arneis (white, dry). In Piemontese dialect, arneis means rascal, rebel, difficult, or stubborn, because it's an unreliable, sometimes exasperating, grape to grow.

The Tradition: Piedmont has surprisingly little tradition of either growing white grapes or drinking the stuff. The most abundant white grape, by far, is the delicious Moscato Bianco, which gets made into the sweet dessert wines Moscato d'Asti (See page 176) or Asti Spumante (See page 48). Then there's the banal dry white wine called Gavi (made from the Cortese grape variety) and the much rarer Erbaluce grape. Neither of these wines is on anybody's list of compelling whites.

All of which makes Arneis stand out. First, it's peculiar to Piedmont, specifically the sandy-soil Roero district that lies between the towns of Bra and Alba. That same sandy soil also grows superb asparagus. Arneis is the only wine I've ever heard producers proudly say goes with asparagus—which it does, in fact.

The odd thing about Arneis is that it almost died out. Only in the 1980s, when the world demanded dry white wine—*any* dry white wine—did Piedmontese producers decide that they'd better offer something in addition to their lavish array of reds. Two producers rescued and revived the almost-forgotten Arneis: Bruno Giacosa and Alfredo Currado (Vietti winery).

What's Arneis got that makes it special—or at least different? It's a delicate dry white that delivers the usual white wine scents of hay and wildflowers along with whiffs of pear and green apple. But what really makes it stand out is a noticeable scent of almonds. All of that, along with an attractive restraint, makes Arneis ideal for simply prepared fish, mild cheeses, and, yes, asparagus.

One last point: Arneis does not age well. You always want the latest vintage, as these delicate scents fade and then almost disappear after just three years or so, at most.

How It's Changed: The big change in Arneis is really in its production. It went from almost extinct in the 1970s to about 1,100 acres today. Since there really was no modern tradition of Arneis wine (the old version, pre-World War I, was slightly sweet), what we drink today is, effectively, tradition-in-the-making.

Because Arneis doesn't age well, nearly every producer avoids aging the wine in oak. Arneis is made in stainless steel vats and bottled young, the better to get it on the market while it's fresh.

Noteworthy Producers: Quite a few producers have climbed on the Arneis bandwagon because it gets a good price on the retail shelves; it's a tasty, original dry white wine, and, well, Piedmont doesn't offer much in the way of whites, especially in the Langhe and Roero zones.

The problem is that too many Arneis bottlings are dilute and insipid, typically because of excessive yields in the vineyard. However, several reliably fine (and well-distributed) bottlings are worth seeking out.

BRUNO GIACOSA—Bruno Giacosa not only pioneered Arneis but also today makes the richest, fullest, most voluptuous version. Giacosa's is the benchmark bottling. When you've had Bruno Giacosa's Arneis, you've reached the end of the line.

CERETTO—The largest producer of Arneis, Ceretto's version, called Blangé (dialect for "white"), is an accomplished, stylish Arneis in a very attractive package. It's always reliably good. And although it's not as rich as Giacosa's version, it is impressively good, especially given the sizable production.

MATTEO CORREGIA—A leading property in Roero, this estate

issues classically good, pure, beautifully defined Arneis.

UGO LEQUIO—A small producer in the Barbaresco zone with an Arneis vineyard Roero. Very fine and rich Arneis from an up-and-coming grower.

VIETTI—Alfredo Currado pioneered Arneis along with Bruno Giacosa (it's unclear quite who came first) and continues to make one of the best versions: clean, pure, and unmistakably Arneis in its light almond scent.

What Do The Locals Eat With This Wine? The Piedmontese are not great fish eaters (the region is landlocked, after all) but when they do eat fish, they reach for Arneis. It's also served with various vegetable antipasti and light pasta dishes.

One Man's Taste—Whose Wine Would I Buy? The best, by far, is Bruno Giacosa. Find his Arneis and you've reached the pinnacle. Happily, his production is considerable and, thus, reasonably available.

Worth Searching For? If you happen to see it

Similar Wines From The Same Neighborhood: Various experimental Chardonnays, Sauvignon Blancs, and Arneis/Chardonnay blends from the Roero and Langhe districts. Few of these are anything special, however.

Asti Spumante

(*ah*-stee spoo-*mahn*-teh)

WHITE

Region: Piedmont (northwestern Italy)

Grape: 100 percent Moscato Bianco

The Tradition: Although it's long since forgotten, in the mid-nineteenth century, Asti Spumante (literally, foaming Asti) was once made in the same fermented-in-this-bottle fashion as French Champagne. But because Asti Spumante was always a sweet bubbly—the Moscato Bianco or white Muscat grape reaches high sugar levels—it was a treacherous method of getting bubbles in the wine because the bottles chronically exploded. The yeasts, feeding on the abundant residual sugar in the finished wine, often created more carbon dioxide than the bottle could withstand and then . . . kaboom! Workers in the cellar would wear wire-mesh face masks, like fencers, to protect themselves. At least one major producer, Contratto, still makes a *méthode champenoise*-style Asti Spumante.

How It's Changed: Today nearly all Asti Spumante is made using the bulk or Charmat method of getting bubbles into the wine. It's called bulk because the process occurs in (very safe) tanks rather than individual glass bottles.

Ironically, Asti Spumante improved because of this technique even though the bulk process is less prestigious than the *méthode champenoise* process. It's also much cheaper. But it's actually a superior technique for Moscato Bianco because it allows the purity of the grape's fragrant, grapey scent and taste to come through resonantly. The French Champagne method, desirable for more neutral grapes such as

Chardonnay, adds extraneous flavors and smells from the enzymatic breakdown of the dead yeast cells inside the bottle (called autolysis). You don't want that with Moscato Bianco, where fidelity to the grape's flavor is everything.

Today's Asti Spumante—now abbreviated to simply Asti since 1994, when the zone acquired DOCG status—is invariably sweet (as it should be), surprisingly refreshing from crisp acidity (ditto), and too often lacking in depth or character. Its popularity (75 million bottles a year) virtually guarantees an industrial wine. The companies that produce Asti Spumante are among Italy's biggest wineries, as they usually produce other big-scale wines such as vermouth. Exceptions exist, however.

Noteworthy Producers: Nearly all of the big Asti Spumante producers are qualitatively equal. And equally mediocre. So it really won't matter much if you get Martini & Rossi, Cinzano, Gancia, Calissano, Bersano, Duca d'Asti, or almost any of the other big houses. They're all good, but unexceptional. The two best Asti Spumante producers for this taster are Fontanafredda and Bera.

BERA—One of the smallest producers of Asti Spumante, which means they can be, and are, more selective in sourcing their grapes. The Bera bottling has lovely finesse and delicacy.

FONTANAFREDDA—Much bigger than Bera (and more famous for its Barolo wines), Fontanafredda owns choice vineyards in the Asti zone, which allows it to create consistently superior Asti Spumante.

What Do The Locals Eat With This Wine? Asti Spumante is, like all bubbly, a wine of celebration. Typically it's served with dessert in Piedmont, which means a sweet flan similar to a crème caramel or with krumiri, a cornmeal cookie peculiar to Piedmont.

Personally, I've discovered (with immense satisfaction from the massive research required) that Asti Spumante is the ideal wine with chocolate truffles. Even though the Piedmontese are great chocolate producers, I don't ever recall this combination in Piedmont itself. Still, it's dreamy.

Asti Spumante is always served refrigerator-cold and in wide-mouthed coupe glasses in Piedmont, the kind we're (rightly) told *not* to use for champagne. So why do the locals use this glass? Because Moscato Bianco is so fragrant that it needs no funneling-up to the nose achieved by narrower, tulip-shaped glasses. Also, since it's low in alcohol, typically just 7 percent, it gets guzzled pretty quickly. So no one's overly concerned about the bubbles dissipating in the wide-mouth coupe.

One Man's Taste—Whose Wine Would I Buy? If I were buying Asti Spumante, I'd reach for Bera or Fontanafredda. Personally I prefer the more lightly bubbling or *frizzante* version called Moscato d'Asti (see page 176).

That said, Asti Spumante is a good choice for a summer party or an event where the guests are not especially interested in wine but would like a little something—a family get-together, for example. It's a crowd pleaser.

Worth Searching For? If you happen to see it

Similar Wines From The Same Neighborhood: Moscato d'Asti

Barbaresco

(bahr-bah-*ress*-koh)

RED

Region: Piedmont (Langhe zone); northwest Italy

Grapes: 100 percent Nebbiolo (red). One of the world's great red grapes, Nebbiolo is exceptionally perfumey with scents of cherries, roses, tar, black fruits, and a sensation of layered dimension. It has high acidity and is frequently tannic. Rarely a stand-alone wine, Nebbiolo shines with food. It's extremely long-lived and can improve for upwards of thirty years in great Nebbiolo wines such as Barbaresco, Barolo, and Gattinara.

The Tradition: The Langhe (*lahn*-geh) zone is home to two of Italy's most famous wine names: Barolo and Barbaresco. They are divided by the Tanaro River, with the city of Alba separating them like a referee between two glaring prizefighters. Barolo is the larger of the two zones; it has two and one half times as much vineyard acreage (3,100 acres of vines in Barolo versus Barbaresco's 1,100 acres).

The tradition of Barbaresco was that, until 1894, it *had* no tradition. Wines from the area were sold as Barolo. After all, wines are both 100 percent Nebbiolo, they both enjoy the same marl (clay with chalk) soil, and they're both in the same set of convulsive, freestanding hills collectively called the Langhe (in dialect, Langa).

So what happened in 1894? That was the year a liberal-minded, upper-class professor, Domizio Cavazza, established a local winegrowers' cooperative, the still-thriving Produttori del Barbaresco. Under his aegis, a wine called Barbaresco under that name first emerged. For the first time ever, Barbaresco had a publicly proclaimed identity.

Worth noting is that even though Barbaresco had no previous public identity until the late twentieth century (see below), that doesn't mean, to use today's psycho-jargon, that it lacked a private identity. The locals *always* knew what they had. And, like Barolo, they long ago identified and acquired a bone-deep folk knowledge of their best hillside exposures.

So today, as in Barolo, we now see numerous Barbaresco bottlings designating single vineyards. Nebbiolo, like Pinot Noir, is immensely expressive, and these vineyard differences are evident and distinctive to local Barbaresco growers. They're also increasingly apparent to interested outsiders who care to study and follow the voices of the Barbaresco landscape.

Among the best named vineyards are Asili (elegant, perfumey); Costa Russi (rich, powerful); Faset (graceful, early-maturing); Martinenga (refined, unusually complete in taste and scent); Moccagatta (meaty, dense); Montestefano (rich, often intense); Ovello (dense, long-lived); Rabajà (basso profundo, robust, rich); Rio Sordo (muscular, forthright); Santo Stefano (exceptionally balanced, intense, long-lived); Sorì San Lorenzo (taut, intense, restrained, long-lived); and Sorì Tildin (detailed, dense, tight, very long-lived). Dozens of other names are seen episodically in addition to many (very good) wines that are offered without a vineyard name appended.

How It's Changed: Barbaresco remained unknown long after Cavazza's radical, power-to-the Barbaresco-people action in 1894. It achieved recognition, then fame, and finally renown only when a wildly ambitious local producer named Angelo Gaja appeared on the world scene starting in the 1970s.

Gaja single-handedly brought Barbaresco to world attention by refashioning the wine using then-unknown-in-Italy small French oak barrels and charging unprecedented prices. While few people know about wine, *everybody's* an expert on money: Could this Gaja (guy-yah) really be worth *that* much money? The sheer chutzpah was captivating; so, too, it turned out, were the wines. Today, Gaja's single-vineyard bottlings ask—and get—$400 a bottle.

The changes in Barbaresco mirror those in Barolo (it's impossible to talk about them separately, so twinned are they in every respect). Foremost among them is emergence of a multitude of small grower estate-bottled wines, which was possible only as prices began to rise starting in the 1980s.

Second is the appearance of single-vineyard names on labels, which was unknown anywhere in the Langhe until (technically) the 1960s and (effectively) the 1980s.

Third, and hardly least, is today's multitude of winemaking styles ranging from oaky/supple to rustic/tannic/no oak traditionalism— and every permutation in between. This makes it tricky to know exactly which style of Barbaresco you're buying.

However, one thing is certain: The odds are greatly in your favor of getting a very fine wine if it says Barbaresco on the label—significantly more so, in fact, than with Barolo. The reason is Barbaresco's smaller size. Where Barolo sprawls across a number of less-than-ideal hillside exposures, Barbaresco's smaller scale ensures a more uniformly high level of vineyard sites. This puts the odds in your favor. Add to that the collectively high standards of its smaller band of producers and you've got a pretty safe bet.

Noteworthy Producers

PIERO BUSSO—A small grower in the Barbaresco zone's biggest town, Neive, Busso is a rising star offering two single-vineyard Barbarescos, both extremely fine. Look for the single-vineyard Barbarescos called Vigna Borgese (refined and austere) and the richer and more complete Vigna Santo Stefanetto.

CA' ROMÉ DI ROMANO MARENGO—A small grower in the village of Barbaresco offering well-made, modern-style Barbaresco. In addition to a good basic Barbaresco, look especially for the Maria di Brun bottling and, best of all, the single-vineyard Sorì Rio Sordo. Elegant, finely detailed wines that drink well young.

CASTELLO DI NEIVE—A large vineyard owner, Castello di Neive issues three versions from its exclusively owned Santo Stefano vineyard: a regular, a Riserva, and the smallest bottling of the three, La Rocca di

Santo Stefano. The style is admirably traditional: austere, detailed, and in justifiable need of aging. Castello di Neive's wines are often in the shadow of the monumentally good Barbaresco "Santo Stefano" made by Bruno Giacosa from grapes purchased from Castello di Neive.

CERETTO—Ceretto's Barbaresco winery is confusingly named Bricco Asili in honor (presumably) of their choice vineyard holding of the same name. (A *bricco* is the sun-catching crest of a hill.) So you have the redundantly named Bricco Asili Bricco Asili (I kid you not). There are two other single vineyard Barbarescos: Bernadot and Faset.

Ceretto's three Barbarescos are surely among this large producer's best wines. Made in a polished, early-drinking style, they are lovely examples of the graceful qualities of Barbaresco. Asili is the best of the three vineyards, creating more complete and finer wine; Bernadot is rich but lacks Asili's elegance and dimensionality; Faset is delicious, with an herbal quality.

GIUSEPPE CORTESE—A tiny producer offering an authentic, slightly rustic style of wine from the fine Rabajà vineyard. Very good quality.

ANGELO GAJA—Gaja used to be a fire-breathing radical in Piedmontese winemaking, having pioneered the use of small French barrels and a comparatively brief fermentation time—a couple of weeks compared to the month-long span in the 1970s and earlier.

Today he's mainstream. Other winemakers make wines that taste far oakier and more drink-now supple (almost fruit-juicy) from ultra-quick fermentations, as well as questionable gizmos such as vacuum concentrators (which mechanically remove water from the grape juice).

In addition to a very fine basic Barbaresco, which is still so-named, Gaja offers three single-vineyard Barbarescos that technically are labeled only as Langhe Rosso rather than Barbaresco. This is because Gaja adds about 6 percent Barbera to the Nebbiolo and the law says a Barbaresco must be 100 percent Nebbiolo. So Gaja said, effectively, "to hell with the law" and labeled his wine as Langhe Rosso, which allows for such blending.

Of course, everyone knows that these three single-vineyard

wines—Sorì Tildin, Sorì San Lorenzo, and Costa Russi—are really Barbarescos. And everyone who can pays dearly for them. They are very great wines. (*Sorì*—pronounced soo-*ree*—is Piedmontese dialect for a south-facing slope.) The wines are oaky when young but profound. They are among the world's—not just Italy's—greatest wines.

BRUNO GIACOSA—The great Piedmontese winemaker issues several Barbarescos, all glorious. Look for a great, robust, muscular single-vineyard Rabajà; a single-vineyard Asili that is easily the finest, richest, and most persuasive made today; and Giacosa's signature single-vineyard Santo Stefano, which is typically the most massive and long-lived of the three.

Bruno Giacosa is a traditionalist producer. You'll find no new oak in his wines and none needed. Should anyone doubt the continuing value and worth of traditional Piedmontese winemaking, they need only taste Bruno Giacosa's wines, preferably when the wines have a respectable amount of age on them, which means a decade or more after the vintage.

UGO LEQUIO—A small grower with just one Barbaresco from the Gallina vineyard. Bright, modern winemaking that improves almost with every vintage. To watch closely.

MARCHESI DI GRÉSY—Marchese Alberto di Grésy owns what many Barbaresco locals agree is the single best vineyard in the district, a thirty-acre site called Martinenga. Di Grésy makes three Barbaresco wines from Martinenga—one simply called Martinenga and two from subplots in that vineyard: Camp Gros (5.2 acres) and Gaiun (5.1 acres). All three are supremely elegant, supple wines made using small French oak barrels, but deftly so. They are beautifully detailed and represent some of the very best of Barbaresco. The two subplots are the pinnacle. In lesser vintages, they are included in the basic Martinenga bottling to achieve a higher overall standard.

MOCCAGATTA—Three single-vineyard Barbarescos: Basarin, Moccagatta, and a recent addition called Colé. Also, an exceptionally good basic Barbaresco. These are all very fine Barbarescos using small, new oak barrels. There's lovely substance to Moccagatta's wines, which serves them well over the long haul.

PAITIN DI PASQUERO-ELIA—A serious producer whose wines keep improving almost annually. Look for an excellent, rich Barbaresco Vecchie Vigne (old vines) and the signature single-vineyard Barbaresco Sorì Paitin, which is dense and layered. Although decidedly modern in style, there's no doubting the seriousness of the wine or the quality of the grapes. This is a producer that shows the possibilities of modernism in pursuit of traditional Barbaresco goodness.

CANTINA DEL PINO—A small producer creating lovely straight-down-the-middle Barbaresco from the superb Ovello vineyard. "Modern Classic" might best describe the style: The wines are clean, deeply flavorful, bright, and devoid of oakiness or winemaking flourishes. Worth seeking out.

PIO CESARE—This mainstay Piedmontese shipper has updated its winemaking in recent years, incorporating small oak barrels and generally freshening and brightening its wines, all for the better in this taster's opinion. The regular Barbaresco is straightforward, good, and largely devoid of apparent oak, while the Il Bricco bottling is richer, denser, and clearly marked by time spent in small new oak barrels. Both are excellent wines.

PRODUTTORI DEL BARBARESCO—The famous winegrowers cooperative is the backbone producer of the district. Its members own roughly 40 percent of all of the great vineyards in Barbaresco. The winemaking here is traditional (no small oak barrels at all) and straight-ahead. If you want a lesson in the true voice of Barbaresco's great single-vineyard *terroirs*, this is where you sign up as a student.

Seven single-vineyard Barbarescos are offered, but only in vintages that merit it. Otherwise they are added to the regular (good) basic Barbaresco that's always offered. Look for such single vineyards as Asili, Ovello, Montefico, Moccagatta, Montestefano, Rio Sordo, Rabajà, and Pora. The winemaking is traditional but modern, clean, and detailed. The single-vineyard bottlings are some of the best Barbaresco made today, as well as a superb value.

PRUNOTTO—This shipper offers two Barbarescos: a regular Barbaresco as well as a single-vineyard Bric Turot. Good, solid wines in a fruity, modern style with noticeable but not especially intrusive oakiness.

ROAGNA—A traditionalist producer whose wines take years to fully express themselves, but they are worth the wait. Roagna offers the single-vineyard Pajé and a special bottling of that same vineyard offered only in the best vintages called Crichët Pajé. These are very dense, rich, tannic-when-young wines that recall the best of another era.

SOTTIMANO—An ambitious producer in the sphere of influence of Bruno Giacosa (both are based in Neive, the biggest town in the Barbaresco zone), but preferring the use of small oak barrels. Nevertheless, the Giacosa influence must still be felt, as Andrea Sottimano's various Barbaresco bottlings are not especially oaky, thanks to excellent density. Look for single-vineyards such as Fausoni, Pajoré, Currà, and Cottà. All are dense, clearly long-lived, and impressively pure.

LA SPINETTA—Giorgio Rivetti is one of the stars of the Langhe, winning acclaim for his serious but decidedly modernistic wines. Although better known for Barbera and Moscato, Rivetti has expanded considerably in recent years, offering a regular Barbaresco and three single-vineyard Barbarescos: Vigneto Gallina, Vigneto Starderi, and Vigneto Valeirano. All are rich, lush wines with noticeable oak yet real backbone from dense wine material under the oak veneer.

VIETTI—The famed Barolo producer makes just one single-vineyard Barbaresco from the Masseria vineyard. But what a Barbaresco it is: dense, spicy, and seemingly limitless in its length. It's one of the finest Barbarescos made today.

What Do The Locals Eat With This Wine? Piedmont's cuisine is seemingly designed for Barbaresco, Barolo, and other red wines of high acidity, wafting perfume, and profound flavor. It's a rich cuisine embracing egg-intense fettuccine pasta (called tajarìn in dialect), braised meats, risotto, and a vast array of antipasti. Since Barbaresco and

Barolo are profound wines, they are reserved for comparably substantial dishes such as pasta, risotto, and, especially, meats such as braised beef, and game birds such as pheasant, rabbit, guinea hen, and the like.

One Man's Taste—Whose Wine Would I Buy? Price no object (or if you're paying), I'd buy Gaja's single vineyard bottlings such as Costa Russi, Sorì San Lorenzo, and, especially, Sorì Tildin. Ditto for Bruno Giacosa's Barbaresco "Santo Stefano" bottling. But in the real world, I actually reach for the single vineyards of the Produttori del Barbaresco, Cantina del Pino, Roagna, di Grésy, and Vietti.

Worth Searching For? Don't die without trying it. Barbaresco is one of the world's greatest red wines, especially if you can have a properly mature (ten-plus years) bottling from a top producer.

Similar Wines From The Same Neighborhood: Barolo, Nebbiolo delle Langhe, and Langhe Rosso

Barbera d'Alba
Barbera d'Asti

(bar-*bear*-ah *dahl*-bah/bar-*bear*-ah *dahss*-tee)
RED

Region: Piedmont (northwestern Italy)

Grape: 100 percent Barbera (red). At its best, Barbera is a deeply colored red wine with lush, plush tastes of cherries, raspberries, blackberries, and a bit of spice. Significantly, it's one of the least tannic red grapes in common production. However, Barbera is noticeably high in acidity, making it ideal for the rich Piedmontese cuisine. The lesser stuff is thin, screechy red wine; top-quality Barbera, however, can verge on being considered truly great wine, with substantial fruit, flavor, and depth.

The Tradition: Barbera is Italy's Cinderella grape. Because it's so vigorous, hardy, and high-yielding, it was widely planted in Piedmont (and elsewhere in Italy) to create a cheap, everyday, scullery-maid sort of wine. But, *à la* Cinderella, there was real beauty lurking beneath, just waiting to be discovered.

Unfortunately, things got worse before they got (much) better. After the sap-sucking root louse called phylloxera devastated Piedmont's vineyards in the late 1800s, Barbera was planted in vast quantities. It was the peasant's grape, growing well in less-than-ideal exposures (unlike Nebbiolo). Its abundant yields were no crime from the starving farmers' point of view. So up until the 1980s, in Piedmont if it was cheap and of no account, it was Barbera.

How It's Changed: A handful of producers always *believed* in Barbera. Despite derisory prices, they grew their Barbera vines in choice sites, creating wines of uncommon depth, dimension, and longevity. Mostly it was for family and friends, along with a small, impassioned coterie of Barbera lovers. ("We few, we happy few, we band of brothers.") These committed producers created a Barbera renaissance, which spawned lavish praise, new appreciation, and—it had to happen—higher prices.

How did they do it? In a word, quality. Yields were slashed, the better to create unprecedentedly rich, intense, concentrated wines. Choice sites that might plausibly have been granted to Nebbiolo were assigned to Barbera (although the very best sites, rightly, are always accorded to the lordly Nebbiolo).

Oh, and there was one other ingredient: oak. In the 1980s and, especially, the 1990s, Piedmont's most ambitious winemakers fell in love with using small French oak barrels.

Putting the lowly Barbera into the oak "glass slipper"—if you'll forgive the mixed metaphor—transformed the scullery maid Barbera into something considerably more aristocratic. Suddenly, *la* Barbera became fashionable. Desirable. Eligible. It was invited to all the best tables. And, of course, it was treated to high prices, too.

Small oak barrels give Barbera textural polish. They're also a kind of make-up, hiding the faint rubber scent that the grape variety can exhibit. The wine's color is deeper and stays that way longer thanks to the tannin molecules of the oak "fixing" the anthocyanins or color pigments of wine, making them more stable and less prone to oxidation.

However, the best Barbera isn't always oaky. Some Barberas see no oak at all—and don't need it. However handled, great Barbera is all about dense, rich fruit, a powerful, faintly spicy perfume, and a brisk, palate-cleansing acidity.

The Difference Between Barbera d'Alba and Barbera d'Asti: Does one exist? Yes. Is it a massive, unmistakable-in-a-blind-tasting difference? It is not. Barbera d'Alba comes from vines in the Langhe zone, a former seabed with chalky clay characterized by a repeating array of freestanding, steep-sloped hills with tight cleavages. Barbera d'Alba from good exposures in the Langhe is dense and meaty and can have a noticeable minerality.

Barbera d'Asti also comes from a hilly, but much more open, land-scape. Compared to the compressed, almost brooding Langhe, the Astigiana, as it's called, is "big sky" country. It's also Barbera country. Where Nebbiolo is king in the Langhe, Barbera reigns in the Astigiana. Barbera is the most widely planted grape in the Asti area. Because of that, the Astigiana is also the source of a lot of crummy Barberas produced by lowest-common-denominator winegrowers' cooperatives content with low prices and mediocre (or worse) quality.

However, precisely because there's so much Barbera grown in the Astigiana, there's also a lot of really good vineyards in choice locations. But only now are these vineyards being segregated and the vines and wine treated respectfully and carefully. Many Piedmontese wine insid-ers believe that in the next decade or two, Piedmont's greatest Barberas will come preponderantly from the Asti zone rather than the Langhe.

Is an Asti-area Barbera different from an Alba-area version? For this palate, Barbera d'Asti seems a little higher in apparent, perceivable acidity than Barbera d'Alba—the wines being of equal quality, of course. Because of this higher apparent acidity, Barbera d'Asti can seem slightly lighter in texture and not quite as meaty as Barbera d'Alba.

At this writing, the absolute pinnacle of the Barbera quality pyra-mid is still occupied by Barbera d'Alba. But Barbera d'Asti is gaining fast—very fast.

Noteworthy Producers of Barbera d'Alba

ELIO ALTARE—Exemplary small oak barrel-aged Barbera, with a single-vineyard Vigna Larigi.

CERETTO—Single vineyard called Piana. Fresh, fruity style Barbera, but no oak. Old vines.

DOMENICO CLERICO—New-style Barbera that's high quality but very oaky, with strong vanilla scent.

ALDO CONTERNO—Single vineyard called Conca Tre Pile. Great vineyard site in Barolo zone. Sees time in small oak barrels. One of the most successful of all new-style Barberas.

GIACOMO CONTERNO—Classic, traditionally made Barbera from old vines in the Barolo district in the Serralunga d'Alba area. Absolutely no oak. One of Piedmont's greatest Barberas.

GIUSEPPE CORTESE—Excellent traditional Barbera from Trifolera vineyard in the Barbaresco district.

BRUNO GIACOSA—Single vineyard called Altavilla. No oak. Superb traditionally made Barbera.

ELIO GRASSO—Single vineyard called Vigna Martina, which is a subplot of the Barolo-zone vineyard called Gavarini. Sees time in small oak barrels but with great deftness. One of the best new-style Barberas.

MARCARINI—Single vineyard called Ciabot Camerano in the La Morra district of the Barolo zone. Traditional. Very concentrated, soft, and rich. A *ciabot* (chah-*booht*) is Piedmontese dialect for a small worker's hut in the middle of a vineyard, used as a refuge and to store tools.

GIUSEPPE MASCARELLO—Two single-vineyard Barberas: Fasana and Ginestra. Both traditional, both superb. Fasana is the lighter of the two; Ginestra (a famous Barolo-zone vineyard near Monforte d'Alba) is fuller, richer, more complete.

MOCCAGATTA—Single vineyard called Vigneto Basarin in the Barbaresco zone. New style, aged in small oak barrels. Excellent vineyard; exemplar of new style Barbera.

E. PIRA DI CHIARA BOSCHIS—Tiny producer offering a rich, intense Barbera d'Alba of exceptional quality.

PRUNOTTO—Single vineyard called Pian Romualdo in Barolo zone. Pian Romualdo is one of the Barolo zone's greatest Barbera sites. Rich, intense, round.

PAOLO SCAVINO—One of the finest of small oak barrel-aged Barberas from two vineyards in the Barolo zone near Castiglione Falletto: Fiasco and Codana. Very rich and concentrated, as well as oak-influenced. A special barrel selection of Scavino's best barrels is proprietarily named Carati, which is indeed superior to Scavino's already very fine regular Barbera d'Alba.

VAJRA—Single vineyard called Bricco delle Viole in the Barolo zone. No oak. Very pure-tasting.

VIETTI—Great Barbera specialist with several offerings. Barbera d'Alba "Scarrone Vyd." is austere, profound, very long-lived. Oaky when young, it absorbs the oak after five years or so. A very small-production old-vine bottling called Scarrone Vigna Vecchia is also offered. It may well be the single best Barbera made anywhere in the Langhe. (See Barbera d'Asti producers.)

ROBERTO VOERZIO—Single vineyard called Pozzo dell'Annuziata in the Barolo zone near La Morra. Huge, very rich, oaky. Bottled only in magnums. Ultra-expensive.

Noteworthy Producers of Barbera d'Asti

BRAIDA DI GIACOMO BOLOGNA—Three single-vineyard Barberas: Ai Suma, Bricco della Bigotta, and Bricco dell'Uccellone. Also a Barbera called La Monella, which is lightly fizzy or frizzante, a once-common style that is fading from use. The late Giacomo Bologna ignited the fashion for small oak barrel-aged Barberas. He single-handedly brought respect to Barbera d'Asti, as well as achieving unprecedented prices. The Ai Suma bottling is fresh and perfumey; Bricco della Bigotta is more austere and finer. The signature wine is Bricco dell'Uccellone, which is rich, intense, and very oaky, as well as the most expensive of the three.

CASCINA CASTLE'T (VIGNA MALABAILA)—Owner-winemaker Maria Borio is well-known in Piedmont for creating lovely wines with a certain modernity. Her beautifully packaged Barbera d'Asti is her signature wine. The label, by the way, is one of the most charming you'll ever see, with a 1950s photograph of four little girls in colorful dresses sitting and standing on an old Vespa scooter. It conveys the light irresistibility of this lovely, smooth, intensely fruity Barbera. Look also for an intense, haunting *passito* (dried-berry) version of Barbera called Passum. Cascina Castle't is one of today's top Barbera d'Asti producers.

LA SPINETTA (CA' DI PIAN)—Very possibly the most ambitious Barbera d'Asti producer today, owner Giorgio Rivetti offers two stunning, decidedly modern Barbera d'Asti wines and a Barbera d'Alba. Barbera d'Asti Superiore is far richer, more intense, and flat-out luxurious than its modest designation would suggest. The single-vineyard Ca di Pian is Rivetti's signature Barbera: dense, oaky, and rich. Look also for a lovely Barbera d'Alba from the Gallina vineyard in the Barbaresco zone. All are quite oaky but substantive.

RENATO RATTI—The famed Barolo producer has purchased vineyards in Barbera d'Asti, creating superb wines.

SCARPA—Three single-vineyard Barbera d'Asti bottlings: Il Piazzaro, La Bogliona, and Bricchi di Castelrocchero. All three are extremely traditional in style and superb examples of old-fashioned Barbera d'Asti at its best. Scarpa is a producer of numerous wines, all old-fashioned in style and substantive.

RENATO TRINCHERO—Two single-vineyards: Vigna del Noce and La Barslina. Vigna del Noce is arguably the greatest traditionally made Barbera d'Asti made today, from old vines dating to 1929. La Barslina is another old vineyard (1936), but unlike Vigna del Nice (they are contiguous), Both rival, in their fashions, the best Barbera d'Alba bottlings.

VIETTI—Two Barbera d'Asti bottlings: Tre Vigne and La Crena. The former is elegant and early drinking; La Crena is one of the great Barbera d'Asti bottlings, capable of rivaling the best Alba offerings.

OTHER GOOD BARBERA D'ASTI PRODUCERS: Bricco Mondalino (Vigna Il Bergantino), Carnevale (Il Crotino), Coppo (Camp du Rouss), La Fagianella (Vigneto Garavagna), Achille Ferraris (Vigneto Nobbio), Renato Rabezzana (Il Bricco), Enrico Vaudano, Viarengo (Vigna Morra)

What Do The Locals Eat With This Wine? Precisely because Barbera was always the "peasant's wine," the foods traditionally paired with Barbera have always been associated with what's known as *la cucina povera*, the cuisine of the poor. A favorite pairing during the late fall and winter was (and is) the warm anchovy and olive oil dip called *bagna cauda*. Tajarìn or tagliatelle is a frequent partner, especially when served with a meat sauce. Polenta, that staple of *la cucina povera*, is almost always partnered with Barbera.

These days, Barbera lovers on both sides of the Atlantic take such pleasure and pride in today's great Barberas that they serve the wine in big Riedel glasses usually reserved for Burgundies or Barolos. And the wine is served with the best aged steaks, braised meats, game, and the like. Of course, you can't go wrong with a good burger, pasta, or pizza, but the best Barberas now deserve headliner status.

One Man's Taste—Whose Wine Would I Buy? The choices are vast, but my top two picks are always the same: Giacomo Conterno and Vietti's Scarrone Vigne Vecchia. Also Elio Grasso's Vigna Martina. In Barbera d'Asti, I love Trinchero's Vigna del Noce, but it hasn't been imported to America for some time.

Worth Searching For? Absolutely worth an effort

Similar Wines From The Same Neighborhood: Any other Barberas from Piedmont such as Barbera del Monferrato and Barbera Colli Tortonesi. Also, various Langhe Rosso bottlings incorporate greater or lesser amounts of Barbera in their blends. Still, nothing beats a 100 percent Barbera.

Bardolino

(bahr-doe-*lee*-noh)
RED

Region: Veneto (northern Italy near Lake Garda)

Grapes: Corvina Veronese (35 to 65 percent); Rondinella (10 to 40 percent); Molinara (10 to 20 percent); Negrara (up to 10 percent); up to 15 percent of any or all of the following grapes: Rossignola, Barbera, Sangiovese, and Garganega

The Tradition: What the gods wish to destroy they first make fashionable. That, in essence, is the story of Bardolino. A small village near tourist-intensive Lake Garda, the light, easy-to-drink and easy-to-like red wine blend called Bardolino was the local tipple at every trattoria in the area. Why shouldn't tourists take home not just a memory of their *dolce vita*, but a bottle or two of the wine that helped make it possible?

You know what happened next. What started out (back in the 1950s, when tourism intensified) as a charming, light red wine of genuine savor grown in the hills became an industrial, bland, utterly banal red wine pumped out in vast quantities from vineyards on the valley floor. (It was the same story for Soave's white wine.)

The old tradition of Bardolino was one of delicacy and real flavor. It wasn't then, and isn't now, a wine to be cellared for decades. But just because a wine isn't stern, time-defying stuff doesn't mean it can't have character. Bardolino *does* have character. To achieve it, yields must be low; the vines should be on hillsides; and the red wine, although lightish in color, should deliver a surprisingly intense cherry-pit taste and scent, which suggests a slightly bitter, mouthwatering quality allied to pleasing cherry-flavored fruitiness.

How It's Changed: Regrettably, not for the better. In the 1980s, the local producers, seeing their sales (rightly) decline thanks to low standards and sheer banality took an even more commercial route: They decided to imitate Beaujolais nouveau. So fermentations got even shorter, and a light, very fruity, utterly uninteresting Bardolino "*novello*" was born. Unless it puts money in your pockets (instead of out of it), I'd suggest you avoid Bardolino *novello*.

I'd like to say that, embarrassed by the error of their ways, Bardolino's producersare grasping their way back to greatness. They aren't. (Their next-door neighbors in Valpolicella are, however. See page 145.) The vast majority of Bardolino bottlings aren't worth your time, attention, or money.

Noteworthy Producers: Few producers deserve commendation. However, precisely because a really good Bardolino is worthwhile, you should certainly seek out the few good, upright producers in Bardolino. Foremost among themis Guerrieri-Rizzardi. Look also for Corte Gardoni. Big producers such as Bolla and Bertani deserve a pass, even if they are, not surprisingly, the most frequently seen versions on the shelf.

What Do The Locals Eat With This Wine? Because of Bardolino's intrinsic lightness, it tends to be the first red wine served, which means it typically accompanies various meats in an antipasto plate such as salami and prosciutto. Or it is served with the pasta course.

One Man's Taste—Whose Wine Would I Buy? Guerrieri-Rizzardi is easily my top choice. I might take a chance on a small producer, especially if it is recommended by a trustworthy merchant who invokes the magic phrase, "This isn't the usual Bardolino." Otherwise, pass.

Worth Searching For? Only if you're there

Similar Wines From The Same Neighborhood: Valpolicella

Barolo

(bah-*row*-loh)

RED

Region: Piedmont (northwest Italy)

Grapes: 100 percent Nebbiolo (red) (See Barbaresco, page 51)

The Tradition: No Italian wine is more significant than Barolo. It carries the banner of Italian red wine greatness the way Bordeaux's first growths and Burgundy's *grands crus* do for France. Until the late twentieth century, Barolo was the only Italian red wine the world viewed as great, although that doesn't mean that many non-Italians actually drank it. Barolo was more heard about than tasted.

Because of this acclaim and (relative) fame, Barolo has the strongest and proudest sense of tradition of any Italian wine district. The cliché about Barolo is that it is the "wine of kings and the king of wines," which propagandistic claptrap the locals actually believed, such was (and is) their pride.

The wine itself, always 100 percent Nebbiolo by law, takes its name from the small town of Barolo, which is located deep within the undulating set of freestanding hills called the Langhe. That name was derived from "tongues" (*lingue*), which the hills were fancifully thought to resemble. (It's sometimes also seen in Piedmontese dialect as Langa.) Two zones—Barolo and Barbaresco—collectively comprise the Langhe.

For centuries, Nebbiolo has been the pride of the Langhe. It's a beast of a grape, highly acidic and ferociously tannic. Its flavors, though, are original and somehow magical. Classically described as having intermingled tastes of tar and roses, only in the Langhe, specifically in its Barolo and Barbaresco districts, is Nebbiolo fully resonant. The Langhe is to Nebbiolo what Burgundy's famed Côte d'Or is to Pinot Noir.

When I was researching my book on Piedmontese cuisine (*A Passion for Piedmont: Italy's Most Glorious Regional Table*), I talked about the old methods of making Barolo with Aldo Conterno (born 1931) who is one of Barolo's greatest winemakers. Conterno recalled how brutally tough their wines used to be, practically furry with tannins from the extended maceration of the fermenting juice with the tannin-rich skins they once used, like a cup of tea where the tea bag was left in far too long.

"I remember when my father, and other winemakers of his generation, used to put their Barolos on the roof to soften them up," he said. "In the old days the Barolos were so tannic, because of how they were fermented. They used to leave the juice and then the brand-new wine in the vat with the tannin-rich grape skins for two months or more. Today, the whole maceration process rarely goes for much more than thirty days.

"After the wines were drawn off from the skins, the Barolo would remain in casks for five, six, seven years, sometimes even more," he said. "And then it would be transferred from the cask into glass demijohns. Even then, the wine could still be pretty tannic. So sometimes, to soften it up, they would put the demijohns outside, on the roof, for the summer and part of the winter. Of course it was oxidized all to hell by then," notes Conterno, "but anyway, they liked that taste."

How It's Changed: Change didn't really arrive in Barolo until the 1970s. And even then, what changes occurred didn't coalesce into a full-scale cultural revision until well into the 1980s. It's as recent as that.

The first change was technical. Instead of fermenting the wine on its tannin-rich skins for one or two months, the maceration period was reduced to weeks and, for a radical few, even mere days. In addition came the use of new small French oak barrels called *barriques*, which hold 225 liters or 60 gallons. These were commonly used in Bordeaux and Burgundy but were unknown in Barolo, where large, old casks called *botte* were employed.

These new barrels gave Barolo a scent of vanilla (from the new oak), as well as fixed the unstable pigments in Nebbiolo, preventing them from quickly shading to a kind of orange-mahogany, which was Barolo's traditional color. So Barolo's "new" color now more resembled Burgundy and Bordeaux, which were and are the world's standard for how an older red wine should look.

The combination of shorter fermentations and the use of small new oak barrels created fresher-tasting and fresher-looking Barolo. Where before Barolo was all about an ethereal but oxidized scent and taste, modern Barolo captures the berryishness of fresh Nebbiolo, along with preserving a brighter, deeper, redder hue.

The other change was a transformation of how the Langaroli themselves viewed—and presented—their own vineyards. Until the 1980s, the great majority of Barolos were given to us by shippers. These shippers didn't own much, if any, land themselves. There was no need. The grapes were theirs for the asking, as Barolo had no tradition of estate or grower bottling. That first arrived only in the 1960s with just a handful of producers. Estate bottling increased slowly in the '70s and only really caught fire in the 1980s and '90s. Indeed, estate bottling in Barolo continues to accelerate to this day.

One of the important effects of the arrival of estate bottling—which means a wine made and bottled by the person growing the grapes—is a greater attention to, and proclamation of, single-vineyard bottlings. Shippers, of necessity as well as convenience, blended numerous vineyard plots into a single commercial wine. They submitted—and still do—that such a blend is superior to its parts. (Shippers everywhere *always* say that. Sometimes it's even true.)

But growers typically have such small holdings (the average vineyard holding in the Langhe is just four acres) that there's not much latitude for blending. And, close to their vineyard plots as they are, there's not much inclination either. So for the first time ever, the world became aware, thanks to single-vineyard-designated Barolos, of the exquisite sensitivity of Nebbiolo as a grape to its site and of the multifaceted, highly localized particularities of the Barolo zone. This was a revelation—and a revolution.

The revolution is now largely accomplished. Today, the challenge that remains is one of incremental but vital gradations of quality, which are achieved through expensive rigor in the vineyard and winery, greater nuance in the use of oak and new winemaking techniques, and willingness for short-term sacrifice in exchange for long-term reputation.

This last factor is noteworthy because the price of Barolo soared in the late 1990s and early 2000s. Not even in their wildest fancies had Barolo producers imagined commanding such prices, equal to those of *grands crus* Burgundies. Inevitably, greed set in, along with an occasional cynical complacency. A subsequent downturn in the market brought some of the younger producers (who had no personal memory of anything other than sunny success) back to earth. Prices remain high, however.

Noteworthy Producers (The Traditionalists / The Modernists): Barolo has numerous producers, the number of which increases almost annually as growers who previously sold their grapes to shippers or the big local winegrowers' cooperative, Terre del Barolo, create their own wines, thereby adding yet another label to Barolo's trove.

Distinguishing among Barolo producers goes beyond just assessing quality. Style now plays a major role. It was easier a decade ago: Modernists were then clearly distinguishable from traditionalists. Today, the middle ground is, if anything, the most heavily populated.

These "centrists" take what they believe are most desirable from the modernist camp (small oak barrels; rotofermenters, which extract flavor and color in a short time through an agitator device; short macerations) and apply those techniques with a traditionalist hand—not too much oak, not too short a maceration, not too vigorous a use of the washing machine-like rotofermenter.

With this in mind, the following producers fall roughly into these camps. Keep in mind that Barolo, more than many zones, is still in a state of aesthetic flux. Producers who enthusiastically pursued certain extremes are now, after seeing the results from a half-dozen or so vintages, recalibrating their techniques and personal palates.

Also, Barolo is more strongly affected than many districts by market demand. Precisely because it gets such high prices and attention—and because this worldwide attention is so new and possibly tenuous—Barolo producers are that much more sensitive to critical and consumer opinion. When you work the high (price) wire, you have to keep a close watch on every little quiver.

The following producers, without exception, are all worth pursuing. They represent the best of their respective camps. And, truth be told, they may very well modulate or revise their winemaking depending upon the vintage, making that year's wines a little more or a little less "traditional" or "modern." So don't let the categories sway you overly. Each has its merits.

Veering Towards The Modern

ELIO ALTARE—One of the most aggressively modernistic Barolo producers, Altare is a believer in short macerations, new small oak barrels, and the creation of supple, pleasing Barolos. His Barolos, all offered in tiny quantities (he makes little more than 3,400 cases divided among various wines, some labeled Langhe Rosso), have a strong international following for they are indeed appetizing, early-maturing, easily accessible wines of genuine quality and depth. Altare's winemaking motto could well be, "Who says you can't have it all?"

AZELIA—Located next door to the Paolo Scavino winery (the family vineyard was divided, with both Azelia and Scavino owning parts of the Barolo vineyard Bricco Fiasco), Azelia was a more traditional winery that signed on to the modernist manifesto in the 1990s. Lovely, intense wines with noticeable oakiness. Look especially for the signature Bricco Fiasco, with the less distinctive Barolo San Rocco a qualitative distance behind.

CERETTO—A large shipper with sizable vineyard holdings. The Ceretto (cheh-*reh*-toh) brothers—winemaker Marcello and marketer

Bruno—were among the earliest and most persuasive of the modernists. Advocates of short fermentations but, interestingly, not in favor of small new oak barrels, the Cerettos pressed the case for Langhe modernity to the world. Quality is high; the wines are supple and pristine; the packaging (and prices) are high-style. The Cerettos have always pursued a certain *bella figura* to better showcase their modernistic cause. Look especially for the Barolos labeled Bricco Rocche and the single-vineyard Brunate, as well as Prapò.

MICHELE CHIARLO—Founded in 1956 and still run by its namesake owner, Michele Chiarlo (mee-*keh*-leh kee-*are*-loh) is one of the largest vineyard owners in the Langhe. He's also one of the most ambitious. Chiarlo's sizable business is based on a substantial wine production from outlying Piedmontese wine zones such as Gavi (bland white wines from the Cortese grape), Asti Spumante, and Barbera d'Asti.

With the wealth generated from these more commercial wines, Chiarlo began buying parcels of such choice Barolo vineyards as Cannubi, Cerequio, and Rocche, among others. Firmly in the modernist camp, employing small oak barrels and moderate fermentation times, the quality of Chiarlo Barolos is steadily improving. That said, these wines—which ask a healthy price—have yet to ascend to the top rank, although that clearly is the aspiration. Look especially for the single-vineyard Barolos: Cannubi, Cerequio, and Rocche. If Chiarlo is ever to be a star, it is with these exceptional vineyards where he will shine.

DOMENICO CLERICO—Another of the Langhe's most resolute modernists, Domenico Clerico creates some of the richest, most opulent and lush Barolos, rivaled only by his colleagues Roberto Voerzio and Luciano Sandrone. A believer in low yields, a lot of oak, and a winemaking style that emphasizes intense fruitiness and soft, almost imperceptible tannins, Clerico's wines are highly sought after and much-praised.

Three single-vineyard Barolos are offered: Pajanà (a plot within the Ginestra vineyard); Percristina (literally "for Cristina," a daughter who died at seven years old; from the Mosconi vineyard in Monforte d'Alba); and Ciabot Mentin Ginestra (another subplot of the Ginestra vineyard; a *ciabot* is dialect for a small hut in the middle of a field or vineyard where a farmer stores his equipment). All are very rich, intense, deeply colored, oaky, and striking. They're also serious and rigorous achievements in contemporary Barolo.

CONTERNO-FANTINO—Guido Fantino has created ever-finer, decidedly modern Barolos from his Barolo vineyards in the Monforte d'Alba zone. (Despite the Conterno name and Monforte d'Alba location, there is no relation to the two more famous Conterno brothers, Aldo and the late Giovanni.)

Conterno-Fantino Barolos represent some of the most attractive of modernistic Barolos: glossy but not overripe or over-extracted. There's some obvious oak, but it's not heavy-handed. There's real balance here. Look for the two single-vineyard Barolos: Vigna del Gris and, especially, Sorì Ginestra.

CORDERO DI MONTEZEMOLO—One of the early, foremost modernists, the Barolos of Cordero di Montezemolo originally emphasized brief fermentations to create supple, early-maturing Barolos of real quality. That was the pioneering path of the late Paolo Cordero di Montezemolo, a gentle, intellectual man of great integrity. After his death in 1987, his two sons, Gianni and Enrico (who joined the winery in 1981), took over.

Today, the wines are as fine as ever, although the use of oak is prominent. Yields remain low, and the wines, despite their suppleness, approachability, and early-drinking affability, actually go the distance better than one might suspect. They age beautifully. Three Barolos are offered, all superb: Monfalletto, Vigna Enrico VI, and Bricco Gattera.

DAMILANO—An old family holding that, starting in 1996, took a sharp turn for the qualitative better thanks to a new generation at the helm. Although a small estate with little more than a dozen acres of vines, the locations are choice, notably with a holding the Cannubi vineyard as well as Liste and Fossati vineyards. Modern, somewhat oaky wines of great intensity and genuine depth. Look especially for the Cannubi. This is a Barolo producer to watch.

ANGELO GAJA—The undisputed king of Piedmontese winemaking, as well as Italy's premier modernist, Angelo Gaja made his name with his groundbreaking use of small new oak barrels with Barbaresco rather than Barolo. Indeed, Gaja didn't even offer a Barolo until the 1989 vintage, with the purchase of a vineyard in the Serralunga d'Alba zone, creating the wine he calls Sperss. ("Sperss" is dialect for "nostalgia," referring to an earlier, pre-1961 era, when the Gaja winery used to make Barolo from purchased grapes, a practice discontinued after Angelo Gaja took control of the family business.)

After 1989, Gaja subsequently bought yet more Barolo property, securing a large parcel of the Cerequio vineyard, which Barolo wine Gaja calls Conteisa. ("Conteisa" is dialect for "quarrel," referring to an ancient dispute between the communes of La Morra and Barolo for possession of the Cerequio land, which was settled by written agreement in 1216.)

Although Angelo Gaja was Piedmont's original wine revolutionary, his winemaking today is now almost—but not quite—centrist, if only because more extremist producers have come along to seize the revolutionary crown. (Using small new oak barrels in Italy today is about as radical as ordering a cappuccino at the local caffè.)

An example of Gaja's near-centrism is the winery's middle road on fermentation times: The Barolos are fermented at a relatively high temperature for one week and then allowed to finish fermenting at a lower temperature for an additional two weeks. The wines age in new small oak barrels for one year, with an additional year in large oak casks. These days, all that is borderline conventional, although certainly modern.

The two Gaja Barolos are noticeably oaky, although their depth and concentration are such that the oak is absorbed and amalgamated over time. Both Sperss and Conteisa are highly polished wines, with supple tannins and well-delineated, precise flavors. Both wines have small amounts (6 to 8 percent) of Barbera added, mostly to deepen the color. This is why neither wine is labeled as Barolo, as Italian wine law requires Barolo wines to be 100 percent Nebbiolo.

SILVIO GRASSO—Grasso is a common name in the Langhe (like Conterno and Giacosa). Sometimes the relations are clear, and often there's no family relation at all, at least not within living memory. Silvio Grasso is a decidedly modern producer who has an uncommonly deft touch in using his small oak barrels. Grasso's Barolos are all lush, intense, concentrated wines, yet there's still a noteworthy restraint. At least six different single-vineyard Barolos are offered by this estate, all surprisingly qualitatively equal or nearly so.

ANDREA OBERTO—Very rich, lush, rather extracted-tasting Barolos with noticeable oakiness. There's no doubting the quality of the three Barolos offered by this small producer (a regular Barolo, plus two single vineyards: Vigneto Albarella and Vigneto Rocche). They are intense and sleek and pop out in blind tastings thanks to a lush, come-hither quality. They are—dare I say it?—flashy. One wishes for a little more detail and restraint because the underlying material is very fine.

ARMANDO PARUSSO—It's hard to know quite where to place Parusso. Until the early 2000s, Parusso threaded between traditionalism and a touch-of-oak modernity. Of late, however, the wines seem to be veering more strongly to a full embrace of many modernistic touches, such as the use of small oak barrels for two years' worth of aging. Perhaps this is related to the completion of a new winery in 2000. Or it's just a palate evolution. Or maybe just good business—or all three.

That acknowledged, Parusso's Barolos exhibit a fine delineation of flavors. Five single-vineyard Barolos are offered. The best bets are Vigna Fiurin and, especially, Bussia.

E. PIRA DI CHIARA BOSCHIS—In 1990, Chiara Boschis took over the tiny (six acres of vines) E. Pira winery, which is literally across the street from her family's venerable winery called Borgogno, run by her brothers. After a bit of experimentation, she has settled into a winemaking style that creates exceptionally intense, lush, slightly oaky Barolo from the great Cannubi vineyard. Chiara Boschis' Cannubi bottling is today among the finest versions of this long-underachieving site. Others own parcels of Cannubi as well, so the competition for the crown is increasing. But E. Pira di Chiara Boschis is currently a benchmark along with (ironically) the staunchly traditionalist producer Giuseppe Rinaldi.

LUCIANO SANDRONE—Sandrone is a persuasive proponent of the lush, intense, soft style of Barolo. He offers two Barolos: a signature Cannubi Boschis (the 85-acre Cannubi vineyard is divided into five subplots: Cannubi, Cannubi Muscatel, Cannubi San Lorenzo, Cannubi Valleta and Cannubi Boschis) and Le Vigne, a blend of several vineyards as the (plural) name suggests. Both Barolos are rich, intense, and decidedly oaky and striking, as well as serious—and successful—attempts at marrying the modern demand for early accessibility with the backbone required for the long-term ageability expected of Barolo.

PAOLO SCAVINO—Enrico Scavino is one of the masters of modernity in the Langhe, constantly tinkering and refining his wines to better showcase his great rigor in his vineyard work. Early efforts with oak in the mid-1980s were heavy-handed (like so many others, in fairness). Today, Scavino has a far more deft touch, delivering flavor intensity and real substance with an oak-influenced stylishness.

Four Barolos are offered: a very fine "basic" Barolo, a much oakier "Carobric," a superb Cannubi vineyard that carries its oak quite well, the flagship Bric del Fiasc bottling that delivers an especially attractive austerity, and the soft, rich, oaky Rocche Annunziata bottling, which is Scavino's most expensive wine. For this taster, the regular Barolo, the Cannubi, and the Bric del Fiasc bottlings represent the best of Scavino's efforts.

GIANNI VOERZIO—Although overshadowed by the acclaim showered upon Roberto Voerzio, the wines of Gianni Voerzio are rightfully among Barolo's best as well. Soft, lush, and noticeably oaky, Gianni Voerzio creates a classic La Serra vineyard bottling from Barolo's La Morra zone.

ROBERTO VOERZIO—One of Barolo's superstars, Roberto Voerzio invariably wins lavish praise for his equally lavish, hugely intense Barolos, of which he offers six: La Serra, Brunate, Cerequio, Bricco

Rocche dell'Annunziata Torriglione, Sarmassa (adjacent to Cerequio), and Vecchie Viti dei Capalot e delle Brunate.

Roberto Voerzio's vineyard yields are famously very low, resulting in Barolos of immense depth and lush intensity, which are given a noticeably oaky veneer from the use of new small oak barrels. These are wines of high, perhaps even excessive, extraction, formidable alcohol from grapes picked at the edge (or over) of ultraripeness and sheer opulence.

Not surprisingly, Voerzio's Barolos make a big impact, especially in tastings where they leap out. The quality is undeniable. There's no calculation here, just an attempt to pursue the flavor limits of Barolo. The resulting wines are very much a matter of taste, as their opulence borders on the flamboyant. They are saved from Liberace-like excess by the serious substance of the wines.

Centrists—Right Down The Middle

ELVIO COGNO POGGIO PETORCHINO—A famous name in Barolo, Elvio Cogno was the longtime winemaker for Marcarini winery in La Morra. After leaving Marcarini in the late 1980s, Cogno founded his own namesake winery in 1990 in another part of the Barolo zone near the town of Novello. Today, the wines are made by Cogno's son-in-law, Walter Fissore. Solid, rich wines with some modernity (oak is used). Two Barolos are offered called Ravera and Elena. Both are muscular, intense, and clearly destined for longevity.

ALDO CONTERNO—One of the great masters of Barolo, Aldo Conterno has consistently navigated a down-the-middle course with his wines, especially the Barolos. The winery is today run by Conterno's three sons. Aldo Conterno raised eyebrows in Barolo when, in the mid-'90s, he began producing Barolos using a rotofermenter, which not only shortens fermentation time but also extracts deep color and flavor.

Conterno insists that with nuanced and knowing use, this computer-controlled device can tease out all of the berryish aspects of the Nebbiolo grape while avoiding the tarry element that comes from Nebbiolo's substantial tannins, which are inevitably drawn out during a long fermentation.

That would put Conterno decidedly in the modernist camp except that Aldo Conterno personally loathes the taste of oak in Barolo. "It may be a good wine, even a great wine," he says of Barolos that see time in small oak barrels. "But for me, if it has oak it's not Barolo." Other Conterno wines, however, such as Barbera and basic Nebbiolo, see oak aging. "Those are my boys' wines," says Conterno, further noting rather gruffly that a winegrower has got to make a living and consumers like oak. Conterno might be best described as a stubborn realist.

The proof is in the tasting, and the new-style Aldo Conterno Barolos are still among the zone's very greatest wines. Time has shown that although the Barolos do seem more supple when young than in the pre-rotofermenter days (before the 1995 vintage), with age they very closely resemble the earlier style. This is because Conterno's vineyard yields are admirably low and the sites themselves superb and distinctive.

Several Barolos are offered: the "basic" Bussia Soprana, two single vineyards Colonello and Cicala, and the only-in-the-best-vintages Granbussia. All are magnificent. For this taster, the standout wines are the single-vineyard Colonello and, especially, Cicala. All are laser-sharp in the flavor delineations and beautifully balanced without obvious extraction. These are benchmark Barolos.

LUIGI EINAUDI—Luigi Einaudi, who died in 1961, was renowned in his day. A Piedmontese, Einaudi was an economist, newspaper editor, and book publisher and in 1948, was elected president of Italy. The winery is located in Dogliani, which is famous for dolcetto. But Einaudi produces several Barolos, including an excellent Cannubi. The wines are deep, rich, even a bit chunky with some oak used, although rarely intrusively so. These are traditionally structured wines that reward considerable aging.

ELIO GRASSO—A relatively new estate in Monforte d'Alba that has gone from strength to strength in recent years. A former banker, Elio Grasso, threw over the paperwork and hopped on a tractor. His wines are pure, direct, and powerful, with no distracting stylistic flourishes. This is the real Barolo thing. Three single-vineyard Barolos are offered: Vigna Chinera, Rüncot, and Casa Matè. All are superb. Worth hunting down.

MARCARINI—A traditionalist producer that once created (when Elvio Cogno was the longtime winemaker) the greatest Brunate and La Serra bottlings produced. Today, owner-winemaker Manuel Marchetti creates admirable, traditional, oak-free Barolos but they are today lighter, more dilute-tasting and less persuasive than the same wines that first created the luster and fame of the Marcarini name in the 1960s, '70s, and '80s.

PIO CESARE—A famous shipper that has slowly transformed its once-admirable, but rustic, traditional Barolos into substantial wines of real refinement. Although Pio Cesare remains traditionalist, it does use small oak barrels, but discreetly so, even though some vintages have the wines mostly in barrique. Indeed, it is an exemplar of how it is possible to be both traditional (in the best sense) and modern (ditto) at the same time.

Two Barolos are offered, both outstanding. The regular Barolo bottling is a benchmark for blended Barolo from several vineyards. Superior (but slower aging) is Pio Cesare's wholly owned single vineyard Barolo Ornato in Serralunga d'Alba. These are wines that deserve extended cellaring.

PRUNOTTO—When Prunotto was run by its former owner and winemaker, Giuseppe (Beppe) Colla, the wines were monuments of traditionalism. They aged for decades and made converts of newcomers to Barolo. In 1989, Prunotto was bought by the Tuscan wine shipper Antinori. The wines under the new ownership have proved to be polished, pleasing but rarely top-rank. Part of the problem, surely, is that the great grapes once available for a pittance to Beppe Colla in the 1960s, '70s, and early '80s are no longer available—or not much anyway—thanks to the explosion of estate-bottling in Barolo. When Antinori bought Prunotto, it bought a famous label, as Prunotto didn't own any vineyards.

RENATO RATTI—The late Renato Ratti was only 54 years old when he died in 1988. He left a vacuum that has never been filled.

Ratti, you see, was not just a winemaker. His real passion was serving as the Langhe's leading wine politician, where he simultaneously headed both the Barolo growers consortium and the Moscato d'Asti/Asti Spumante growers consortium.

Ratti represented the area's interests in the endless bureaucratic wine wrangling in Rome. He was the zone's foremost intellectual, issuing a first-ever map showing single-vineyard boundaries, as well as one of the earliest advocates (and producers) of single-vineyard-designated Barolos.

Not least, he was a pretty good winemaker, too. Ratti believed that Barolo had to modernize, become more accessible, cleaner-tasting, and supple. He was not, however, persuaded by the use of oak, despite his friendship with, and admiration for, Angelo Gaja, who so forcefully advocated the use of small oak barrels.

Today, the winery is capably run by his son, Pietro. And they are still supple, forward Barolos of great polish and come-hither invitation. They are lovely, pure, and true. And, yes, there's some oak in the wines today. But nothing too intrusive. Worth seeking out.

VIETTI—Four superb Barolos are offered by this small, brimming-with-ambition producer. Luca Currado took over the winemaking from his pioneering father, Alfredo, who was among the first in the 1960s to issue single-vineyard bottlings and almost single-handedly brought the white Arneis grape back from near-extinction. Under his son's hands-on winemaking, the wines have acquired more polish and flavor definition. Vietti is a classic right-down-the-middle producer with its willingness to use both barriques and large casks.

The five Barolos are all terrific. There's a "basic" Barolo Castiglione that is a blend of as many as five vineyards plus single-vineyards such as Brunate, Lazzarito, Rocche, and Villero. The single vineyard bottlings are, not surprisingly, the standouts, with Rocche and Villero the superstars. All are wines that reward and deserve extended cellaring. Vietti makes some of Barolo's greatest wines.

Holding The Traditionalist Line

FRATELLI CAVALLOTTO—A sleeping beauty of a Barolo estate that seemed, finally, to get an awakening kiss in the early 2000s. For too long, this producer, which owns significant acreage in choice sites, offered wines that only could be called old-fashioned. Too often the wines were less than clean-tasting, with a unwelcome scent of less-than-perfectly clean old wood casks. Happily, that's all gone down. Cavallotto Barolos in recent vintages are still traditional (large casks, long fermentations), but the wines are cleaner, brighter, and fresher-tasting. They're still not for early drinking, as the tannins are substantial. But these are worthy Barolos—and the "comeback" is still a bit of a secret.

GIACOMO CONTERNO—The late Giovanni Conterno (he died in 2004 at age 75) was, along with Bruno Giacosa and the late Bartolo Mascarello, one of the masters of traditional Barolo. He was a traditionalist *par excellence* and had no truck with small oak barrels, controlled fermentations, or seemingly anything that smacked of modernity. And he made flat-out great Barolos. (His brother is the more modern-minded Aldo Conterno; Giacomo was their father.)

That said, there did seem to be a bit of "freshening" in the wines starting in the mid-'80s, although no radical stylistic changes. (Stainless steel fermenting vats are used, for example.) Perhaps it was the influence of Giovanni's son, Roberto, who has made the wines for years now. Perhaps it was his brother Aldo's example (the brothers, although not close, were not estranged as some people thought). Maybe it was the evolution of an already highly refined palate, which unconsciously kept up with the times, even if the "ideology" remained seemingly unchanged. Winemaking, after all, is a summation of numerous small decisions, many of which are intuitive, especially at Giovanni Conterno's elevated level.

Only two Barolos are offered, both monuments: Barolo Cascina Francia and Barolo Monfortino. The latter is a collector's item and sells for hundreds of dollars. There's sometimes confusion about what

Monfortino is. It's simply a selection of the best subplots in Conterno's 35-acre Cascina Francia estate in Serralunga d'Alba. Where the regular Cascina Francia Barolo is bottled after four years, Monfortino is bottled only after seven years. Both wines are aged in large oak upright casks.

Barolo Cascina Francia is the more readily available wine and invariably ranks among the top ten Barolos of any given vintage. Monfortino is less often seen and commands a collector's premium. These are very great, long-lived Barolos that deserve to be sought out and cherished.

FONTANAFREDDA—One of Barolo's largest estates, Fontanafredda has been owned since 1931 by the Tuscan bank Monte de Paschi, which acquired it from the estate of the illegitimate son of King Vittorio Emmanuelle II. It is a stunner of an estate, with more than 170 acres of vines and a magnificent horizontally striped structure that is a landmark in the area. It is arguably the greatest single winery jewel in all of Piedmont.

Unfortunately, Fontanafredda is also a dinosaur. While it's surely a very profitable business (it issues far more wine, including an excellent Asti Spumante, than just those from its own vineyards), Fontanafredda seems lost in a reverie of traditional Barolo that doesn't serve it well.

For too long the wines were musty and dried out. That problem now seems a thing of the past, but there's still a lack of vibrancy in the wines. They should be thrilling, given Fontanafredda's great vineyard resources. Instead they're workmanlike and uninspired, lacking vibrancy.

Today's Barolos from Fontanafredda are good and admirably traditional, but they could be much better yet.

BRUNO GIACOSA—With the recent passing of Bartolo Mascarello and Giovanni Conterno, Bruno Giacosa is today the king of Barolo traditionalism. Giacosa is also unusual in that he owns very little vineyard land, with the notable exception of Falletto vineyard in Serralunga d'Alba, which he bought in 1982. It is the source of his Barolo wines today.

Bruno Giacosa Barolos are great, classic wines. No new oak here.

No hokey-pokey in the winery. Instead, he practices a rigorous, almost monastic purity involving long fermentations and impeccably clean large casks. And great fruit, of course.

Giacosa makes a regular Barolo, a single-vineyard Falletto bottling, and, starting in 1997, a special best-of-the-best Rocche di Falletto Riserva bottling from selected subplots in Giacosa's Falletto vineyard. These are very great wines that need ten years in the bottle to really shine. They are very much worth the wait—and the hunt.

BARTOLO MASCARELLO—Every sizable wine zone of any venerability has its local, revered "character," and Bartolo Mascarello was Barolo's. When the Langhe was in a convulsion of change in the 1980s and '90s, Bartolo Mascarello was more vociferously traditionalist than ever. He loved describing himself (in Italian; he spoke no English) as the "last of the Mohicans." With Giovanni Conterno and Bruno Giacosa, he was the third of the trinity of Langhe's great traditionalists.

Unlike the other two, for whom the word "taciturn" was invented, Bartolo Mascarello was voluble. He loved polemics. And he was much more of an intellectual than any other winegrower of his generation. Since he was wheelchair-bound by multiple sclerosis, he relished the unending stream of visitors who stopped by to pay homage and listen to him expound like some Greek oracle. (For years you took your chances on whether he was available to receive visitors, as he refused to install a telephone. His daughter finally insisted that he get one.)

Mascarello's winemaking was—and in the hands of Alessandro Fantino, whom Mascarello made a partner when Fantino was just thirty years old—still is resolutely traditionalist. He felt that small oak barrels verged on the sinful, never mind rotofermenters, short fermentations, or anything else smacking of "progress."

No matter. Mascerello's wines have stood the test of time in every sense. A blend of several vineyards (Cannubi, San Lorenzo, Rue, and Rocche), they are dense, austere, and absolutely in need of ten to fifteen years of age. And they also demand food, as they are not lush, vanilla-scented, "stand alone" wines. But a mature Bartolo Mascarello Barolo, displaying a deep mahogany hue and a paradoxical scent of tar and violets, is a transport into the best of Barolo's laudable tradition.

GIUSEPPE MASCARELLO—Mauro Mascarello, the fourth-generation owner-winemaker of this small, traditionalist estate, is a delicious anachronism. Like his fellow traditionalists, he eschews small oak barrels, rotofermenters, vacuum concentrators, and pretty much anything that prevents Nebbiolo from tasting the way it did decades ago, at its best.

In fairness, Mauro Mascarello is no knee-jerk antiquarian. He uses stainless steel tanks for fermentation, transferring the Barolos to large, upright oak casks for aging. His yields are low, and the winemaking careful and attentive, with no filtering. His are clean, strong, delineated wines. But the aesthetic is different—and powerful.

Mascarello's signature wine is the single-vineyard Barolo Monprivato. Starting in 1993, a special subplot bottling (using only one Nebbiolo clone called Michet) from Monprivato called Ca' di Morrisso is issued. Both wines are superb. Look also for excellent Barolo Santo Stefano di Perno, Barolo Villero, and Barolo Bricco. But Monprivato is the star.

ODDERO—An old estate on the comeback trail. Previously rustic, ultra traditional wines have shown greater depth, refinement, and vibrancy in recent years. Competition appears to have awakened the Oddero family to the possibilities of creating traditional Barolos with all their unvarnished virtues without rusticity. This is a good thing because Oddero is one of the Langhe's largest landowners with parcels in some especially choice vineyards. Look for Barolo Rocche de Castiglione, Barolo Mondoca di Bussia Soprana, and Barolo Vigna Rionda, among others. This is a sleeping beauty of an estate that's still in the process of waking up. To watch.

FRANCESCO RINALDI—A resolutely traditionalist grower with some fine Barolo vineyards such as Cannubi (which is labeled Cannubio) and Brunate. Elegant, slightly lighter-style wines that beg for food as well as the better part of a decade's aging.

GIUSEPPE RINALDI—Although little-known outside of connoisseur circles (thanks mostly to the tiny production), the wines of this small grower are among Barolo's greatest. Rinaldi uses upright oak casks for his fermentation and for aging the wine. Most unusually, he also adds the skins of Barbera grapes to the Barolo while the wine is fermenting, to create a deeper color. (How odd that ever-modernist Angelo Gaja—who adds 6 to 8 percent Barbera to his Barolo—and ultra traditionalist Luciano Rinaldi should find common ground.)

Two Barolos are offered, each a blend of two named vineyards: Barolo Brunate-Le Coste and Barolo Cannubi San Lorenzo-Ravera. Both are simply splendid wines, monuments to the continuing greatness of Barolo traditionalism. They have flesh, vibrancy, intensity, and lovely delineation. They also need years in the bottle, along with hearty food, for their virtues to be fully revealed. They are among Barolo's greatest wines.

What Do The Locals Eat With This Wine? In the Langhe, Barolo is the wine pinnacle of the meal. You start with a Dolcetto, move to a Barbera and then cap the dinner with Barolo. Typically, Barolo is paired with braised beef (in the old days, when Barolo was dirt cheap, the beef would be braised in Barolo), game birds such as guinea hen or pheasant or even pasta dishes (always a first course) when fresh white truffles are in season (October through January). Barolo is a wine that deserves meats, big glasses to allow its perfume to collect, and an appreciative audience. It's also an autumn and winter wine. Somehow, Barolo in the summer just doesn't taste right,

One Man's Taste—Whose Wine Would I Buy? The choices are agonizing. I would reach for anything from Aldo Conterno, Giacomo Conterno, Bruno Giacosa, Elio Grasso, Bartolo Mascarello, E. Pira di Chiara Boschis, Giuseppe Rinaldi, and Vietti. But really, I would happily drink any of the producers cited previously—and many others who names are absent only because of space reasons. (Really, Barolo deserves a book of its own.)

Worth Searching For? Don't die without trying it

Similar Wines From The Same Neighborhood: Any Nebbiolo wine such as Nebbiolo delle Langhe, Langhe Rosso, and Barbaresco, and in northern Piedmont, such wines as Ghemme, Gattinara, and Lessona, among others

Bolgheri

(*bowl*-geh-ree)
RED AND WHITE

Region: Tuscany, specifically a small section of coastal hills and flatlands close to the sea

Grapes and Wines: Numerous varieties planted, notably Cabernet Sauvignon, Merlot, Sangiovese, and Syrah for the reds and Vermentino and Trebbiano for the whites. Other red varieties planted include Canaiolo and Cabernet Franc; for whites, Chardonnay and Sauvignon Blanc. Rosé or rosato is also made from the various red grapes.

Red Bolgheri wines are almost always blends, very often with a sizable Cabernet and Merlot component. They are always big, often luscious, sun-rich red wines, often made in a style employing noticeable oakiness. Sometimes they can be quite tannic, but mostly the style is buffed to a high polish with smooth tannins and a supple mouth feel.

White Bolgheri is rarer, with the best examples employing the local Vermintino grape to great effect. A good white Bolgheri can be intensely herbal, crisp, and wonderfully original.

The Tradition: Amazingly, for Italy, there *is* no tradition in Bolgheri— at least not for winegrowing. Bolgheri's tradition was sheep-, horse-, and cattle-grazing. Grapevines came to the area only in 1944, when the late Marchese Mario Incisa della Rochetta (a Piemontese who married into the great landowning family of Bolgheri, the della Gherardesca clan) planted Cabernet Sauvignon and Cabernet Franc on his hillside horse farm. It was a hobby, really, like raising orchids. He got the vine cuttings from his fellow aristocrats at Château Lafite-Rothschild. All this while World War II was raging, no less.

For two decades, Mario Incisa della Rochetta made a Bordeaux-style wine for his family's private use, which he christened Sassicaia. (Sasso refers to rocks; the local Tuscan dialect suffix "aia" is like adding a "y" in English, thus, literally, "rocky" or "rocky place.") He commercialized Sassicaia only in 1968.

Finally in 1978, the then-unknown Sassicaia vanquished several big-name red Bordeaux in a well-publicized tasting conducted by *Decanter* magazine in London. Sassicaia—and the utterly obscure Bolgheri zone—rocketed to wine fame. Sassicaia now sells for about $150 a bottle. An "untraditional" wine of great critical and commercial success, it ushered in the phenomenon known as "Super Tuscan" wines.

How It's Changed: It's essential to know that Bolgheri has always been an aristocratic land preserve. For centuries, dating to at least the 1400s, the gentle coastal hills and the flat, sandy plain abutting the Mediterranean Ocean were owned almost entirely by the Counts della Gherardesca and their relatives. They planted now-towering umbrella pines and installed a fortresslike castle in the one town of the area called—you guessed it—Bolgheri.

The della Gherardescas shaved off portions of their vast landholding in Bolgheri as they needed money, usually selling it to aristocratic friends or family relations. So until very recently—and even today— it's not easy to purchase any kind of sizable property in the zone.

For example, the next wine to become famous in Bolgheri after Sassicaia was called Ornellaia. It was created in the late 1970s by Lodovico Antinori, who happened to be Mario Incisa della Rochetta's nephew (and Piero Antinori's brother, who owns and runs the famous Antinori wine house). The Antinoris are Florentine aristocrats; they, too, own extensive property in Bolgheri.

Only now is Bolgheri transforming itself from exclusively grazing land to a significant grape-growing district. Property ownership is passing into newer hands, such as the hundreds of acres bought and developed into vineyards by Piemontese winegrower Angelo Gaja, who liked the possibilities of the place.

And what are those possibilities exactly? In a word, Californian. Bolgheri is the California of Italy. It's free of any burdensome traditions (so you can make any kind of wine you like). The climate is sunshine-rich but moderated by cooling ocean breezes, creating an ideal environment for warmth-loving but sensitive grapes such as Cabernet Sauvignon, Merlot, and Syrah. Bolgheri is quite dry, but winter rains supply the necessary water. In short, it's ideal not just for winegrowing, but for *freedom*. Bolgheri is a rare blank slate in a country where seemingly everything was long ago inscribed.

Noteworthy Producers: For the red wines, a handful of producers really stand out:

ORNELLAIA—Ornellaia, originally founded by Lodovico Antinori, was sold to California's Robert Mondavi Winery, which in turn sold it in 2005 to Tuscany's aristocratic Frescobaldi family. Ornellaia offers four bottlings: the namesake Ornellaia (65 percent Cabernet Sauvignon, 35 percent Merlot, and 5 percent Cabernet Franc); Le Serre Nuove (75 percent Cabernet Sauvignon and 25 percent Merlot); Le Volte (50 percent Sangiovese, 35 percent Merlot, and 15 percent Cabernet Sauvignon); and Massetto (100 percent Merlot). The top picks are the rich, luscious Ornellaia bottling and the intense, striking 100 percent Merlot wine called Massetto.

GRATTAMACCO—Grattamacco makes both an impressive red wine (a roughly equal Cabernet/Merlot blend) and one of Bolgheri's best whites (100 percent Vermentino). More than some others in Bolgheri, Grattamacco's wines are infused with real character, not just the intense fruit that the sunshine and cool climate of Bolgheri seem able to tease out of whatever's planted there. Grattamacco has been at it a little longer than some others, so older vines help.

CA' MARCANDA (GAJA)—Ca' Marcanda has three Cabernet/Merlot offerings called Promis, Magari, and the most expensive—and best—the repetitively named Ca' Marcanda Ca' Marcanda. Of the three, the last-named is easily the best. All of these wines are works in progress.

Collectively, they are beautifully made, sleek, refined, and rich-tasting but not yet quite as characterful as one might hope. But then, the vines are still young and it's early days for nearly everyone in Bolgheri.

MICHELE SATTA—Michele Satta, an ambitious producer, offers five reds and three whites. Look for Piastraia (25 percent each Cabernet Sauvignon, Syrah, Merlot, and Sangiovese) and the Costa di Giulia white (65 percent Vermentino and 35 percent Sauvignon Blanc). Very fine wines across the board. The Costa di Giulia white is especially persuasive.

SASSICAIA—This is the wine that started it all. And it's an example of one of those wines that, like Gucci shoes or Tiffany jewelry, has achieved a kind of self-sustaining fame that transcends whatever intrinsic quality it might offer. It's now a symbol, rather than, in this case, a wine. Sassicaia is certainly good, but the hoopla notwithstanding, there's nothing terribly special about it, especially at its high asking price and the abundance of terrific Cabernets available from seemingly everywhere today. It was a revelation in its day, but now Sassicaia coasts to commercial success on a luster achieved when the competition—both in and outside of Italy—wasn't quite so compelling.

What Do The Locals Eat With This Wine? Tuscans are big steak eaters, preferably their prized white steers from the ancient Chianina breed. They like it simply grilled over a wood fire and given a condiment splash of Tuscany's fabulous olive oil. Bolgheri reds are certainly the ticket for that memorable dish. The whites are served with seafood, which again is cooked with typical Tuscan simplicity where freshness is prized over complication.

One Man's Taste—Whose Wine Would I Buy? My first pick is Grattamacco, both red and white. I find its wines among the most characterful of any in Bolgheri and better-priced, too. Angelo Gaja's Ca' Marcanda Ca' Marcanda is very good, if pricey. Ornellaia is certainly pleasable, as well as perhaps the easiest to find. Not least is

Michele Satta's superb white Bolgheri. Satta's wines are always worth investigating, if you spot them.

Worth Searching For? If you happen to see it

Similar Wines From The Same Neighborhood: Any of the many Super Tuscan blends; also, Morellino di Scansano (See page 171.)

Brunello di Montalcino

(broo-*neh*-low dee mohn-tahl-*chee*-no)
RED

Region: Tuscany (north-central Italy)

Grapes: 100 percent Sangiovese (a local clone called *brunello*, the "little brown one")

The Tradition: Although the most famous wine of Tuscany is surely Chianti—a district name—the most prestigious and expensive Tuscan wine is a relatively recent creation called Brunello di Montalcino.

Brunello di Montalcino is new only by Italian standards, where if your family or its winery isn't at least 500 years old, you're a Gianni-come-lately. The earliest wines from the vineyards surrounding the exceptionally steep hilltop town of Montalcino date only to the 1880s, at least under the name Brunello di Montalcino.

Sangiovese has been grown in Montalcino for centuries. But it wasn't until 1870, when Ferruccio Biondi-Santi segregated a clone of Sangiovese that had smaller, more rot-resistent berries, that we saw the first stirrings of a new wine. He called this clone or strain the "little brown one" or *brunello*. It created a wine that was richer, darker, and more powerful than any Sangiovese in neighboring Chianti.

Give the Biondi-Santi family credit: Not only did they single-handedly create a new Italian wine name, but they also relentlessly, implacably insisted on a high price. Above all, they consistently made a wine that, unlike anything in neighboring Chianti, could age and improve for decades. And over several generations they developed a family *hauteur* such that they pretended, anyway, that they didn't care if their wine sold or not.

Brunello's ability to age for decades is the key. Back in the 1880s, red Tuscan wines were frequently made to taste softer, the better to be drunk young. Ferruccio Biondi-Santi instead created his own style, something sterner and more "important." He felt that he had the right stuff with his "little brown one." He was right. He called his wine Brunello di Montalcino. An 1888 bottling—the first great vintage of his new wine—is occasionally tasted today and still found alive and rewarding. (The oldest Biondi-Santi Brunello I've personally had was a 1955, tasted after a half-century of cellaring, and it was impressively youthful.)

All this history is important simply because the luster—and, especially, the high price—of Brunello di Montalcino today uniquely derives from this Biondi-Santi "Big Bang."

How It's Changed: Despite the historically high price asked by Biondi-Santi, the fact is that Brunello di Montalcino was virtually unknown to the world until the 1970s. Barolo was Italy's most famous and prestigious red wine; Brunello was like a small-town rodeo champion, a strictly local pride.

Then the Italian wine boom happened starting in the 1970s. Seemingly out of nowhere, rumors emerged about a fabulous wine called Brunello di Montalcino that could age for decades and, in the specific case of Biondi-Santi, was said to be the most expensive red wine in Italy.

The buzz was such that in 1978, Banfi Vintners (an American wine importer that made its bundle selling sweet, fizzy Riunite Lambrusco) began buying and cobbling together several decrepit old Montalcino farms. Today, Castello Banfi occupies 7,100 contiguous acres in Montalcino, one-third of which are vineyards.

By the 1990s, Brunello di Montalcino became one of Italy's most sought after prestige wines. New producers emerged, many with brand-new vineyards of untested quality and, of course, very young vines. To put this in perspective: In the late 1960s, there were fewer than 200 acres of Brunello di Montalcino. Today there are 4,893 acres of vines in the Brunello di Montalcino appellation.

This is both good news and bad. Never before have we seen so many Brunellos. Yet the quality is distressingly variable. Simply put, too many of today's Brunellos aren't worth the invariably high price being asked. You would have to be very trusting indeed, especially at $75 to $300 a bottle, to assume that, just because the label says Brunello di Montalcino, it must be exceptional. The potential exists, as do some consistently superb achievements. But inevitably, what with some 150-plus producers, many of them new, the annual results are spotty.

Part of the unreliability of Brunello di Montalcino rests with a new stylistic experimentation, as well as young vines and new producers. Biondi-Santi set the template by aging its wine in large casks for three years or longer before bottling. This was not uncommon everywhere in Italy well into the 1960s.

In great vintages a Brunello could withstand such long oak-aging. In lesser vintage the fruit was sapped, losing freshness and vitality. Nevertheless, the original appellation requirement called for three years of aging in cask. It created old-style wines that were fast going out of fashion.

Finally, only in 1998 did the law change, reducing cask aging from three years to two. (It was made retroactive to the 1995 vintage.) This being Italy, the change really reflected only what was happening anyway, as producers were already privately rebelling. However, the original requirement that Brunello di Montalcino not be released until four years after the vintage still stands—and is easily enforced.

Noteworthy Producers (The Traditionalists / The Modernists): The big change in Brunello today, apart from all of the young vines and new producers, is the increased emphasis on small new French oak barrels (called *barriques*) and an ever-greater California- and Australia-like fruit intensity creating wines with an almost liquorous texture. As always, when done well, some beautiful wines can emerge. But too often, one regrets to say, the wines lack finesse and distinction. They're just big and oaky and syrupy.

A top Brunello di Montalcino should retain Sangiovese's distinctive dustiness. The Brunello clone, however, seems to add its own twist: a whiff of orange peel. Not every Brunello has this, but then again, no

other Sangiovese wine seems to have it. So I always look for that signature dusty/orange peel scent. Acidity should be noticeable, although
not intrusive. A Brunello di Montalcino shouldn't taste fruity-sweet.
(Some of the more massive, extracted versions do.) Tannins should be
present, but they needn't be mouth-clenching in their astringency.

Traditionalists can be identified not so much by their insistence on
adhering to a three-year cask-aging regimen as by an absence of obvious new oak, by a lack of highly extracted fruitiness, and by the finesse
that comes from good acidity allied to the sort of fruit density that
comes from low vineyard yields. You get an undefinable sense that the
wine is a statement of the land rather than the winemaker. This can be
achieved equally well in a so-called "modern" style (which emphasizes
freshness and fruit vibrancy) as by a more "traditional" bottling that
sees long cask-aging.

Producers that fit the preceeding description include Biondi-Santi,
Canalicchio, Canalicchio di Sopra, Costanti, Fattoria dei Barbi, Il
Marroneto, Il Poggione, Talenti, and Val di Suga, among others.

Modernists, so-called, are an increasingly large group, as this style of
Brunello attracts high praise from critics who taste Brunellos in large
numbers where the wines' massive richness and oaky, fruit-dense
sweetness leaps out in a big tasting. Such wines are, to be sure, very
pleasurable drinking. The challenge is restraint, which some versions
forgo in exchange for power, richness, and scale.

Among the best producers creating Brunellos of real interest that fit
the best of the preceeding description are Altesino, Antinori, Caparzo,
Case Basse, Castello Banfi, Ciacci Piccolomini d'Aragona, Fanti,
Fuligni, Pertimali, Pieve di Santa Restituta, Poggio Antico, Siro
Pacenti, Tenuta La Fuga, and Valdicava, among many others.

What Do The Locals Eat With This Wine? Brunello di Montalcino is
one of Italy's most serious red wines, deserving of many years of cellaring. Consequently, it's often the centerpiece wine of a meal. In
Tuscany, where the cuisine is simple, Brunello would be served with

the local wild boar (*cinghiale*), beef from the local, ancient Chianina breed, or a roast of any kind such as beef, pork, goat, or lamb.

One Man's Taste—Whose Wine Would I Buy? My traditionalist tendencies come out strongly with Brunello. Although I do enjoy the flamboyance of the so-called modernists, I usually reach for Costanti, Canalicchio, and Il Poggione. Not only are these three producers unusually consistent, but they're also better-priced than some others.

A WORD ABOUT ROSSO DI MONTALCINO: The appellation called Rosso di Montalcino was created in 1983 as an (intelligent) alternative to the Brunello designation. It gave producers of Brunello a vehicle by which to "declassify" lesser lots of Brunello or to divert part of the production from expensive long aging. (A Rosso di Montalcino wine can be released as soon as one year after the vintage compared to Brunello's four years.) Also, a fair amount of acreage in the Montalcino zone is not entitled to create Brunello di Montalcino. But growers in these sites can grow Sangiovese to create a Rosso di Montalcino. Some 1,400 acres of vines in Montalcino fall into this category.

Knowing all this, you can see why Rosso di Montalcino is sometimes called the "baby Brunello." It's not really. But it is an early-drinking Sangiovese that can, with the right producers, be an exceptional value. Not surprisingly, the best Brunello di Montalcino producers are, natch, the best bets for exceptional Rosso di Montalcino. A good Rosso in a top vintage, by the way, will age beautifully for upwards of a decade, its early-drinking ability notwithstanding.

Worth Searching For? Don't die without trying it (especially a well-aged, well-cellared version from a top producer and vintage)

Similar Wines From The Same Neighborhood: Rosso di Montalcino (see above); and any 100 percent Sangiovese wine from Tuscany, especially in the Chianti zone

Chianti Classico

(kee-*ahn*-tee *clah*-see-koh)
Red

Region: Tuscany (north-central Italy)

Grapes: Sangiovese up to 100 percent; Canaiolo Nero up to 10 percent; other red grape varieties up to 15 percent, both indigenous (such as Colorino and Mammolo) and "invited" (such as Cabernet Sauvignon, Merlot, and Syrah, among others)

The Tradition: When Italians refer to a zone as "classico," it invariably means the heart of something. That's certainly so with Chianti Classico. The legally defined Chianti Classico appellation was created only in 1966. But some vineyards in the zone have been growing grapes and making much praised wine for nearly a thousand years. Above all, everyone in Tuscany always knew that this zone was the choicest.

There is such a thing as generic "Chianti." It can come from anywhere in quite a large area surrounding the Classico zone. Within that large area are seven subzones, of which Classico is one: Classico, Colli Arentini (the hills around Arezzo), Colli Fiorentini (the hills around Florence), Colli Senesi (the hills around Siena), Colli Pisane (the hills around Pisa), Montalbano, and Rùfina. All can, and do, put the name "Chianti" in front of their subzone designation, e.g., Chianti Colli Senesi.

Nobody disputes that Chianti Classico is *il vero cuore*, the true heart, of Tuscan wine. It's the finest of all of the various Chiantis. It's also where Chianti has seen the most protracted, intense struggles from which, only now, is it emerging with any clear sense of destiny and purpose.

Allow me to explain. More than anywhere else in Italy, Chianti seems susceptible to rulemaking. In 1716, for example, Grand Duke

Cosimo III de Medici created the first controlled appellation of origin, drawing boundaries on a map of decreed wine zones.

Vast tracts of the surprisingly wild Chianti countryside were (and still are, although less so) owned by aristocratic Tuscan families based in Florence and Siena that go back eight hundred years or more. Many of them sold their farms only in the 1960s and '70s with the decline of mezzadria (see page 29). Some, such as Antinori and Frescobaldi, remain prominently active in wine today.

Keep in mind that, unlike Burgundy, the Loire, parts of Germany, or even Piedmont, Tuscany never developed a tradition of single-variety wines. Its native red grapes Sangiovese, Canaiolo Nero, and Mammolo were always blended together, along with other varieties, including white grapes.

Modern troubles actually began a long time ago with—isn't it always?—the best of intentions. In the 1850s, Baron Bettino Ricasoli, an influential aristocrat (the newly united Italy's second prime minister after Cavour), was interested in agricultural improvements.

Based at his still-thriving Chianti Classico estate called Brolio, he proposed what he believed was an improved mixture of grapes for a superior blend. Sangiovese, the great red grape of Tuscany, along with the still unheralded red grape Canaiolo, was the backbone of the blend. But to soften the wine and make it more fragrant, Ricasoli recommended adding as much as 30 percent of such prone-to-oxidation white varieties as Trebbiano and Malvasia.

Because of his personal interest and prestige—and because the blend did suit the tastes of his time, which was for early-drinking reds—the Ricasoli blend became the default definition of Chianti. So much so, in fact, that in 1966 Italian wine bureaucrats actually codified Ricasoli's century-old formula into law, which was like designing a mid-twentieth century roadway based on the width of a horse.

Making matters even worse was the often-unnoted fact that this new legal codification didn't prescribe the *wine* blend. Rather, it prescribed what growers had to plant in the *vineyards*. The formula of

Sangiovese at 50 to 80 percent, Canaiolo Nero at 10 to 30 percent, and Malvasia and Trebbiano at 10 to 30 percent was a decree about the percentage of each variety that could—indeed, must—be planted in Chianti vineyards.

It was a disaster for quality, if only because it was also an invitation for greed. Sangiovese is a relatively low-yielding grape. But Trebbiano is generous to a fault. So not only did growers, when they replanted, install high-yielding clones or strains of Sangiovese, but they also loaded up their vineyards with Trebbiano. The result was a flood of Chianti wines with grossly disproportionate amounts of white wine (Trebbiano) in the actual blend, sometimes as much as half. And the Sangiovese itself was already pretty thin stuff thanks to the high-yielding, poor-quality clone chosen at the time.

So the wine bureaucrats saw the error of their (outdated) ways and moved to correct their mistake, right? Wrong. They defended their legal turf, insisting that *this* was Chianti. And the law was the law.

In the meantime, Tuscan agriculture had reached a low point. The mezzadri had long since fled to the cities for better-paying jobs. And the farmers who stayed scratched out only a subsistence living. The old aristocratic landowners, for their part, were inert. They were devoid of ambition, as well as capital with which to make improvements, even if they were so inclined. To them, their estates were burdens, not assets.

What saved Chianti was a freeway: Autostrada 1. Completed in the 1960s, A-1 was Italy's first high-speed toll road, connecting Milan to Rome, passing through Bologna on its north-south run. Chianti lay right in its path.

New urban wealth spawned in Milan and Rome suddenly had fast, easy weekend access to the gorgeous Chianti countryside. This new wealth wasn't the old landed aristocracy. Instead, they were the new Italian meritocracy, who made fortunes in small manufacturing, design, and trading companies. They wanted retreats from their hectic urban work lives.

The stone houses of the Chianti countryside were ideal.

Restoration was needed, but that was no problem. These people had money and ambition. Almost invariably, these same country houses came with vineyards attached. They, too, needed work. So the same ambition that made their new owners so successful in the city was applied to their new vineyards.

The new owners knew nothing about winegrowing. So they turned to consulting winemakers or enologists. Chianti probably has more such consultants than any other wine region in the world. These consultants told the new owners that if they were ever to make fine wine, they had to invest money in new vineyard plantings and modern equipment and strive for a much higher standard of wine quality than was then in effect. And, by the way, they had to market the wine when it finally appeared.

The new owners were undaunted. After all, they had made just such efforts in their own professions, so why not wine? A few aristocrats, to their credit, dusted themselves off and gave chase. Most just gave up, selling off their properties.

How It's Changed: The transformation of Chianti, starting in the 1970s, was pretty rocky. There were too many new vineyards using the worst sort of Sangiovese clones. The wine that emerged from these high-yielding clones was dilute and lacked color intensity.

When the new owners tasted their wines from the newly planted, high-yielding Sangiovese vines, they were dismayed. The wines were too light in color and dilute in flavor. They had to do *something*. Also, they wanted, as in their own professions back in Milan and Rome, to be modern and international.

The kill-two-birds-with-one-stone solution arrived with the idea of planting such "international" grapes as Cabernet Sauvignon, Merlot, and Syrah. Adding one or more of these to the wine blend easily solved the color intensity problem, as these varieties are nothing if not color-intense. Ditto for flavor. They can be massively fruity, almost bullying even. And not least, their use signaled modernity, an open, international outlook. Take *that*, Baron Ricasoli!

The authorities huffed and puffed, occasionally threatening puni-
tive action. The local Chianti Classico growers' consortium, for its part,
tried simultaneously to mollify the wine bureaucrats while pleading
with its members—who were threatening to leave the consortium—
not to be too provocative.

By the 1980s, it all came to a boil. The most ambitious, quality-ori-
ented growers told both the government *and* the Chianti Classico
growers' consortium to take a hike. They were abandoning not the
Chianti Classico land but the name itself.

From now on, they would label their wines as Vino da Tavola, table
wine, the lowest and humblest of all legal wine designations. It also
conveniently had the fewest constraints. You could blend anything you
wanted under that name. These new wines—almost invariably boast-
ing significant inclusions of Cabernet Sauvignon, Syrah, or Merlot—
became known as Super Tuscans.

It was classic *Alice In Wonderland*: ("It's no use going back to yesterday because I was a different person then," said Alice.) Chianti Classico's
finest and most expensive wines—heralded by critics and pursued by
consumers—were sold, almost laughably, as mere Vino da Tavola. The very
definition of Chianti Classico, never mind its prestige, was under siege.

The authorities, for their part, came up with what they hoped was
a pacifying set of new rules. In 1984 they proposed new regulations: You
could use up to 90 percent Sangiovese if you liked. But 5 percent
Trebbiano or Malvasia was still required. (The past must still be respect-
ed.) And you could use up to 10 percent of "nontraditional" grapes.

The collective response was the Tuscan version of a Bronx cheer.
After all, practically everyone in Chianti Classico was already doing
this anyway, like kids carousing at a purportedly banned party. The
adults came home, saw the situation, and declared, "All right, we give
you permission to party." Chianti Classico shrugged and rocked on.

Above all, the new rules didn't address the fundamental element of
Chianti's crisis: What, exactly, is Chianti Classico? The modernists said
Chianti Classico is anything they want it to be. "Super Tuscan now,

Super Tuscan forever! We don't need no Chianti Classico," they sneered.

The only problem, then and now, is that these wines didn't (and don't) taste much like anything associated with Chianti. Above all, their very Sangiovese soul is lost, subsumed under the invasive taste and scent of Cabernet Sauvignon or Syrah. They were "international" in the same boring way that all airports, however well designed, look alike.

While this was happening, a smaller, less vocal—but no less committed—group recognized that the soul of Chianti Classico is Sangiovese. And that at its best, Sangiovese could also be its salvation. After all, no one else in the world could grow this tricky grape variety with anywhere near the success as Tuscany in general and Chianti Classico in particular.

Starting in 1988-89, the Chianti Classico consortium, in concert with governmental authorities (and their funding), initiated a first-ever Sangiovese clonal selection program called Chianti Classico 2000. Such clonal investigations are nothing new, having long since been performed for Cabernet Sauvignon and Chardonnay in California and for Pinot Noir and Chardonnay in Burgundy. But for Sangiovese and Chianti it was new—and desperately needed. The indigenous grapes Canaiolo Nero and Colorino were also included.

The project, now concluded, is widely seen as a success—or at least a good start, anyway. It was, if nothing else, a substantive proclamation of the primacy and desirability of Sangiovese.

Creating hundreds of small batches of segregated wines grown in several locations across Chianti Classico made from 239 presumed clones of Sangiovese, Canaiolo Nero, and Colorino, researchers winnowed the best strains to seven clones of Sangiovese and one clone of Colorino deemed superior. Called the "Chianti Classico 2000 clones," they were immediately approved by the government for commercial propagation.

Oh, and what happened to the rules? In 1995, the authorities returned to the "party," issuing a new, "Come home, all is forgiven" decree. In an attempt to deflate the growing prestige and perceived desirability of the Super Tuscans, the new rules declared that Chianti

Classico can be made from 100 percent Sangiovese, a blend of Sangiovese and Canaiolo Nero, or Sangiovese and Canaiolo Nero *and* up to 15 percent of any other grape you'd care to include.

Whether this makes any difference remains to be seen. What is happening, however, is that Sangiovese is regaining respect, even in the eyes of the most committed Super Tuscan sorts. A new Chianti aesthetic now seeks to praise Sangiovese, not to bury it.

The clear-eyed reality, though, is that today there is no such thing as a "true" Chianti Classico. It could be 100 percent Sangiovese. But it might also be deeply affected by Cabernet Sauvignon, Merlot, or Syrah. Some producers are returning to the Chianti Classico designation, while others remain resolutely out of the fold, preferring to employ the broad, vague designation "Toscana" on their labels.

Noteworthy Producers (The Traditionalists / The Modernists): Few Italian wines are more complicated to negotiate than those from Chianti Classico producers. Many of the more than six hundred producers are underachievers, for starters.

In addition, nearly every producer rings the changes from a Chianti Classico *normale* to a Riserva bottling (released later; always more expensive; often oaky) to one or more "special" non-Chianti Classico-designated wines with proprietary names. These are their "Super Tuscan" bottlings. They are almost always wines with significant percentages of Cabernet Sauvignon, Syrah, or Merlot. And almost always, they see significant time in small French oak barrels and are invariably the highest-priced wines in the winery's portfolio.

What's a seeker of Chianti Classico "truth" to do? Or, for that matter, what's a savvy shopper to do? The answer is as simple as it is economical: Buy the producer's basic Chianti Classico. Too often the Riserva wines are only marginally superior to the regular bottling, and they're always pricier. You're usually paying for time in oak barrels as much as the (presumed) higher quality of the wine itself. Granted, this is a broad generalization. But it's more true than it ought to be.

The following producers represent a high-end slice of some of Chianti Classico's best. It's by no means an exhaustive list—that would take an entire book in itself—but with any of these producers you'll get a good, true, and above all, Sangiovese-based taste of some of the best in Chianti Classico today.

ANTINORI—Basic wines are designated Pèppoli; one step up is the Chianti Classico Riserva. They're good wines, but not great. Antinori's famous Super Tuscans are Tignanello (80 percent Sangiovese and 20 percent Cabernet Sauvignon) and Solaia (75 percent Cabernet Sauvignon, 20 percent Sangiovese, and 5 percent Cabernet Franc).

BADIA A COLTIBUONO—An ancient estate creating strongly traditional wines. Basic Chianti Classico is good, but not a head-turner. Improving quality every year. Best bet is their Sangioveto, a 100 percent Sangiovese wine. (It can't be designated as Chianti Classico because it employs a grape name, Sangioveto being a local term for Sangiovese.)

CAPANNELLE—An elegant, if expensive, Chianti Classico producer, although none of the wines is so designated. Still, the basic "Vino da Tavola" is entirely Sangiovese and very refined.

CASSAFRASSI—A still-unknown very high-end producer with superb Chianti Classico normale. The wine labeled XXI Seccolo (twenty-first century) is mostly Sangiovese with some Merlot. It is exceptional.

CASTELLARE DI CASTELLINA—Very good producer with high-elevation vineyards. Basic Chianti Classico is mixed: In warm vintages it's very fine, less so in cooler years. Here, the two Riserva wines are indeed superior: a regular Riserva and, especially, the single vineyard Vigna Il Poggiale. The signature wine is I Sodi di San Niccolò, which is 85 percent Sangiovese and 15 percent Malvasia Nera. It's oaky but impressive. A Merlot and Cabernet are nods to the market in this otherwise tradition-minded estate that has actively—and rightly—campaigned for Sangiovese.

CASTELLO DEI RAMPOLLA—A good, solid producer of equally

good, solid, if a bit mundane Chianti Classico wine. This producer's acclaim comes from its two much-praised Super Tuscans: Vigna d'Alceo (85 percent Cabernet Sauvignon and 15 percent Petit Verdot) and Sammarco (85 percent Cabernet Sauvignon and 15 percent Sangiovese). They are massive, oaky wines that show well in tastings.

CASTELLO DI AMA—An exceptional Chianti Classico producer issuing multiple, single-vineyard bottlings touched with a bit of modernity (small oak barrels, the use of modest amounts of Merlot). But the end results are inspiring. The basic Chianti Classico is consistently one of the best in the field (80 percent Sangiovese, 8 percent Canaiolo, and 12 percent a mix of Malvasia Nera and Merlot). It's intense, lush, and rewarding. Vigneto Bellavista is a very high elevation vineyard (1,500 to 1,700 feet) that's mostly Sangiovese with traditional grapes (Canaiolo, Malvasia Nera) added. It's a bit oaky, but layered and dense. Their Super Tuscan is the 100 percent Merlot called L'Apparita. It's very oaky and unpersuasive to this taster. But the Chianti Classico wines are worth pursuing.

CASTELLI DI BOSSI—Superb Chianti Classico (90 percent Sangiovese, 10 percent Merlot). The Riserva, called Berardo, sees 15 percent Merlot and more oak. Girolamo is their 100 percent Merlot Super Tuscan, along with Corbaia (70 percent Sangiovese, 30 percent Cabernet Sauvignon). The deal is the regular Chianti Classico.

CASTELLI DI CACCHIANO—Good, if not compelling, Chianti Classico (85 percent Sangiovese and 15 percent Merlot). The Riserva is called Millennio. These are structured wines that show best only with food. Owned by the Ricasoli family. Also, don't miss the Cacchiano olive oil. It's one of Tuscany's best, which is saying something considering the competition.

CASTELLO DI FONTERUTOLI—An ancient estate that's been in the Mazzei family since 1435. Fonterutoli (fohn-teh-*roo*-toh-lee) is one of the leading properties in Chianti Classico. It very effectively treads a careful line between modernity (use of Cabernet Sauvignon and Merlot, along with small oak barrels) and tradition (an austere,

Sangiovese-inspired winemaking style).

The wine simply called Fonterutoli is 100 percent Sangiovese. It's lovely stuff: detailed, balanced, and authentic. That called Castello di Fonterutoli is a more modern blend: 85 percent Sangiovese with 10 percent Cabernet Sauvignon and 5 percent Merlot. It's denser, richer, and darker. The Sangiovese material is substantive enough not to be bullied by the oft-times intrusive Cabernet. Much more modern yet is Siepi, which is half Sangiovese and half Merlot—and all shiny new modernity and oakiness.

The ticket here are the two Chianti Classico wines. Fonterutoli's style is impressively austere. These are wines that deserve and reward aging, up to a decade or more.

CASTELLO DELLA PANERETTA—One of the most underrated estates in Chianti Classico, perhaps even in all of Italy. The structure is more of a fortress than a castello or castle, which makes sense when you learn that the thousand-year-old property sits astride the line where the warring factions of Siena and Florence engaged in periodic battles. Not the best neighborhood, at least socially.

But for grapegrowing, Castello della Paneretta occupies choice land. It's a small valley with two other properties, both renowned: Monsanto and Isola e Olena. All three estates create wines that share similar taste characteristics: a meaty, solid quality to the Sangiovese, unusual longevity, and a certain smack of iron in the taste.

Paneretta's wine is the least-famous of the three, yet easily just as good as the others. The regular Chianti Classico is 90 percent Sangiovese, with 10 percent Canaiolo Nero. It's exceptionally rich, substantial wine that rewards aging. Two other, more expensive, oak-inflected Chiantis are offered: Torre a Destra (the tower to the right), which is 100 percent Sangiovese, and Terrine, which is half Sangiovese and half Canaiolo Nero. The latter two wines are dense, succulent, and modern-smooth. And very seductive.

Castello della Paneretta is one of Chianti's greatest properties. Yet oddly, its light still remains hidden under a bushel of modesty—or maybe just a reluctance to engage in the necessary public relations. Worth seeking out.

Castello di Verrazzano—A winery on the comeback trail. The name is indeed *the* Verrazzano: Giovanni Verrazzano, who discovered the entrance to New York harbor (and a lot of the rest of the East Coast), was born at this property in 1485. Good Chianti Classico with sometimes overly discernible oakiness, especially in the Riserva and the wine called Sassello (the name of a thrush). Still, good wines that deserve attention.

Castello di Volpaia—A great estate occupying a rather remote and high elevation. The tiny village of Volpaia is the estate: The Stianti family owns the entire village, and the winery, so called, is actually shoehorned into various small structures in the village. (In Tuscany, you can't change the outside appearance of an old structure by even a brick.) During harvest you can see flexible pipes snaking through the narrow streets, transferring juice or newly fermented wine from vats from one building to another.

Volpaia's Chianti is informed by the high elevation of the vineyards (greater delicacy) and owner Giovanella Stianti's dedication to the classical tastes of Sangiovese and traditional blending grapes such as Canaiolo Nero. The regular Chianti Classico is lovely: delicate, pure, and almost ethereal. Sterner, more substantial, and long-lived Sangiovese comes from the Riserva bottling. Most impressive of all is Coltassala, which is almost entirely Sangiovese with some Mammolo, an indigenous red grape. It sees some oak, but very deftly so. Very great wines, among the best in Chianti Classico.

Dievole—The Schwenn family keeps tinkering with Dievole (dee-*eh*-voh-leh), attempting to squeeze from this impressive and ancient estate near Siena ever-better wines. It's a hard property to keep track of, if only because the restless owner issues a stream of proprietarily labeled wines with names like Pinocchio and Primadonna.

The key to nearly everything done at Dievole is an interest in the estate's heritage and that of Chianti as a whole. Sangiovese rules here.

The wines are variable, but always improving. Worth watching.

FATTORIA DI FÈLSINA—One of Chianti Classico's greatest properties. Located near Siena, Fèlsina is one of those rare properties where seemingly everything they do is invariably first-rate. This is where Sangiovese finds one of its finest expressions in three different yet clearly related versions. The "basic" wine is Chianti Classico "Berardenga." There's nothing basic about it, as it's better than probably 90 percent of all other Chianti Classicos. It delivers a purity of Sangiovese, all dust and minerals lubricated by a black cherry fruitiness.

Better yet is the Riserva bottling, which is exceeded in turn by Fèlsina's two signature bottlings: the single-vineyard Chianti Classico "Rancia" and a proprietarily named wine called Fontalloro. Both are nearly 100 percent Sangiovese. Both are massive, organ pipe-deep rich wines that demonstrate just what Sangiovese can deliver when the yields are low and the winemaking deferential. There's no need (or use) for new French oak barrels in these two wines. The minerally/dusty/tarry fruit of these wines say it all. Both wines need the better part of a decade to reveal their full dimensions. Very great wines, across the board.

FATTORIA LE FONTI—A winery on the upswing in recent years. Strong Sangiovese presence in the wines along with a noticeable oakiness that—given the sheer substantiality of the raw material—may well become seamlessly incorporated in the wine over time. Chianti Classico *normale* is a lovely rendition, with persuasive delicacy allied to real substance. The Riserva is significantly richer, more powerful Sangiovese with noticeable oak from small barrels. The label called Vito Arturo (100 percent Sangiovese) is muscular, intensely fruity wine redolent of dried black cherries and can probably take the apparent oakiness it displays when young in its stride as it ages. All are marvelous wines that deserve close attention.

FONTODI—Another of the great Chianti estates that championed the primacy of Sangiovese, Fontodi is easily one of the most reliably good estates in Chianti Classico. There has been some rearranging of the portfolio in recent years. Where once there was a Riserva, since 1999, Fontodi has issued only one wine labeled Chianti Classico. The grapes that previously were reserved for, well, the Riserva now go into the flagship Chianti Classico. Not surprisingly, the wine is the better for this welcome addition. It's strong, black cherry/dusty, intense Chianti, a benchmark.

Instead of the Riserva is the single vineyard Chianti Classico "Vigna del Sorbo," which sees a small amount of Cabernet Sauvignon added to the Sangiovese. There's also a good lather of small new oak barrels too, giving the wine a noticeable, but not overpowering, oakiness.

Most powerful of all is Fontodi's most famous wine, the 100 percent Sangiovese bottling called Flaccianello. Aged in small oak barrels for at least sixteen months, it emerges as sweet-smelling as a baby from its bath. However, Flaccianello is a wine of considerable substance. It shakes off the oak over time. Sometimes it can be so powerful that it borders on the brutish, however.

The best bet, for this taster, also happens to be the smallest (price) bet: Fontodi's terrific Chianti Classico *normale*. It's the real, pure, Chianti Classico thing.

ISOLE E OLENA—One of the most admirable of all Chianti Classico estates. Owner-winemaker Paolo de Marchi is one of Chianti's most insightful winegrowers, someone who has—like so many others—toyed with using Cabernet Sauvignon and Syrah only to eventually conclude that Sangiovese is supreme. He planted those other varieties but now prefers to play it straight with Sangiovese whenever he can. (De Marchi is not an ideologue, however, and if a vintage weakness calls for it, he's willing to add a dollop of Syrah to his Chianti for color or to punch up the fruitiness.)

That said, today Isole e Olena is an exemplar of the greatness of Sangiovese. Worth noting is that the vineyard is in a location where Sangiovese can really shine, as Isole e Olena is in an apparently distinctive (or so the wines tell us) subdistrict that includes Castello della Paneretta and Monsanto, both of which also shine with Sangiovese.

The basic Chianti Classico from Isole e Olena is annually one of Chianti Classico's finest: powerful, intense, long-lived yet graceful. It is suffused with the dusty, brambly, minerally scent and taste of Sangiovese (about 80 percent), with the balance being Canaiolo Nero. A little Syrah (5 percent) might be added, if de Marchi deems it necessary.

Better yet is Isola e Olena's signature wine, the 100 percent Sangiovese bottling called Cepparello (cheh-pah-*rel*-loh). Cepparello was the name of an ancient castle in the valley that was destroyed by the Florentines in 1260. Consistently one of Tuscany's finest Sangiovese wines (and I'm including Brunello di Montalcino when I say "Tuscany" here), Cepparello is profound, powerful, dense, and long-lived—a benchmark wine.

Isole e Olena also issues Cabernet Sauvignon, Syrah, and Chardonnay wines under a separate label called Collezione de Marchi. The Syrah, called L'Eremo, is noteworthy and has a devoted following.

FATTORIA LA MASSA—Founded in 1992 by Naples-born Giampaolo Motta (who was then only 31 years old), La Massa made a very big impact in Italian wine circles in a very short time, winning numerous awards and accolades. Motta is a talented winemaker with a decidedly modern taste. His wines are glossy and luxurious, with an unmistakable influence of small oak. (Motta is also a proponent of a winemaking technique now popular in Bordeaux, where he studied chemistry, called micro-oxygenation, in which oxygen is gently infused, as with a fish tank bubbler, into a barrel of wine. It's thought to create softer, more gentle tannins.) Perhaps La Massa's wines are a little *too* polished and soft. But the underlying raw material, and integrity, are indisputable. La Massa's signature wine is called Giorgio Primo, a blend of Sangiovese (85 percent) and Merlot (15 percent). It's very rich, oaky, intense, and supple.

LE CINCIOLE—Another newcomer to Chianti Classico, Le Cinciole was founded in 1991 by a Milanese couple (Luca and Valeria Orsini) fleeing the pressures of the big city. They brought with them not only money and ambition but also rigor. Cinciole's is not the easiest site in

Chianti Classico if only because the vineyard is quite high in elevation, upwards of 1,200 feet. Superb Chianti Classico made almost entirely from Sangiovese with a small amount of Canaiolo Nero. It's as delicate and powerful as a cable on a suspension bridge, thanks to the high elevation (delicacy) and low yields (the wine's "tensile" strength). A single-vineyard, 100 percent Sangiovese, Chianti Classico Riserva from its Petresco vineyard is richer and more intense yet, along with being a bit oaky from time spent in small barrels. It is superb and gives every indication of being long-lived. Worth seeking out.

MONSANTO—One of a trio of wineries in a small subdistrict (Val d'Elsa, the narrow valley of the Elsa River), along with Isole e Olena and Castello della Paneretta. Owned by the Bianchi family, originally from Milan, Monsanto has been carrying the banner for classical Sangiovese-proud wine since the mid-1960s. The Bianchis were on the scene long before most other "foreigners" (Italian and otherwise) road to rescue Chianti from the doldrums.

All three wineries in this almost magical zone share certain taste characteristics, namely a rich, beefy, meaty Sangiovese wine with noticeable iron-like, even medicinal, notes. They're all unusually long-lived wines. And they are like no others in Chianti Classico.

At one time Monsanto reigned supreme. Today, of this privileged trio, Monsanto's wine is the least of the three, eclipsed by the intensity and power of Isole e Olena and the ever-ratcheting ambition of neighboring Castello della Paneretta. Monsanto's style, in comparison to its neighbors, seems a little too desiccated, sapped of the fruit intensity this zone can uniquely deliver. Still, it remains a lovely wine. One would like a greater freshness, though—to see the jewel better-faceted, as it were. But the material is certainly there. Monsanto is a wine always worth watching.

MONTEVERTINE—The story of Montevertine, one of Chianti Classico's finest estates, is the story of the transformation of Chianti Classico since the 1960s. The late Sergio Manetti (he died in November 2000 at age 79) was a man at odds with the Chianti wine establishment he first met when he bought his small estate as a weekend retreat in 1967. (He owned a steel mill in the industrial Tuscan town of Poggibonsi.) Like so many others, Manetti became enthralled by winegrowing and subsequently appalled by the regulations then in place, requiring the use of white grapes such as Malvasia.

So Manetti struck a blow for quality and against bureaucratic myopia: He withdrew from the Chianti Classico Consorzio growers' organization. Then, in 1981, he effectively ripped the Chianti Classico epaulets off his label: His Montevertine wine no longer bore the Chianti Classico designation. Instead it declared "Vino da Tavola da Radda in Chianti" (red table wine from Radda in Chianti). At the time it was a delicious outrage, especially since by then his wine—first released in 1971—was already seen as one of Chianti's best.

From there, this small estate (41 acres of vines today) went from strength to strength. Manetti issued not just a Montevertine and Montevertine Riserva (his two stealth Chianti Classicos) but also his signature single-vineyard wine called La Pergola Torte (the twisted pergola), a 100 percent Sangiovese aged in small oak barrels. When first released in 1977, it caused a sensation. To this day, it is one of the best 100 percent Sangiovese Chiantis made.

Subsequently, another single-vineyard bottling, called Il Sodaccio, appeared. (Originally the entire production went to the Michelin three-star restaurant Pinchiorri in Florence. Now, the restaurant has an exclusive on a bottling called Il Cannaio.) Then came a third wine called Pian del Ciampolo. All are Sangiovese with small amounts of Canaiolo Nero. None sees any nonindigenous grapes.

Today, in the eyes of some, the formerly-at-the-ramparts revolutionary Montevertine is *behind* the times. This is because Manetti was unalterably opposed to the use of "international" grapes such as Cabernet Sauvignon, Merlot, or Syrah. No matter. The wines of Montevertine are as superb as ever. Also, they are unusually perfumey, even delicate—a Volnay among Chiantis. This is partly the result of the vineyard site in Radda in Chianti, which tends to create more delicate, even ethereal, Chiantis. However, time has proved the Montevertine wines, especially

La Pergola Torte, age magnificently. They are wines to seek out.

IL PALAZZINO—A small producer creating powerful, persuasive Chianti Classico and, especially, a 100 percent Sangiovese blockbuster called Grosso Sanese. Yes, there's the seemingly inevitable oakiness, but not so much so as to detract from the intense flavors and stern spine of these wines. To watch closely.

QUERCIABELLA—A New Wave producer of very good Chianti Classico and Riserva along with several proprietarily named blends such as Palafreno (55 percent Merlot and 45 percent Sangiovese); Camartina (55 percent Sangiovese, 45 percent Cabernet Sauvignon, and 5 percent Syrah and Merlot); and a white called Batàr (65 percent Chardonnay and 35 percent Pinot Biano). Stick with the two Chiantis. They're lovely wines, especially the Riserva.

RIECINE—A small producer whose intense, powerful, beautifully balanced Chiantis fill me with admiration—and fill my cellar too. Created in 1971 by a British advertising executive, John Dunkley, and his Italian wife, Palmina, Riecine was in the forefront of Chianti Classico's fueled-by-outsiders renaissance. Dunkley sold the winery to his winemaker Séan O'Callaghan and majority owner Gary Baumann, an American executive for one of the big multinational accounting firms. He lives in Milan.

O'Callaghan has proved to be a superb winemaker, crafting 100 percent Sangiovese Chianti Classico and Riserva wines, along with an oakier, more barrique-influenced Sangiovese called La Gioia. All are consistently, unerringly superb. If anyone should need a demonstration of what Sangiovese can achieve, you can do no better than to put a glass of Riecine Chianti Classico *normale* or, better yet, Riserva, in front of him. And then let the wine do the (eloquent) talking.

SAVIGNOLA PAOLINA—A very small producer with just seventeen acres of vines, the most in its centuries-old history. (The Fabbri family has owned the estate since 1780.) But yields are low because the soil is sparse and water is scarce.

Owner-winemaker Ludovica Fabbri says that by harvest time in September, water is in such short supply—and needed for cleaning the winery every day—that they often forgo showers. "I don't want to think what we smell like during harvest," she laughs.

But what's in the bottle is best described as perfumed. Savignola Paolina makes an exceptionally suave, elegant Chianti Classico and Riserva, both almost entirely from Sangiovese. These are superb Chianti Classicos, filled with a berryish quality that could legitimately be described as Burgundian, so Pinot Noir-like are they. The trick is finding the wine, which is, happily, sent disproportionately to America.

TERRABIANCA—A New Wave Chianti Classico estate created by a former Swiss jewelry shop owner, Robert Guldener. Although perhaps a little over-polished, Terrabianca's Chianti Classico and its Riserva bottling called Croce (97 percent Sangiovese and 3 percent Canaiolo Nero) are lovely renditions, with elegance and balance. Also worthy is the 100 percent Sangiovese Piano del Cipresso and Scassino (97 percent Sangiovese and 3 percent Canaiolo Nero).

Various other proprietarily named bottlings, such as Campaccio (70 percent Sangiovese and 30 percent Cabernet Sauvignon); Ceppate (75 percent Cabernet Sauvignon and 25 percent Merlot); and Il Tessoro (100 percent Merlot) reflect the estate's modernist approach. Stick with the Sangiovese-based wines and you'll be happy.

VILLA CAFAGGIO—Lovely, austere Chianti Classico and Riserva from a rigorous estate. Owner-winemaker Stefano Farkas creates long-lived, deeply fruity wines that deliver an intensity rivaled only by a handful of other Chianti producers. Some oakiness is present, especially in the Riserva bottling called Solatio Basilica, which is nevertheless a terrific Chianti Classico made from very low yields. Look also for the oaky but massive San Martino, which is 100 percent Sangiovese but, unusually for Chianti Classico, made in part (one-third) from the Brunello clone of Sangiovese. A very oaky 100 percent Cabernet Sauvignon called Cortaccio is also made. Stick with the Chianti normale or Riserva.

What Do The Locals Eat With This Wine? Tuscan cooking is the simplest, very possibly even the crudest, in all of Italy. The soil is poor and unlike, say, lush Piedmont, which thinks nothing of serving as many as a dozen different antipasti, a place like Chianti sings a tune with fewer octaves. So Chianti is served with various salamis and preserved meats (a Tuscan specialty), bean stews, and the big hunks of blood-rare meat, preferably from the ancient Chianina breed. Tuscany is unique in Italy for liking beef in large portions, American-style, and Chianti wine surely does go well with it.

One Man's Taste—Whose Wine Would I Buy? Given the array of Chiantis on the market, I would be remiss in not encouraging you to be adventurous. There are always new or newly revived estates that deserve to be tasted. That said, I'd certainly reach for Riecine, Castello della Paneretta, Fèlsina, Fontodi, Savignola Paolina, Castello di Volpaia, and Castello di Ama if they were at hand.

Worth Searching For? Absolutely worth an effort

Similar Wines From The Same Neighborhood: Any of the other six Chianti appellations, especially Chianti Rùfina (look for Selvapiania and Frescobaldi).

Collio
Colli Orientali del Friuli
Isonzo

(koh-lee-oh/koh-lee aw-ree-on-*tah*-lee del free-*oo*-lee/ee-*sawn*-zoh)
RED AND WHITE

Region: northeast Italy (the easternmost section of the Friuli region on the border of Slovenia, north of Venice)

Grapes: Numerous varieties both red and white. Whites include Pinot Bianco, Sauvignon Blanc, Chardonnay, Riesling Italico, Tocai Friulano, Traminer, Traminer Aromatico (Gewürztraminer), Verduzzo, Malvasia, Pinot Grigio, and Picolit. Reds include Cabernet Sauvignon, Cabernet Franc, Merlot, Refosco, Pinot Noir, Schiopettino, and Pignolo.

The Tradition: What we're dealing with here are three small, separate-but-contiguous districts, each of which certainly has its own attributes, but they share a common local wine culture, similar grapes, comparable climates, and not least, a vaulting ambition.

Although the locals take pains to distinguish their wine as being from Isonzo or Colli Orientali del Friuli or Collio, the reality is that for the rest of us, they're really just one zone. Lumping them together is no injustice. They share far more than they differ. Also, the total land area is small: Collio Orientali del Friuli has 5,700 acres of vines, Collio has 4,000 acres of vines, and Isonzo has 2,500 acres of vines.

To best understand the area—as well as grasp the skyrocketing success achieved starting in the 1980s and continuing today—it helps to get a sense of the lay of the land. Along the border with Slovenia (the former Yugoslavia), the land is hilly and plumped with chalky clay and sandstone because it was an ancient seabed.

These hills (between 300 and 1,500 feet) fringe the western and northern part of the zone. They quickly diminish into what was an ancient flood plain and basin of the Isonzo River. The flatter part is alluvial gravel from the river; the part that greets the diminishing hills shares the chalky clay (marl) of the hills proper.

Such soils and exposures, along with a maritime-influenced cool-ness from the Adriatic Sea, which is just a dozen miles or fewer to the south as the seagull flies, invites a broad array of grape varieties. This helps explain why the area offers so many different wines: The soil and the climate are exceptionally hospitable.

That was the longtime good news. The equally longtime bad news was that until the 1970s, the area was a backwater: isolated, insular, and rustic. The vast majority of its wines was crudely made and equally crudely sold, typically in bulk demijohns. It was a Sleeping Beauty badly in need of an awakening kiss of ambition and technical sophis-tication. Italy's fine-wine renaissance in the 1970s and, especially, the 1980s provided just the right smooch.

Everywhere in Italy the hunger for modernity led to ravenous appetites for change, improvement, and recognition. Nowhere was this appetite keener than in this one-time backwater. Old winemaking equipment was discarded in favor of new, temperature-controlled vats. Yields were lowered, almost radically. Not least, the old bulk sales in demijohns were replaced by proudly labeled estate-bottled wines.

The old ways were forcefully, sometimes harshly, rejected. It caused a lot of family dissension. Superstar winemaker Silvio Jermann, for exam-ple, was in such profound disagreement with his father that he simply upped and left for Canada, returning only years later to claim the fami-ly winery and turn it into an icon of the area. I still recall seeing Wanda Gradnik, a rare female winemaker in the 1980s, flatly forbidding her father—actually an ambitious fellow in his own right with hands thick-ened by a lifetime of vineyard labor—from literally *entering* her winery. He hung about the edges of the cellar like a reprimanded dog.

How It's Changed: As much as any region in Italy, the districts of Collio, Colli Orientali del Friuli (the eastern hills of Friuli), and Isonzo are constantly tinkering with their identities and wines.

Originally it was all about making clean varietal wines. This was pioneered by the late Mario Schiopetto, who more than anyone else inspired a new generation of young winemakers to pursue quality over quantity, rigor over complacency. He started his eponymous winery in 1965, consecrating it to a new, technologically sophisticated standard inspired not by the local bulk production but by the best producers in France and Germany. His striving for flavor purity is still today respectfully cited by younger winemakers as a continuing inspiration.

Then came a renewed interest in indigenous grapes such as Tocai Friulano, Ribolla Gialla, and the difficult, low-yielding Picolit, which creates a memorable sweet wine. Reds such as Refosco and the rare, indigenous Schiopettino were pursued.

This phase shifted into a new interest in creating blended wines, spurred by the critical acclaim and marketplace reward lavished on Silvio Jermann's proprietarily named Vintage Tunina, a kaleidoscopic blend of Chardonnay, Sauvignon Blanc, Ribolla Gialla, Malvasia, and Picolit. (It was named after the poorest of Casanova's lovers, who worked as a housekeeper in Venice.) First appearing in 1975, it soon became a critical sensation. By the early '80s, others were inspired to imitate its aesthetic and, of course, its marketplace success.

By the late 1980s, success caused its own problems. The "dog can talk!" excitement of the area's fresh, new white wines gave way to a perception that these same wines were too light and thin. Indeed, yields were too high, with too few vines per acre growing too many clusters per vine.

The best producers improved their game. They planted more densely spaced vineyards where each vine sported fewer clusters, the better to make more texturally dense and flavorful wine. Small oak barrels became increasingly common, along with late harvesting. These changes, among others in both the vineyard and the winery, did not so much transform the wines as amplify them. Today they are denser, richer, and more substantial.

Although the almost tumultuous experimentation of the 1980s and early '90s has now subsided, there's still a surprising zest to the area. Producers continue to tinker with new or different blends. Red wines are getting more refined; whites have become more intense and substantial. The market has unequivocally endorsed all of this: Prices for these wines are strikingly high—and have been for nearly two decades.

Above all, the variety of wines offered from the best growers in Collio, Colli Orientali del Friuli, and Isonzo make this area a kind of winelover's playground. You pick up a bottle from one of the producers to follow and you're sure to find something different, original, and more often than not, memorable. The style usually is fresh, clean, and even zingy, with an unexpected depth of flavor. They are not weighty wines, but instead trade on great finesse, lovely balance, and precisely delineated flavors. That's why these wines have a following.

A WORD ABOUT CARSO: A separate zone near, but different from, Collio, Isonzo, or Colli Orientali del Friuli is Carso. It's a narrow strip of land that serves as a terrestrial "bridge" between Trieste and the Italian mainland. The soil is heavily limestone, which makes it hard to work for a farmer, but gives wines a decided minerality much sought after by winegrowers everywhere.

Even though technically Italian, Carso really is Slovenian in its language, cuisine, and culture. It grows most of the same grapes as its neighbors directly north in Collio & Co., with the notable indigenous exception of a white variety with the Slavic-sounding Vitovska. Carso also takes pride in growing a grape it calls Terrano, which, only a few miles north in Collio, is called Refosco.

One producer, above all others, put Carso on the world wine map: Edi Kante. See below for details.

A WORD ABOUT SLOVENIA: Many winegrowers in Collio and Colli Orientali del Friuli, both of which rub the border with Slovenia, freely concede that some of the best vineyard sites lie across that border in

Slovenia. The differences between them and their neighbors in the hills across the border are, linguistically and viticulturally, almost no differences at all. The cuisines are similar; so, too, are their dialects.

Historically, what is today Slovenia had a wine industry once indistinguishable from its Italian neighbor. Only as Italy became wealthier and more worldly, starting in the 1960s, did the local winegrowers pull away ever more strongly, even radically, from their across-the-border winegrowing neighbors.

Slovenia's day will come, doubtless in direct proportion to its own political stability and economy. Winegrowers there are already making the effort. No one—neither the Slovenians nor the Italians—doubts the aptitude of the land. After all, a border is as meaningless to a grapevine as it is to a bird.

Noteworthy Producers: Numerous growers crowd this zone. And there's a certain amount of qualitative shapeshifting that goes with wineries that once were at the pinnacle somehow sliding down. Generational changes, along with complacency, seem to account for much of this fluidity. Not least, there's always a new (or newly inspired) winegrower rising in the ranks.

The following producers all have a track record. Not every wine they make is of equal quality, but they can be relied upon to issue something at minimum interesting and at maximum original and exciting.

BASTIANICH (COLLIO)—A new and very good producer owned by the Bastianich family in New York, which owns Felidia restaurant (the mother, Felidia) and a fine retail shop called Italian Wine Merchants (the son, Joseph). Across the board, the wines are very good, with the standout being the signature wine blend, white and red, called Vespa (wasp). The Vespa white is frankly modeled on Jermann's Vintage Tunina, which it rivals. Very fine Tocai Friulano and interesting Tocai Plus using partially dried grapes. Look also for Calabrone Rosso, a red blend also made using partially dried grapes. A strong producer.

BORGO CONVENTI (ISONZO AND COLLIO)—A large estate with,

inevitably, an extensive set of offerings. Look especially for Tocai Friulano and the red Schiopettino. A mixed bag, qualitatively.

BORGO DEL TIGLIO (COLLIO)—A small, biodynamic grower. Not widely distributed, but worth looking for because the overall quality here is very high. Look especially for a tasty Chardonnay and a "Bianco" blended from Chardonnay, Tocai Friulano, Malvasia, Riesling Italico, and Sauvignon Blanc.

LA CASTELLADA (COLLIO)—A limited production keeps this superb producer from becoming better known. There used to be just two wines (a bianco and a rosso), but more varietally labeled wines have appeared in recent years. All of the wines see oak, usually deftly so. Worth seeking out.

GIROLAMO DORIGO (COLLIO)—A small producer with very good Tocai Friulano.

LIVIO FELLUGA (COLLIO)—A well-distributed producer issuing extremely good wines across the board. Look especially for a terrific Tocai Friulano and a benchmark Picolit dessert wine. The white blend called Terre Alte is top-notch, as is the red blend of Refosco, Merlot, and Pignolo called Sossò. Various other blends, red and white, are offered. Worth pursuing.

MARCO FELLUGA (ISONZO AND COLLIO)—The largest estate in the area with a complicated array of offerings. Really, two estates are involved: Marco Felluga with 320 acres of vines in Isonzo and Russiz Superiore with 173 acres of vines in Collio. With such extensive landholdings, the wines are numerous and, inevitably, varied.

Under the Marco Felluga label, look for good Ribolla Gialla, Pinot Grigio, and an excellent white blend of Ribolla Gialla, Tocai Friulano, and Pinot Bianco called Molamatta.

Under the Russiz Superiore label, the offerings are stronger: an excellent Sauvignon Blanc and an opulent white blend of Tocai Friulano, Pinot Bianco, Ribolla Gialla, and Sauvignon Blanc called Col Disôre. Look also for a good (and rare) Verduzzo. Reds are stronger under this label, reflecting Collio's greater aptitude for growing red varieties. A red blend of Cabernet Sauvignon, Cabernet Franc, and Merlot called Rosso Riserva degli Orzone is a standout.

GRAVNER (COLLIO)—One of Italy's most original (and controversial) winemakers. Josko Gravner's wines are not for everyone—and they are like no one else's. He uses old-fashioned open-top wood vats to ferment the wines, including the whites. Then, more strangely yet, Gravner ages his white and red wines in massive terracotta amphorae that are buried up to their necks in the earth. It's a system that's been used in Georgia, in the Caucasus mountains, for thousands of years.

Also, Gravner ferments his whites wines with their skins, a practice abandoned by nearly everyone, everywhere, in the last forty years. Consequently his white wines are uniquely deep gold in color. (It looks like oxidation, but it's not.) In addition, Gravner is biodynamic in his grapegrowing and winemaking (a kind of ultraorganic methodology).

What results from all this is puzzling, dazzling, mind-opening, and palate-changing. The white wine called Breg is the signature wine, a blend of Sauvignon Blanc, Chardonnay, Riesling Italico, and Pinot Grigio. It's deeply colored with glints of orange (!) in the hue. A spicy, rich, deep scent. Really, it's like no other white you've likely ever tasted. Look also for a Ribolla Gialla treated similarly, as well as a Rosso (red). But it's the Breg that stands out.

Worth noting is that Josko Gravner has become a bit of an icon to several other winemakers, notably fellow Collio grower Damijan Podversic and Andrea Sgaravatti of Castello di Lispida in the Eugani hills between Venice and Verona. See also Radikon and Edi Kante.

JERMANN (ISONZO)—Whenever anyone compiles a list of the area's best producers, Silvio Jermann is on it and not infrequently leads it. One thing is certain: Few producers in the area are as consistently good as Jermann. Collectively, his wines are dense, fully ripe, and surprisingly powerful given their elegance and finesse. The famous white blend Vintage Tunina is Jermann's signature white, as well as a rather oaky blend of Tocai Friulano, Ribolla Gialla, Malvasia, and Picolit called Capo Martino. There's also a superb Sauvignon Blanc, a good

Pinot Grigio, and a terrific Ribolla Gialla sold under the name Vinnae.

Silvio Jermann has a penchant for ever more barmy names for some of his blends. First came (in 1987) his barrel-aged Chardonnay bafflingly called "Where The Dreams Have No End." That morphed into "Were Dreams Now It Is Just Wine!," which then almost wistfully contracted into "Were Dreams . . .". It's a good Chardonnay, but not as compelling for this taster as, say, Vintage Tunina. Look also for intriguing reds such as Pignacolusse (100 percent Pignolo); the dialect-saturated Mjzzu Blau & Blau (90 percent Franconia, a.k.a. Blaufränkisch or Lemberger, and 10 percent Pinot Noir); and Red Angel On The Moonlight (100 percent Pinot Noir).

EDI KANTE (CARSO)—The great cult producer of Carso. Kante is an exceedingly fine, rigorous producer who, like Josko Gravner, marches to the beat of a drummer almost no one else hears. He pioneered the revival of the near-extinct indigenous white grape called Vitovska, which is pleasing and minerally, although hardly earth-shaking.

But then Kante decided to make the wine differently, not only fermenting it on the skins (which makes it look like apple cider) but also including much of the sediment in the bottle—with instructions on the back label telling you to shake the bottle several times before pouring to distribute the sediment! The wine, called Vitovska Extra, is amazingly good—and superior to his more conventionally made Vitovska (which he continues to make). Go figure. There's also a lovely Malvasia, redolent of orange blossoms, and a superb Sauvignon Blanc.

MIANI (COLLIO)—Owner-winemaker Enzo Pontoni is a giant in every sense (he's nearly seven feet tall). A former engineer, he took over the family vineyards and lowered the yields to what are arguably the lowest in Friuli. He produces so little that his total annual production is just seven hundred cases a year. Finding Miani wines is nearly impossible. Affording them is yet another matter. However, should you run across any of his bottlings (Sauvignon Blanc, Chardonnay, Tocai Friulano, Ribolla Gialla, a blend called Bianco, among others) you certainly should grab it. They are uniformly intense, rich, and memorable.

DORO PRINCIC (COLLIO)—Good Pinot Grigio and Tocai Friulano. A solid producer, but not in the top rank.

PUIATTI (ISONZO AND COLLIO)—An evolving winery with newly acquired vineyards in Collio. Steadily improving wines that are assiduously oak-free (a point of pride for owners Giovanni Puiatti and his sister Elisabetta). A new category of wines, red and white, called Archétipi (archetypes) is the most promising. Look also for the grouping called Ruttars, which is their newly purchased Collio vineyard. To watch.

RADIKON (COLLIO)—Stanislao Radikon is yet another of Friuli's cult producers. Like his colleague Josko Gravner, his white wines are like few others. Vine density is high; yields very low. Radikon doesn't (yet) use terracotta amphorae. But he's such a restless producer that it wouldn't be surprising if he did someday. At present, he prefers large oak casks and small barrels. But he does ferment his white wines on their skins, with the inevitable deep, ciderish honey-gold hue that results.

Radikon's wines are . . . different. They are intensely flavorful, but in a fashion like no other. The dark hues are initially off-putting. And there seems to be some bottle variation, perhaps because Radikon does add any sulfur in his winemaking, which can lead to instability in a wine. Nevertheless, you don't want to miss a Radikon wine, if only for the mind-opening, palate-expanding experience of it. Look especially for the Ribolla Gialla, which is possibly unique on the planet in Radikon's hands. A white blend called Bianco Oslavje is a mix of Pinot Grigio, Chardonnay, and Sauvignon Blanc

RONCHI DI CIALLA (COLLIO)—You don't see much of this producer, but it's very much worth pursuing. A small producer high on the hill within literal sight of the Slovenian border, Ronchi di Cialla makes an outstanding Schiopettino, the rare indigenous red of Collio. Look also for outstanding Refosco and the white variety called Verduzzo. A red blend called Cialla Rosso is a rewarding fifty-fifty combination of Refosco and Schiopettino. Good Picolit, too.

RONCO DEL GNEMIZ (COLLI ORIENTALI DEL FRIULI)—A small producer delivering an overall high standard of quality with Sauvignon

Blanc, Chardonnay, and a white blend called Bianco di Jacobo. Small size (forty-two acres of vines) precludes wide distribution, but if you see some, they're worth grabbing.

RUSSIZ SUPERIORE—See Marco Felluga

SCHIOPETTO (COLLIO AND COLLIO ORIENTALI DEL FRIULI)—More than any other producer in this zone, the late Mario Schiopetto (he died in 2003 at age 72) was the guiding light for two generations of winegrowers around him. It was Schiopetto, in his pursuit of flavor purity and a desire to elevate the standards of the zone to something competitive with the best of France and Germany, who pioneered the use of temperature-controlled fermentations and significantly lower yields in what was, effectively, a bulk wine zone. His example, starting in 1964, succeeded spectacularly. It is more impressive because Schiopetto was personally a modest man. It was his example and dedication that inspired, rather than exhortation.

Schiopetto's wines, now made by his family, are still today among the very best of the area. Look for top-rate Tocai Friulano, Sauvignon Blanc, and especially Pinot Bianco. There's also the inevitable (good) white wine blend called Blanc des Rosis, as well as several whites that see some time in small oak barrels. Overall, Schiopetto is, if not necessarily in a league of its own, certainly a leader of the pack.

TENUTA VILLANOVA (ISONZO AND COLLIO)—A large producer of good but not spectacular whites and reds. The full range is present here. Prices are reasonable, and these wines make a pleasant introduction to the possibilities of the zone.

VENICA & VENICA (COLLIO)—A very good producer issuing the usually panoply of whites and reds. Look especially for very precise, well-delineated Sauvignon Blanc and Pinot Bianco. A blend of Tocai Friulano, Chardonnay, and Sauvignon Blanc called Tres Vignis is a worthy competitor in the seemingly vast field of Friuli's proprietarily labeled white wine blends. Also a good Merlot called Perilla.

LA VIARTE (COLLI ORIENTALI DEL FRIULI)—A small producer with fifty-three acres of vines in terraced hillsides, it offers no fewer than fifteen wines at last count. La Viarte is a contender. (*Viarte* is Friulian dialect for "springtime.") The red wines here, especially the Schiopettino and the wonderfully named local grape called Tazzelenghe (literally, "tongue cutter" because of its once-rustic hardness). Excellent Ribolla Gialla and Tocai Friulano, among others. Worth seeking out.

VIE DI ROMANS (ISONZO)—Incontestably the finest producer in the Isonzo district and easily one of the very best of the entire area. The winery name originally took that of the family name, Gallo, but California's giant Gallo winery—which assiduously guards its trademark rights—threatened to sue for trademark infringement. Faced with that kind of economic might, they changed the name to Vie di Romans (vee-eh dee roh-*mahnz*), literally Roman roads, as the cellar is sited over an ancient Roman road.

Gianfranco Gallo is a superb, perfectionist winemaker with eighty-four acres of meticulously tended vines. Specializing in whites—which seem suitable for the flat, gravelly, alluvial flood plain of the Isonzo River area—he has fashioned some of the finest Chardonnay, Pinot Grigio, and especially Sauvignon Blanc anywhere in Italy.

Different versions of these varieties are offered, usually delineated by the use of oak barrels or no oak at all. Chardonnay "Champagnis Vieris" sees no oak at all, while Chardonnay "Vie di Romans" is barrel-fermented and aged in small French oak barrels. Sauvignon Blanc "Pierre" is a pure play, no-oak rendition, while the Sauvignon "Vieris" is barrel-fermented and aged in small French oak barrels.

Which are better? Impressively, both the stainless steel and the oak renditions are persuasive. This taster's preference goes toward non-oak versions, but truly, that is just one man's taste. Gianfranco Gallo knows how to create great white wine either way. The Pinot Grigio "Dessimis," for example, spends time in oak barrels, which is unusual for the area. Yet it's a benchmark bottling.

Look also for the white wine blend called Flors di Uis, which is a rich mix of Malvasia, true Riesling, and Tocai Friulano. It's one of the most original-tasting of the area's many white wine blends.

VILLA RUSSIZ (COLLIO)—A winery that has improved steadily over the years and has never been better than it is today. Concentrating mostly on white varieties—there are several quite good reds—Villa Russiz achieves impressive concentration in its wines. Look for two excellent Sauvignon Blancs. That called Sauvignon de la Tour spends ten months on its lees or sediment, which adds a greater depth and thick mouth feel. A Chardonnay called Gräfin de la Tour sees the same treatment. Pinot Grigio here is ripe and rich as well.

Several reds are offered, included two good, rich Merlots, the one designated Graf de la Tour aged in small oak barrels. This is a producer worth pursuing.

VOLPE PASINI (COLLI ORIENTALI DEL FRIULI)—A producer on the escalator upward. For a while, Volpe Pasini seemed to coast along, issuing good, solid commercial wines. But a new line in this producer's wide-ranging portfolio called "Zuc di Volpe" promises greater achievements. Look for an excellent Ribolla Gialla under this designation, as well as multiple other varieties, red and white. The new Zuc di Volpe lineup is what you want to look for from this newly energized producer.

ZUANI (COLLIO)—Patrizia Felluga of Russiz Superiore, with her son Antonio, has started yet another winery in the Collio zone, called Zuani. So far, just two wines are offered, both white wine blends. The unoaked bottling called Zuani Vigne is a fresh white of good quality. More impressive is the barrel-fermented and small oak barrel–aged white simply called Zuani. The blend of Tocai Friulano, Pinot Grigio, Chardonnay, and Sauvignon Blanc is an impressive wine and a promising start for a new label. But then, the Felluga family has got the grapes and the know-how.

What Do The Locals Eat With This Wine? Italians everywhere, including in Collio & Co., see white wines as accompaniments to food rather than meals in themselves. The powerful, often oaky, flavors of California Chardonnays and white Burgundies seem bullying to the Italian palate. Just as they like their fish simply prepared and as fresh as possible—the better to exalt and revel in the fish itself—so too do they like their white wines to respectfully partner the fish and not push past it in a bid for glory.

In other words, the locals serve their wines, both red and white, with a certain insouciance that comes from the recognition that the very subtlety of these wines allows them to accompany all sorts of dishes. Varieties like Ribolla Gialla, with its lush texture and rich flavor, are served with cheeses and white meats such as pork or chicken. Sauvignon Blanc and Pinot Grigio seem reserved almost exclusively for fish. But if you wanted either, especially the Sauvignon, with your cheese, nobody would raise an eyebrow.

The reds, especially Refosco and Schiopettino, are certainly reserved for meats, especially game. They are rich, slightly rustic red wines and pair best with various spicy/fatty salamis, braised dishes, and red meats of all kinds, especially game.

One Man's Taste—Whose Wine Would I Buy? Although there are numerous worthy wines and wineries to choose from, I find it quite easy to point to Vie di Romans, Schiopetto, and Jermann as my top picks. You almost never go wrong with just about anything these three superstars offer.

More radically, I am entranced by the peculiar but compelling wines of Josko Gravner. Those of Radikon are intriguing, but I find Gravner more persuasive. Edi Kante is worthy as well.

Worth Searching For? Absolutely worth an effort

Similar Wines From The Same Neighborhood: Many of the same varieties grown in this easternmost section are grown elsewhere in the much larger Friuli region. Only rarely do they equal or even rival those from Collio, Colli Orientali del Friuli, or Isonzo.

Dolcetto

(dohl-*che*-toe)
RED

Region: Piedmont (northwest Italy)

Grapes: 100 percent Dolcetto (red)

The Tradition: For centuries, the everyday tipple in Piedmont, especially in the Langhe zone (which also creates Barolo and Barbaresco from the Nebbiolo grape), was Dolcetto. It still is. But prior to the arrival of the phylloxera root louse in the 1880s, which devasted all of the vines, necessiating replanting, Dolcetto was *the* everyday red. But after phylloxera, a great deal of the higher-yielding Barbera grape was installed. So there was (and still is) much more cheap Barbera in Piedmont than Dolcetto. It usurped Dolcetto's place as the cheapest everyday red.

This centuries-old tradition of daily Dolcetto drinking is revealed by the improbable number of named Dolcetto appellations. After all, nobody ever said, then or now, that Dolcetto was a great red wine. It's a crooner of a grape, not an operatic to-the-rafters voice like Nebbiolo. The deferential respect of a Dolcetto-specific appellation therefore reflects more the extensiveness of Dolcetto cultivation rather than the seriousness of the resulting wine.

This is why Piedmont has seven named Dolcetto districts: Dolcetto d'Acqui, Dolcetto d'Alba, Dolcetto d'Asti, Dolcetto di Diano d'Alba, Dolcetto di Dogliani, Dolcetto delle Langhe Monregalesi, and Dolcetto d'Ovada.

Of these, only three really stand out: Dolcetto d'Alba, Dolcetto di Dogliani, and Dolcetto di Diano d'Alba.

Dolcetto d'Alba stands out because so much is produced. This is the zone that also grows Nebbiolo for Barolo and Barbaresco. But not every hillside exposure works for the finicky Nebbiolo. So the same growers also plant Dolcetto. A good Dolcetto d'Alba is an intense, meaty Dolcetto, often with noticeable intrinsic tannins.

But insiders acknowledge that Dolcetto d'Alba is not the source of Piedmont's best Dolcettos. That distinction belongs instead to the two (relatively small) zones that specialize in, and make their reputations from, this grape variety: Dolcetto di Dogliani and Dolcetto di Diano d'Alba. Here you can really taste some differences.

Dolcetto di Dogliani is always the biggest, ripest, and above all silkiest of any Dolcetto. It's suave stuff, with exceptional fruit intensity. In comparison, Dolcetto di Diano d'Alba (which alone has the right to also say just Diano d'Alba with no mention of Dolcetto) is a sterner, more structured wine. Where Dogliano is silky and lush, Diano d'Alba is detailed and tailored. It ages exceptionally well.

The local Piedmontese affection for Dolcetto remains strong, which is reflected in its consistently high price (for an everyday wine). The price remains high not only because it's still widely consumed but also because locals buy the *grapes* to make the wine themselves. Dolcetto is an easy variety to make into wine, and everywhere in Italy there's a nostalgic affection for making a bit of your own wine for family consumption. Dolcetto is Piedmont's favorite variety for that purpose.

City dwellers foray into the countryside to buy Dolcetto grapes for a bit of home winemaking. The reason they choose Dolcetto is that it's drinkable—and meant to be drunk—quite young. Dolcetto is fruity, only moderately acidic (especially compared to Barbera), neither needs nor wants aging in new oak barrels, and you can slurp down your homemade wine mere months after making it. And it always tastes good: grapey, vibrant, with a faint whiff of almonds and berries. Not least, it's pretty easy to make into wine unlike, say, notoriously cranky Nebbiolo.

How It's Changed: Inevitably, there's a trend toward making Dolcetto into a more "serious" wine. Where once Dolcetto was relatively light (compared to Barolo, anyway) and cheerfully cheap, today an increasing number of Dolcettos are more powerful than ever, with alcohol levels approaching 15 percent, thanks to ultraripe grapes grown by ultra-ambitious growers. Prices, too, are higher than ever. And these "serious" Dolcetto wines are sometimes subjected to new French oak barrels, which adds wood tannins to the wine. Traditionally, Dolcetto never displayed much tannic structure. (Who needs astringent tannins in a wine originally meant to be drunk within a year?)

The good news is that the best Dolcettos made today are very likely the best Dolcettos *ever* made. These exemplars are pure, often from named single vineyards, free of oak, and a joy to drink. And yes, they can age well for several years in bottles, gaining at least a little complexity. But Dolcetto is really meant to be enjoyed for its vibrant, youthful—dare one say ebullient?—fruitiness.

Noteworthy Producers (The Traditionalists/The Modernists): After it was discovered that Barbera responded admirably to time in small oak barrels, a number of experimental producers decided to do the same for Dolcetto. It doesn't work, or at least not nearly as persuasively so as for Barbera. The oak flavor (vanilla) adds nothing to Dolcetto's violet- and almond-scented fruitiness. And the oak tannins amplify Dolcetto's own, usually submerged-under-the-fresh-fruit tannins, resulting is a rather furry-textured wine. Who needs that? (Barbera has fewer tannins than Dolcetto.)

This once, the traditionalists are clearly on the angel's side. Happily, they are numerous. An easy rule of thumb for buying Dolcetto—especially the widely seen Dolcetto d'Alba—is that good producers of Barolo or Barbaresco also make pretty swell Dolcettos.

For Dolcetto d'Alba, look for: Vietti, Silivio Grasso, Cantina del Pino, Marcarini, Elio Grasso, Sorì Paitin, Poderi Colla, Aldo Conterno, Cordero di Montezemolo, Renato Ratti, Marchesi di Gresy, Bruno Giacosa, Moccagatta, Ettore Germano, Giuseppe Cortese, Pio Cesare, Ceretto, Luciano Sandrone, Vajra, Enzo Boglietti, Prunotto Domenico,

Clerico, Azelia, Paolo Scavino, E. Pira, Icardi, Luciano Sandrone, and Vajra, among many others.

For Dolcetto di Dogliani, look for Luigi Einaudi (get the regular bottling and pass on the tannic and expensive "Vigna Tecc" bottling), Pira, Francesco Boschis, Quinto Chionetti, Fratelli Pecchenino, and Anna Maria Abbona.

For Dolcetto di Diano d'Alba, look for Claudio Alario, Bricco Maiolica, and Gigi Rosso.

What Do The Locals Eat With This Wine? Dolcetto is always the first red wine served in a traditional multiwine Piedmontese meal. (Barbera comes next, then something from Nebbiolo such as Nebbiolo delle Langhe, Langhe Rosso, Barbaresco, or Barolo.) Consequently, Dolcetto is the common accompaniment to any of Piedmont's famously extensive antipasti courses, where as many as six separate antipasti are served. Dolcetto is much liked with *carne cruda*, the finely chopped or very thinly sliced raw veal that is a specialty in the Langhe zone. Any meat or vegetable dish pairs beautifully. Dolcetto is an easygoing red—and so are its drinkers. It's not a wine that invites agonizing over just the right food and wine "marriage."

One Man's Taste—Whose Wine Would I Buy? Dolcetto do Dogliani and Diano d'Alba are my first choices. For Dolcetto di Dogliani, I look for Quinto Chionetti and Einaudi's regular bottling. In Diano d'Alba, my first choice is Bricco Maiolica.

Among the many (and good) Dolcetto d'Alba offerings, I look for Vietti, Renato Ratti, Marcarini, Marchesi di Gresy, and Elio Grasso. But many good Dolcettos are made.

Worth Searching For? Absolutely worth an effort

Similar Wines From The Same Neighborhood: Any of the other Dolcetto districts not emphasized above, such as Dolcetto d'Acqui, Dolcetto d'Asti, Dolcetto delle Langhe Monregalesi, and Dolcetto d'Ovada.

Falanghina
Fiano di Avellino
Greco di Tufo

(fah-lahn-*gheen*-ah/fee-*ah*-no dee ah-veh-*lee*-noh/*greh*-koh dee *too*-foh)
WHITE

Region: Campania (southern Italy, east of Naples)

Grapes: All three are ancient white varieties from the Campania region around Naples that have been very successfully revived in recent years. The law allows up to 15 percent of a lesser white grape called Coda di Volpe (literally, fox tail) to be blended with these three grapes.

The Tradition: Few areas of Italy have a more ancient wine tradition than the zone around Naples, the region of Campania. It was in Campania that the ancient Romans grew their most prized wines, most famously, Falernian.

The ancient Romans were the original wine geeks. They even had wine writers, most notably Pliny, who felt free to hold forth in distinguishing the quality of one prized wine from another, most famously in his book *Natural History*, which he wrote in AD 77, two years before his death while observing the eruption of Mount Vesuvius.

The most famous wine was called Falernian. In a fashion that we would describe today as Burgundian in its specificity, Pliny said three categories of Falernian wines were distinguished: Caucinian, which was grown on the higher slopes; Faustian (grown on the estate of Faustus, the son of the dictator Sulla) was grown on the mid-slope; and then there was plain Falernian from the lower slope. (Similar top/middle/lower distinctions are still made today for Burgundy's Clos de Vougeot vineyard.)

Falernian was praised unreservedly and was considered at its best after fifteen or twenty years of age. Hearing this, the modern mind automatically assumes that Falernian was a red wine, as white wines are notoriously fragile.

But, in fact, Falernian was white. It was made from what was then called the Aminean grape, which has every possibility, according to modern historians, of being the same grape that today we call Greco di Tufo. What's more, it was quite high in alcohol, probably around 15 percent, which would certainly help it keep. This was achieved by allowing the grapes to get very ripe before being picked. And then some or all of the grapes were placed on straw mats and allowed to raisin. In short, Falernian was a *passito* wine, which of course are still being made today (see Recioto della Valpolicella, page 192, and Vin Santo, page 259).

The wine was aged in small (seven gallons) clay amphorae, which were sealed with wax and pitch. The pitch—really a resinous sap—would seep into the wine over time, and the Roman wine fanciers discovered that they liked this flavor addition. Indeed, wine was never served, as the Italians would say today, *in purezza,* or a pure state. It was instead a vehicle for other flavorings such as seawater (they liked the tang) or pine sap (think of the Greek wine Retsina).

Because of the long aging and expense of creating a *passito* wine, as well as the limited amount of juice dried grapes offer, Falernian was hugely expensive. It was strictly for the wealthy, much like Chateau d'Yquem is today.

All of which gives some inkling of Campania's unrivaled history as a fine-wine region. Regrettably, this pedigree of fine winegrowing lapsed in the zone not just for centuries, but millennia. Wine certainly continued to be grown without interruption. But the audience, and the ambition, declined with the fall of Rome, which Gibbon dated to AD 476, when the last Roman emperor was deposed by the Germanic invaders.

Campanian wine soldiered on as a local item, with the occasional attention of the international market for the poetically named Lachryma Christi (Tear of Christ) wine from the slopes of Mount

Vesuvius southeast of Naples. Offered as both a red and sweet white, it was much prized in the 1800s and early 1900s. But mostly the wines of Campania were local and rustic.

What's more, Campania's extraordinary wine history once made it a repository of hundreds of grape varieties, most of which have disappeared or become so obscure that tracing their ancient lineage is difficult or impossible.

This, in effect, is the story of Falanghina, Fiano di Avellino, and Greco di Tufo, all three white grapes having nearly gone extinct until brilliantly revived in the late twentieth century. The story is not as uncommon in Italy as one might imagine, as nearly every region has varieties or strains within a variety that are now lost or reduced to a mere few acres. Or they're anonymously intermixed in a vineyard with other varieties, a practice called, in California wine jargon, a "field blend."

How It's Changed: The great change everywhere in Campania started in the 1970s, as it did in so many other Italian wine zones. The revival of Italy's economy after World War II reached the south later than it did the north (and is still reaching it). But by the 1970s, the opportunity to think about wine as something more and better than a cheap demijohn to be sold in bulk began to penetrate.

The producer who responded first, and for decades afterward, best, was the Mastroberardino family. The brothers Antonio and Walter Mastroberardino (who, since 1994 after a family "earthquake," have gone their own ways, with Antonio retaining the family label and Walter starting a new winery called Terredora di Paolo) pioneered the revival.

The Mastroberardino family is exceptionally historically minded and was long aware of Campania's great wine grape heritage. The family claims, likely rightly so, that they single-handedly revived Fiano di Avellino, rescuing it from extinction in 1940 by identifying single vines intermixed in vineyards, gathering the clusters, and producing all of thirty bottles' worth of wine.

The example of the Mastroberardino family, as well as their acclaim and financial success, was not lost upon their neighbors, although it was slow in coming (on both sides). By the 1980s, the renewed attention to Campania's native varieties became a kind of rallying cry, as well as a source of local pride. More than in, say, Sicily, growers in Campania seem convinced that their only worthwhile future rests with the grapes that are uniquely theirs.

Are these three white wines world-beaters? Not really. But all three really are worth the devoted attention of their producers as well as more than merely a glance from wine lovers everywhere. All three wines are distinctive, rewarding, and above all, a great pleasure to drink. No, they do not rival great white Burgundies or a magnificent Riesling. In fairness, I have never heard a Campanian producer suggest that they do. But they do deliver something rare in its own right today: a distinct personality.

Falanghina is a dry white with an exceptionally luscious texture. The name derives from the Latin *falanga*, or stake, the wooden support that allows a vine to grow upright. Falanghina is an unusually aromatic dry white wine, with come-hither hints of honeysuckle, peach, white pepper, and spices. That sounds like a lot, too much even, but this succulent dry white also delivers surprisingly crisp acidity. There's a definite citrus note, more so than in Fiano di Avellino. It's the sort of white wine that, unlike others, goes beyond the obvious pairing with fish. If anything, it's better with something creamy: pasta, risotto, soups. Or it's terrific just on its own as an aperitif or a sunset-sipper.

Fiano di Avellino is the variety rescued from oblivion by Antonio Mastroberardino in the 1940s. The grape variety once enjoyed considerable appreciation, very like because it ripens to an unusually high sugar content. Indeed, traditionally Fiano di Avellino (Avellino is a province in Campania) was always a sweet wine. Today's ubiquitous dry version is, in fact, a new twist. The most common, and accurate, descriptor of Fiano di Avellino is an attractive scent of hazelnuts allied with a whiff of pears, honey, and beeswax. It's a soft, ripe, almost Rubenesque white wine that's ideal as an aperitif or sunset-sipper. Because of its ripe richness, this is a white wine best served with pork, chicken, veal, or anything in a cream sauce. It's got better acidity than you might suspect, which becomes apparent when partnered with food.

Greco di Tufo is arguably the finest of the three great Campania whites, if only because it displays a minerality largely absent in Falanghina and Fiano di Avellino. There's more "backbone" in Greco di Tufo, a Matisse of a wine compared to Falanghina's Monet and Fiano's Rubens. (All three wines are quite sensual, as these fanciful comparisons suggest.)

No one disputes that Greco di Tufo is the oldest vine, the "greco" (*grieco* in local dialect) clearly referring to the ancient Greeks who first brought it to Italy; Tufo refers to the commune of Tufo where it thrives. Originally it was grown on the slopes of Mount Vesuvius, where it is better known as the white wine version of Lachryma Christi.

As with Fiano di Avellino and Falanghina, Greco di Tufo was traditionally a sweet wine. Campania's volcanic soils and generous sunshine encourage grapes to ripen fully, and these varieties respond willingly. However, planting any of these varieties at higher elevations checks that tendency thanks to greater coolness. (Remember the "normal lapse rate": For every thousand feet in elevation, the temperature drops three and one-half degrees. For a grapevine, that's huge.)

Greco di Tufo is today almost always made into a fully dry wine delivering restrained scents of almonds, apricot, peaches, pear, minerals, and herbs such as mint. At its best, it's fuller, richer, and somehow a more encompassing wine than Falanghina or even the naturally opulent Fiano di Avellino. This makes it an especially good choice for veal or chicken, as well as anything creamy and rich, including cheeses.

Noteworthy Producers (The Traditionalists / The Modernists): Although Campania has an ever-increasing number of producers, many of whom are spurred to greater achievement by the success of a handful of the best-known names, only a few producers really matter in the American market. Happily, this select group are the leaders. They make the benchmark wines, and they're well-distributed. If you try wines from any of the producers that follow, you're assured of getting the best of Campania made today.

FEUDI DI SAN GREGORIO—Although Mastroberardino gets pride of place (and great respect) for its pioneering efforts at celebrating Campania's heritage varieties, as well as issuing some of the best renditions, today the producer to beat in Campania is the relatively new and ambitious winery Feudi di San Gregorio.

Founded only in 1986 by Vicenzo Ercolino and his wife, Mirella Capaldo, Feudi di San Gregorio is the superstar of southern Italy. Everything about the quite large (250,000 cases and growing) winery speaks of ambition. Nearly all of the growing array of wines, red and white, offered by Feudi di San Gregorio is among the best of its kind, as well as modern-tasting in its cleanliness, depth of flavor, and delineation.

And, amazingly, although there are plenty of small oak barrels present in Feudi's ultra-modern, Japanese-designed $25 million winery and visitor center (the modernity of which is almost shocking in the otherwise conventional small hill town of Sorbo Serpico), they have the sense to leave their white wines well away from these barrels.

Committed to indigenous Campanian varieties, Feudi di San Gregorio offers all three whites: Falanghina, Fiano di Avellino, and Greco di Tufo. All three are benchmarks. Indeed, I have not tasted better. The Falanghina, especially, seems to lead the pack. This is a great producer, which demonstrates that size is no impediment to quality if the necessary rigor is present. They've got it (see also Taurasi, page ___).

MASTROBERARDINO—As previously mentioned, Mastroberardino is the lighthouse of Campania, the winery (and family) that showed the way. The fraternal breakup in 1994 resulted in a loss of some vineyards, which seemed, initially, to affect the quality of the wines. Today, however, the winery seems back on track. Its Fiano di Avellino and Greco di Tufo—both sporting the proprietary name Radici, or roots—are superb: detailed, flush with fruit, yet restrained and balanced. Falanghina Sannio (Sannio is a district name) is equally sublime. Also very good Lachryma Christi del Vesuvio in both the white and red versions—very likely the best made today.

OCONE—Domenico Ocone is much less well-known than Mastroberardino or Feudi di San Gregorio and much smaller than either of those two powerhouses as well. But in matters of quality, Ocone occupies the same pinnacle.

Like nearly everyone else in the area, the Ocone family originally sold its wine locally to demijohns to private clients and in bulk to local shippers. But starting in the late 1960s, when Luigi Ocone took over the winery with a desire to estate-bottle the family's production, the Ocone wines became more ambitious.

Today, the son, Domenico, is committed to biodynamic grape-growing and winemaking, which is an extreme, and rigorous, form of organic agriculture. Ocone's Falanghina di Taburno (Taburno is a district name) is superb, as is their Greco di Taburno. An oak-aged single-vineyard Falanghina called Vigna del Monaco is also offered, although I don't recall ever seeing it in America.

TERREDORA DI PAOLO—The "other" Mastroberardino. Although founded in 1994, it's hardly surprising that Terredora di Paolo (Paolo is one of Walter Mastroberadino's sons) quickly rocketed to the top rank. For one thing, Walter Mastroberardino had half of the original family vineyards, about half of which were planted to Greco di Tufo and the rest to Fiano di Avellino and the red Aglianico. Needless to say, the two white wines were the strongest contenders in the new winery's portfolio.

Today, Terredora di Paolo has more vineyard acreage (about 340 acres at last count) and more stocks of wines, especially reds, aging in their cellar. As with the other shining lights of the zone, their Falanghina is top notch, as is their Fiano di Avellino. There's also a single-vineyard Falanghina of striking intensity called Campore. Not least is a Greco di Tufo that's very likely the finest bottling of any in the zone, especially the two single-vineyard versions, Loggia della Serra and Terre degli Angeli.

Walter Mastroberardino, as much as his brother, Antonio, is committed to indigenous varieties. So the entire lineup of Terredora di

Paolo wines is made exclusively from indigenous grapes. There's very good Lachryma Christi, red and white, too. This is a very great producer with yet more to come given its newness.

What Do The Locals Eat With This Wine? Campanian cuisine, as anyone who's been in Naples can attest, is lusty fare. No lingerie-thin slip of raw fish for these folks. The same applies for their wines. All three of these whites are full-bodied, fairly rich, and capable to taking on a far greater array of foods than, say, an austere French Chablis. As previously noted, all of these wines are commonly paired with fish (which in the area often see the addition of olives, garlic, tomatoes, and other sun-kissed items). But cheeses are ideal, as are white meats such as chicken, pork, and veal.

One Man's Taste—Whose Wine Would I Buy? Really, any of the producers cited previously are equally good. I like the pricing of Feudi di San Gregorio, which is significantly less expensive than Mastroberardino. Ocone is less easily found, but when I see it, I grab it. Ditto for Terredora di Paolo.

Worth Searching For? Absolutely worth an effort

Similar Wines From The Same Neighborhood: Various local varieties such as white Coda di Volpe and the very obscure Pallagrello Bianco, as well as reds such as Piedirosso, Aglianico and the extremely rare Casavecchia and Pallagrello Nero. (These last two red varieties are made by Vestini Campagnano, a winery founded in 1990 for the express purpose of reviving these previously uncommercialized antique varieties. A small amount does trickle into the United States.)

Gattinara

(gah-tee-*nah*-rah)
Red

Region: Piedmont (northwest Italy)

Grapes: Nebbiolo (minimum 90 percent) and Bonarda (maximum 10 percent) (both red)

The Tradition: Whenever anyone mentions Piedmont or Nebbiolo (or both), everyone's mind instantly turns to Barolo and Barbaresco. But there was a time, a half-century ago and more, when the district and wine called Gattinara was as prestigious and highly regarded as Barolo. Both wines are Nebbiolo; both are famous for aging and improving for decades. Indeed, a good Gattinara will easily outlast a good Barolo—for a reason.

Even though they're both made entirely (well, a minimum of 90 percent for Gattinara) from Nebbiolo, the two wines *are* different. The difference comes from two sources: temperature and soil.

Barolo and Barbaresco are both in the Langhe hills, which is in southern Piedmont. But Gattinara is roughly 75 miles north of the Langhe. It's in the Vercelli and Novara hills, which are the real *piemonte*, or foothills, of the towering Alps. The climate is noticeably cooler, which means growing Nebbiolo there is a bit of a stretch.

And even when it ripens, Nebbiolo doesn't ripen quite as fully as it does farther south in the Langhe. This is why all of the Nebbiolo-based wines in the *colli Novaresi* and *colli Vercelesi* traditionally blend other red grapes with their Nebbiolo, which the law reflects to this day. Proof of Gattinara's privileged (meaning warmer) site is found in the fact that it must be at least 90 percent Nebbiolo, which is far higher than for wines from nearby districts such as Ghemme, Fara, Sizzano, Boca, or Lessona. Its localized warmth is unique.

142

This northerly location, even in Gattinara, means the wine is slightly more acidic than Barolo and Barbaresco. In lesser vintages that's a bit daunting as Nebbiolo is already an intrinsically high-acid variety. That alone tells you that vintages *really* matter with Gattinara.

But the real difference, the informing one, comes from soil. For once, this business of soil is easily traced and understood. The Langhe hills are a former seabed. This is why its soil is chalky clay, thanks to eons of sediment (the clay) and uncounted generations of dead sea critters (the calcareous chalk).

But the Novara and Vercelli hills are glacial in origin. The soil is granitic. No prizes for guessing what the nearby Alps are composed of.

This soil difference is potent for an ultrasensitive grape variety such as Nebbiolo. Translated into wine it means that, all other things being equal (ripeness, sugar content, winemaking technique), a Gattinara will always taste harder, be less fleshy and more austere, convey a distinctive minerality, and take longer to mature than a Barolo. Soil has much to do with these distinctions, along with the area's more ripeness-inhibiting coolness.

The granite soil and cooler climate means growing Nebbiolo in the zone is no easy undertaking. The area's centuries-old separation from the more intensive "Nebbiolo culture" to the south is underscored by language. In the Novara and Vercelli hills, Nebbiolo is called *Spanna* in dialect. That word is unknown in the Langhe. Indeed, for centuries and still today, local growers offer an inexpensive Nebbiolo wine simply called Spanna.

How It's Changed: Despite its once-lustrous reputation (the Swiss were big Gattinara connoisseurs), Gattinara has steadily declined in vineyard area, price, and overall quality since World War II. What happened in Gattinara was the same desertion from unremunerative farms as happened throughout Italy (see "Mezzadria—How Sharecropping Profoundly Affected Italian Wine," page ___).

But this flight from the fields was extreme in the Novara and

Vercelli hills for the compelling reason that the cities and towns of the area—Novara, Ivrea, Biella, and many others—were precisely where Italy's Industrial Revolution began before World War I. It was and still is the heart of Italy's thriving textile industry. (If you're looking for a Giorgio Armani "second," this is where you have to go.) Ivrea, for example, was home to the Olivetti manufacturing and computer business.

The hard-to-cultivate granitic hills of Gattinara and its satellite wine zones—Ghemme, Fara, Sizzano, Boca, Lessona, and Bramaterra—were not just depopulated but actually reverted to scrub.

To this day you can easily spot former vineyards long since gone fallow: The scrub is all of a certain height, as it's all about the same 50-year-old age. And you can still see the odd, now-wild, grapevine clambering its tendrils and shoots up the scrubby trees. (The trees are so stunted because the granitic soil is so poor in nutrients.)

Gattinara never recovered. To this day it persists as a lack-of-success story among great Italian wines. Gattinara not only has nowhere near as much vineyard acreage as its famous competitors—Gattinara has just 222 acres of vines compared to Barolo's 3,100 acres and Barbaresco's 1,100 acres—but worse, it suffers an underachiever's lack of ambition and conviction that the future holds promise.

Does it? Sure it does. There are a few very good to borderline great Gattinaras. And when you taste one, especially if it's at least a decade old from a good vintage, you'll have no doubt in your mind or palate. Gattinara at its best is a very great wine. But it's still waiting for its Messiah. Most of the producers there are content to be merely commercial, rather than obsessive about quality and evangelical about the area.

Noteworthy Producers (The Traditionalists/The Modernists): The distinction between traditionalists and modernists in Gattinara is a small one, if only because there aren't many producers (thirty at most) and the real delineation is between commercial quality and something finer.

Gattinara's best producers can be counted on the fingers of one hand: Antoniolo, Travaglini, Dessilani, and a small newcomer, Anzivino. And that, believe it or not, is about it.

The best producer, by far, is Antoniolo. It is the standard-bearer for the zone, offering three single vineyard bottlings: Le Catelle, Osso San Rato, and San Francesco in addition to a regular Gattinara bottling. Their winemaking is modern with just a touch of oak. But in Antoniolo's wines, especially the Osso San Rato and San Francesco bottlings, you can taste really fine Gattinara, with its faint scent of violets allied to various berry notes and a certain stoniness in scent and taste.

A much larger producer, Travaglini, issues two wines, both in a rather bizarre, lumpily squarish bottle that Travaglini has used for decades. The regular Travaglini Gattinara is good but far from great. However, the denser, richer Riserva version really is very fine, as well as classically long-lived.

The rather commercial producer Nervi makes a reasonably good single-vineyard bottling called Vigneto Molsino.

Dessilani, for its part, has always issued reliable Gattinara. But somehow it never achieves greatness, although it's certainly a satisfying wine.

What Do The Locals Eat With This Wine? Like their fellow Piedmontese, the locals reserve Gattinara for the highlight of the meal, which usually means the meat course. Game is a great favorite, although an older Gattinara (twenty years or more) may well be reserved for the cheese tray.

One Man's Taste—Whose Wine Would I Buy? There's no question about it: You want Antoniolo, preferably one of its single-vineyard bottlings. Barring that, I'd look for Travaglini Riserva.

Worth Searching For? Absolutely worth an effort

Similar Wines From The Same Neighborhood: Ghemme, Boca, Fara,

Sizzano, and Bramaterra. Look also for the generically labeled Spanna (Nebbiolo). Of these, the best by far is Ghemme, especially from the producer Cantalupo, whose wines are outstanding (and imported to America). Ghemme was long considered second only to Gattinara in quality and distinction. Cantalupo's wines show why. They are worth a search.

Lagrein

(lah-*grine*, rhymes with *spine*)
RED / ROSÉ

Region: Trentino/Alto Adige (northern Italy near the Austrian border)

Grapes: 100 percent Lagrein (red)

The Tradition: One of the opportunities of today's active appreciation of Italian wines is that previously obscure bottlings are now coming to our attention. Lagrein is one of these. It's grown only in the Trentino/Aldo Adige region of northern Italy, mostly and best in the higher elevations of Alto Adige/Südtirol.

   A word about the Alto Adige/Südtirol: This is the northern part of the region. Because it was once part of Austria, the local and much-preferred language is German. After World War I, the region was ceded to Italy. (During World War II, the Germans took it back, but it was ceded yet again to Italy at the war's end.) Today it's now part of Italy.

   To the locals it's Südtirol or South Tyrol; to Italians it's Alto Adige (ahl-toe *ah*-dee-jeh), literally the upper part of the Adige River. Official usage decrees both languages, hence Alto Adige/Südtirol.

   The southern portion of the Trentino-Alto Adige region is the province of Trento (which confusingly is also the name of the main city of the province). Inhabitants of Trentino are Italian speakers. They've always looked south to Italy rather than north to Austria.

   Not surprisingly, tensions ran high for decades after World War II. Both provinces, especially Alto Adige/Südtirol, have been granted unusual governmental autonomy by Italy. This was to defuse separatist tensions, which became increasingly violent in Alto Adige/Südtirol in the 1950s, '60's, and '70s. Today, Alto Adige/Südtirol is very nearly a state within the larger Italian state, so extensive are its autonomous powers.

Now, where was I? Oh yes, Lagrein. Although grown successfully in the southern (Trentino) part of the region—specifically in Campo Rotaliano plain near the city of Trento, which is better known for Teroldego (see page 238)—Lagrein is really an Alto Adige/Südtirol specialty.

A red grape, Lagrein appears in two kinds of wines: a deep, rich full-blown red wine called Lagrein *dunkel* (German) or *scuro* (Italian). Both mean "dark." And Lagrein also takes a turn as an exceptionally delicious rosé or *rosato*.

In Alto Adige/Südtirol, the locals call the rosé (which can also be made into a sparkling wine) a Lagrein *kretzer*. The name stems from *kretze*, a kind of woven basket used long ago to sieve the must (the just-fermented wine with the grape skins).

Both the red and the rosé are worthy, with the full-blown red wine being, of course, the more serious of the two.

A good Lagrein *dunkel* is deeply colored, almost opaque and—given the formidableness of the color—surprisingly rich and soft. It typically offers scents of ripe blackberries and plums, along with hints of nutmeg, anise, and violets. Often there's a distinct minerality thanks to the limestone soils commonly found in Alto Adige/Südtirol. The very deep color is deceptive in that you expect a somewhat "flabby" wine from overripe grapes, yet Lagrein usually has a bright acidity, which makes it a fine partner with food.

The *rosato* Lagrein, for its part, is one of the world's better rosés. A good one delivers a zippy flavor intensity, as Lagrein is so intensely fruity even when coming to the ball barely dressed, as it were.

How It's Changed: The biggest change to Lagrein has been the introduction of small new oak barrels to the winemaking. This, of course, is hardly unique in Italy. But unlike some other grape varieties that can be—and often are—overwhelmed by oak, Lagrein can handle it. Indeed, the vanilla scent of new oak marries nicely with Lagrein's blackberry scent. (Think of a fruit cobbler with a pastry crust endowed with the tiny seeds of a vanilla bean and you won't be far off.)

The other big change is sheer seriousness of purpose. When Lagrein was strictly local—which it was until the 1980s—its admirers gave it respect but hardly insisted on putting Lagrein up against the world's great reds. However, in today's permanent wine revolution (to borrow from Marx and Engels), Lagrein has been thrown into competition with the Big Reds from France and California, as well as against other Italian contenders. Consequently, ambitious producers lowered their vineyard yields, used small new French oak barrels, and selected the choicest sites. They treated Lagrein as if company were coming—which, in a way, it was. The results are now the finest Lagreins ever tasted.

Noteworthy Producers (The Traditionalists/The Modernists): Even though the total acreage of Lagrein is fairly limited (roughly five hundred acres in the southern Trentino province, much of it new since the 1980s, and seven hundred acres in Alto Adige/Süd Tirol, much of it old), the number of good producers is gratifyingly large. Really, very few poor Lagreins are sent to the United States, if only because it's an obscure (to us) variety and the demand is elitist, in the best sense. These producers are all admirable: Hofstätter (especially the Steinraffler Vineyard), Alois Lageder, Elena Walch, Tiefenbrunner, Mayr-Nusser, Tenuta Waldgries, Bottega Vinaia, Ignaz Niedrist, Klosterkellerei Muri Gries, Cantina Tramin, Cantina Santa Maddalena, Castell Salleg, and Colterenzio.

What Do The Locals Eat With This Wine? As with, say, Teroldego (see page 238), the cuisine associated with Lagrein is decidedly Germanic and hearty. The real Lagrein fanciers are in Alto Adige/Südtirol. And there, high in the mountains hard against the Austrian Alps, the cooking is nothing if not substantial. You see a lot of *speck* (a salted and cold-smoked cured pork with a generous amount of fat, similar to pancetta or bacon); you're treated to bread dumplings (*canederli*) and various meats, especially game. Since Lagrein is certainly one of the heartiest reds of the area, and well-regarded, a Lagrein *dunkel* will take pride of place with the main—inevitably meat—course.

A Lagrein *rosato*, on the other hand, serves during the antipasto, as a chilled summer red or any other time when the food is lighter. More than most rosés, a Lagrein *rosato* has real depth and can pair well with all but the most forcefully flavored, e.g., smoked or braised, meats.

One Man's Taste—Whose Wine Would I Buy? Several producers consistently issue terrific Lagrein *dunkel*. All are in Alto Adige/Südtirol, as that northern province is the true home of this variety. My first choice would be the oak-kissed (but not heavily smooched) Lagrein "Steinraffler Vyd." from Hofstätter. It's a real benchmark bottling: rich, structured, intense, yet graceful.

In fairness, the greatest single Lagrein producer is surely Klosterkellerei Muri Gries, which issues no fewer than three different bottlings. In 1845, Benedictine monks from the monastery of Muri in Switzerland took over the abandoned Canons Monastery of the Gries (originally started in the twelfth century), and from then on, the monastery was known as Muri-Gries. The monks still perform most of the work in the vineyard, hand pruning the vines and hand harvesting the grapes.

Lagrein is this winery's great specialty, so much so that they've identified as many as one hundred strains or clones of Lagrein in their ancient vineyard. Look especially for the Lagrein "Abtei Muri" bottling, grown inside the monastery's walls (in Latin, *muri*). It is their most significant bottling and easily one of the greatest Lagreins made today. (Note: "Gries" refers to a zone near the city of Bolzano, a gravelly plain. If the Lagrein grapes come from vineyards in this zone, the wine can be labeled Lagrein di Gries or Griser Lagrein.)

Worth Searching For? Absolutely worth an effort

Similar Wines From The Same Neighborhood: Far less known, although much more extensively grown, is the local red grape called Schiava (skee-*yah*-vah), also called Vernatsch in German. A fruity red wine, Schiava is much liked in Alto Adige/Südtirol. Although similar to Lagrein in its fresh berry flavors, it tends to be lighter and less intense than Lagrein and is often drunk when very young. But perhaps that's because it hasn't been lavished with the same ambition now bestowed on Lagrein. Or maybe the locals know that Schiava is a simple draft horse to Lagrein's thoroughbred. Whatever the reason, I've yet to taste a Schiava as substantial and dimensional as the best Lagrein. That said, Schiava is a pleasing red and worth trying if you see it.

Lambrusco

(lahm-*broos*-koh)
RED

Region: Emilia-Romagna (north-central Italy, between Milan and Florence)

Grapes: Lambrusco (red); several strains such as Lambrusco di Sorbara, Lambrusco Salamino, and what's generally acknowledged as the best strain, Lambrusco Grasparossa (so named because its stems and pedicles turn red in autumn)

The Tradition: Italy has a longstanding, and widespread, tradition of drinking red wines that are semi-sparkling, what the Italians call *frizzante*. When you pour them into a glass, they froth and then settle down into something very close to a "regular" wine. But *frizzante* wines nevertheless retain a slight, refreshing prickle in the mouth. Historically, many Italian reds (and even more whites) were made in both still and *frizzante* versions, such as Brachetto and Freisa in Piedmont and Aglianico in Campania in southern Italy, among many others.

The reason previous generations liked *frizzante* red wines was the richness (or fattiness, anyway) of their food. Bubbles cut through rich food, whether it's a slice of salami or a lavish feast with cream sauces.

Knowing this, it's easy to see why Lambrusco—which can fairly be described as Italy's great frizzante red—has survived. Emilia-Romagna has what is indisputably Italy's richest, creamiest, fattiest cooking. (Need I say that it's scrumptious?) The frothy, brightly acidic, richly fruity Lambrusco is just the ticket—or rather, the knife—to take on the local dishes.

That said, the taste for frizzante extended to dessert as well. One of Lambrusco's great traditions, still in effect today, is a *dolce* or sweet version. It, too, has its place on the table (especially with fruits and fruit tarts). And sometimes, on a hot summer days, nothing beats a cool *dolce* Lambrusco.

How It's Changed: Because the various strains or clones of the Lambrusco grape variety are all generous in their yields, Lambrusco had two informing traditions: It was frequently made by farmers for their own consumption, and these same farmers saw no reason to lower their yields and thus reduce their yearly supply of their beloved Lambrusco wine.

Many local Lambrusco lovers in Modena and Bologna will go out to farms in the region to buy their yearly supply of artisanally made *Lambròsc*, as they say in dialect. These wines—unlike commercial bottlings made in big stainless steel tanks—are fermented in the bottle like French Champagnes. I've had some over the years. Sometimes they're terrific, reflecting low yields, good grapes, and fine winemaking. Other times they're, shall we say, rustic.

What this means is that Lambrusco has always been a wine, whether commercially produced or rustic, that has not enjoyed a demanding audience. It was expected to be cheap, frothy, and pleasant. It was not expected, as it were, to go to college.

This approach still remains today, with some wonderful, noteworthy exceptions. The great majority of Lambrusco wines today are made by one of at least seven winegrowers' cooperatives in the zone. All are professional; few create anything much beyond the commercial.

One of these is the Lambrusco that most wine-drinking Americans know: the Lambrusco brand-named Riunite, named after the winegrowers' cooperative of the same name (Cantine Cooperative Riunite) that creates the wine. It's made for its American importer Villa Banfi in vast quantities to Banfi's carefully calculated specifications.

Riunite is a sweetish or *amabile* version of Lambrusco; it's very light in color and weight—closer to soda pop than "real" Lambrusco. Nevertheless, Riunite is one of the world's best-selling and best-distributed wines. Although a far cry from its original model, the success of this very particular version of Lambrusco says something about the fundamental appeal of both the Lambrusco grape and the *frizzante* style.

Noteworthy Producers (The Traditionalists / The Modernists): As noted previously, most Lambrusco bottlings are simple commercial items. It's all about quantity (15 million bottles a year) and low price. Lately, one or another winegrowers' cooperative announces a new "elite" Lambrusco, designed to win more respect and fetch a higher price. But such offerings are more about *bella figura* than conviction.

That said, a handful of Lambrusco producers are truly serious about this long underrated wine. They typically use the Lambrusco Grasparossa strain, which is lower yielding and creates a richer, dense wine. And they prune these vines more severely yet, resulting in few clusters per vine that create wines of greater character, concentration, and depth.

Foremost among these ambitious producers is the small family estate called Villa di Corlo. They produce several versions of Lambrusco, including a delicious *dolce* bottling. But the signature wine, really a benchmark bottling, is the dry, dense, and full-bodied Lambrusco called Corleto.

Almost as good is a larger company called Medici Ermete. Their best Lambrusco is bottled in an unusually attractive bottle shaped somewhat like a bowling pin. It's called Concerto and it too delivers a rare quality.

Look also for a small producer called Barbolini.

There surely are other, small, producers whose wines trickle into America, brought in by impassioned importers after their own epiphanies drinking a local, artisanal Lambrusco during a lunch or dinner in Emilia-Romagna.

None of these exemplars costs much money; both are meant to be savored with food joyously rather than "seriously." Yet their respective producers are themselves serious, knowing the obstacles they have to overcome in order to convince the world of Lambrusco's real capacity for goodness.

What Do The Locals Eat With This Wine? Rich or deliciously fatty is the ticket with Lambrusco. The locals have it with salami, a rich lasagna, cheesy pizza, various dishes braised in red wine such as braised rabbit or beef, and not least, the local world-famous cheese, Parmigiano-Reggiano. Sweeter versions are served with fruits and with various almond-flavored cakes. A favorite pairing with *dolce* Lambrusco are soft amaretti or macaroons. It also tastes great with roasted chestnuts.

All Lambruscos should be served cool but not refrigerator-cold.

One Man's Taste—Whose Wine Would I Buy? My first choice is Villa di Corlo's bottling called Corleto, which has a small but growing distribution in the United States. Look also for Medici Ermete's Concerto bottling. And if you spy an obviously small-grower Lambrusco brought in by an ambitious local importer or merchant, by all means give it a try. After all, you're not going to be risking much money. And the pleasure possibility is in your favor.

Worth Searching For? If you happen to see it

Similar Wines From The Same Neighborhood: As always, various local wines can be found, if only on the spot. Look for such wines as Fortana (a dark, frothy red grown near the city of Parma) and a rarely seen frothy white called Montuni del Reno.

Langhe Rosso

(*la'hn*-geh *roh*-so)
RED

Region: Piedmont (northwest Italy)

Grapes: Possible 100 percent named-varietals for reds: Nebbiolo, Dolcetto, and Freisa; for whites: Arneis, Favorita, and Chardonnay. For blends (Langhe Rosso), anything can be blended. Typical blends include such grapes as Nebbiolo, Barbera, Syrah, Pinot Noir, and Cabernet Sauvignon, among others. "Langhe Bianco" is a blend that might include Chardonnay, Sauvignon Blanc, Arneis, and Favorita, among others.

The Tradition: As elsewhere in Italy, in the 1980s and '90s Piedmont saw considerable rebellion against what were perceived (often rightly) as overly restrictive wine regulations. Again, as elsewhere, regulations regarding permitted varieties and unpermitted blends were often flouted, usually discreetly but sometimes quite publicly.

Increasingly, the most ambitious (or revolutionary) producers turned their backs on the traditional label designations about place (Barolo, Barbaresco, or in Tuscany, Chianti Classico) and instead used the humblest, least specific designation possible: Vino da Tavola. This was really cocking a snoot. A category once associated with the cheapest, coarsest, lowest sort of bulk wine was employed for Italy's most ambitious, sometimes finest, and often most expensive wines. That it also conveyed a reverse snobbery *bella figura* made it more attractive yet.

To the authorities, however, it was insubordination of the worst sort, a flouting of their carefully constructed pyramid of class and quality. The legalities they so carefully, voluminously, and oppressively put forth were being used against them, like gleeful high-school students finding a loophole in an oppressive principal's ever more restrictive regulations.

A less-nuanced culture might have insisted on a crackdown. But Italy is Italy for a reason: Experience long ago taught Italians that you can just as easily conquer your opponent with subversive accommodation as by unyielding resistance. So the authorities simply changed the law.

They said, "OK, *basta* with this vino da tavola business. We'll create a new category that allows you to legally blend what you like. In Piedmont you must call it 'Langhe.' *Then* you will be in compliance with the law!"

So in good Italian style, everybody won. The authorities had their putative authority restored to them (very important, if only to save face), and the winegrowers got to do what they wanted (which they were doing anyway) without harrassment.

How It's Changed: The legal appellation called "Langhe" became effective in 1994. There are two sorts of "Langhe" bottlings. First, there are those with a grape name appended, e.g., Nebbiolo Langhe, Dolcetto Langhe, Chardonnay Langhe, etc. These wines must come from the legally defined zone for the "Langhe" designation (including the Roero district, which is not, in fact, in the actual Langhe hills). These variety-qualified Langhe labels must be composed exclusively from the grape variety specified.

The other "Langhe" bottling is not qualified by a grape name. It's called just Langhe Rosso or Langhe Bianco. Here, anything goes. You can blend as you like, which is precisely what nearly all producers using the "Langhe Rosso" or "Langhe Bianco" designation do. Since the zone is dominated by red grapes, the vast majority of "Langhe" wines are Langhe Rosso.

A typical Langhe Rosso, if such a thing could be so characterized, employs Nebbiolo to which one or more of the following grapes are added: Barbera, Syrah, Pinot Noir, Merlot, Dolcetto, or Cabernet Sauvignon. Often there's a lavish dose of new French oak added as well. And prices are rarely at the low end. These are *bella figura* bottlings, after all.

One effect of the new Langhe designation is that it has all but snuffed the old Nebbiolo d'Alba designation, which is more prescriptive and restrictive than the new Nebbiolo Langhe label. Still, some more traditionally minded producers prefer the old Nebbiolo d'Alba designation and continue to use it (see page 182).

Noteworthy Producers (The Traditionalists/The Modernists): It is all but impossible to generalize about Langhe Rosso bottlings except to say they represent a producer's philosophy or experimentalism. In most cases, they are unpredictable in taste.

Take, for example, the wine called Quartetto from the producer Aldo Conterno. It's a blend of Nebbiolo, Barbera, Cabernet Sauvignon, and Merlot, hence Quartetto. Does it taste Piedmontese? Hardly. It's a big, rich red wine that's meant to appeal to a so-called international market, as opposed to Conterno's great Barolos, which appeal to, well, an international market.

Then you have Piedmont's most expensive wines: the various Barbaresco bottlings of Angelo Gaja. They used to be labeled Barbaresco. Now, with the sole exception of Gaja's "regular" Barbaresco bottling, which still uses the appellation name, all of Gaja's other wines, red and white, are technically Langhe Rosso or Langhe Bianco. Yet Gaja's famous single-vineyard Barbarescos—excuse me, Langhe Rossos—are in fact 95 percent Nebbiolo and 5 percent Barbera, give or take a few percentage points.

Why does Gaja use the Langhe Rosso designation? Because he wants to add a little Barbera, mostly for its color-enhancing quality, and the regulations for Barbaresco insist on 100 percent Nebbiolo. So Gaja—whose name is more famous than Barbaresco—takes refuge in Langhe Rosso. His worldwide fan base doesn't care. They're buying "Gaja" after all, rather than mere "Barbaresco."

And so it goes. Here are some of the more noteworthy Langhe Rosso bottlings. Each is different and can—and very likely will—change in its blend of grape varieties or their proportions from vintage to vintage. You can usually be sure of a little, or a lot, of vanilla-scented oakiness from the use of new small French oak barrels.

ELIO ALTARE VIGNA "ARBORINA"—Nebbiolo (100 percent)

ELIO ALTARE "LARIGI"—Barbera (100 percent)

ELIO ALTARE "LA VILLA"—Nebbiolo and Barbera

ENZO BOGLIETTI "BUIO"—Nebbiolo (80 percent) and Barbera (20 percent)

CERETTO "MONSORDO"—Cabernet Sauvignon, Pinot Noir, Merlot, and Nebbiolo

DOMENICO CLERICO "ARTE"—Nebbiolo (90 percent), Barbera (5 percent), and Cabernet Sauvignon (5 percent)

PODERE COLLA "BRICCO DEL DRAGO"—Dolcetto (85 percent) and Nebbiolo (15 percent)

ALDO CONTERNO "IL FAVOT"—Nebbiolo (100 percent)

ALDO CONTERNO "QUARTETTO"—Nebbiolo, Barbera, Cabernet Sauvignon, and Merlot

CONTERNO-FANTINO "MONPRA"—Nebbiolo, Barbera, and Cabernet Sauvignon

MATTEO CORREGIA "LE MARNE GRIGIE"—Barbera (75 percent) and Nebbiolo (25 percent)

ANGELO GAJA "SITO MORESCO"—Nebbiolo (35 percent), Merlot (35 percent), and Cabernet Sauvignon (30 percent)

ANGELO GAJA "CONTEISA"—Nebbiolo (92 percent) and Barbera (8 percent)

ANGELO GAJA "COSTA RUSSI"/"SORÌ SAN LORENZO"/"SORÌ TILDIN"—Each is Nebbiolo (approximately 95 percent) and Barbera (approximately 5 percent)

ANGELO GAJA "SPERSS"—Nebbiolo (94 percent) and Barbera (6 percent)

ANGELO GAJA "DARMAGI"—Cabernet Sauvignon (95 percent), Merlot (3 percent), and Cabernet Franc (2 percent)

ETTORE GERMANO "BALÀU"—Dolcetto (65 percent), Barbera (25 percent), and Merlot (10 percent)

MARCARINI "DONALD"—Barbera (60 percent), Nebbiolo (30 percent), and Syrah (10 percent)

FIORENZO NADA "SEIFILE"—Nebbiolo (70 to 80 percent) and Barbera (20 to 30 percent)

GIORGIO RIVETTI "PIN"—Nebbiolo, Cabernet Sauvignon, and Barbera

LUCIANO SANDRONE "PE MOL" (PEG LEG) LANGHE ROSSO—Barbera (60 percent) and Nebbiolo (40 percent)

PAOLO SCAVINO "CORALE"—Nebbiolo (50 percent), Barbera, Cabernet Sauvignon, and Merlot

CA' VIOLA "BRIC DU LUV" ("luv" is dialect for *lupo* or wolf)—Barbera and Pinot Noir

GIANNI VOERZIO "SERRAPIU"—Nebbiolo and Barbera

ROBERTO VOERZIO "FONTAN"—Merlot (100 percent)

What Do The Locals Eat With This Wine? The "international" nature of these wines, along with their very newness, means there's no local tradition of pairing these wines with anything in particular. Almost invariably, the Langhe Rosso blends are deeply colored, intensely fruity, and vanilla-scented from new oak barrels. So, like all other wines of this sort, whether French, Californian, Tuscan, or Piedmontese, the best food bets are strongly flavored meats such as beef, lamb, or game. Of course, the Langhe Rosso wines that are really Barolos or Barbarescos in disguise are paired with many traditional Piedmontese dishes.

One Man's Taste—Whose Wine Would I Buy? Setting aside wines such as Angelo Gaja's Barbarescos-in-all-but-label-name wines and other wines like it, I can't say that I would choose any of the Langhe Rosso blends. A Nebbiolo Langhe, sure. That's just the new guise for the old Nebbiolo d'Alba appellation. But the blends leave me unmoved. They're usually very expensive and smell more of the marketplace than of Piedmont.

Worth Searching For? Only if you're curious—and someone else is paying.

Similar Wines From The Same Neighborhood: None.

Montepulciano d'Abruzzo

(mawn–teh–pool–chee–*ah*–noh dah–*broo*–tzoh)

RED

Region: East-Central Italy (Abruzzo is a mountainous area that borders the Adriatic Sea. If you drive directly east from Rome across the Apennine Mountains, you'll be in Abruzzo.)

Grapes: Minimum of 85 percent Montepulciano; Sangiovese up to 15 percent (red)

The Tradition: Everybody who writes about Montepulciano d'Abruzzo feels compelled—is obligated, really—to point out that Montepulciano is the name of the grape variety and it has nothing to do with the confusingly similar name, and utterly different wine, called Vino Nobile di Montepulciano. That Tuscan wine is actually made from Sangiovese. And there, Montepulciano is the name of a town, rather than the local grape.

No one really knows why the red grape native to the Abruzzo area got tagged with the name of a Tuscan town. The Sangiovese and Montepulciano grape varieties are not at all related (although in the nineteenth century, it was once thought so).

Montepulciano is a red grape that creates one of Italy's most easily liked wines. Even the most commercial Montepulciano d'Abruzzo from one of the zone's several big winegrowers' cooperatives is an enjoyable quaff. At minimum, a Montepulciano d'Abruzzo is always a deeply colored, soft, lush red wine with a juicy fruitiness and soft tannins. At maximum, a great Montepulciano d'Abruzzo is a massive, inky-black red wine with a fjord-like depth of fruit, although never with as many layers or as much finesse as, say, a Brunello di Montalcino or a Barolo.

Traditionally, this was a wine that suffered not just from bulk sales but

162

a bulk mentality as well. The Montepulciano grape is a robust variety that willingly gives high vineyard yields. The impoverished growers of Abruzzo (until recently, a brutally poor region, even by Italian standards) were grateful for Montepulciano's fruitful generosity. They still are.

To this day, too many—most, even—Montepulciano d'Abruzzo wines are made from vines that yield far too many clusters per vine for real quality. This has been a problem for the increasing number of serious-minded producers who cut their yields in exchange for better quality. If a consumer sees one bottle of Montepulciano d'Abruzzo for $6.95 and another, identically labeled, for $15, which do you think gets bought?

The irony, in fairness, is that the $6.95 bottle is still pretty good, which shows just how attractive this wine really is. Still, the better growers, selling at a higher price, do deliver superior goods that are worth seeking out.

How It's Changed: Precisely because the Montepulciano grape is so generous in its yields, and because Abruzzo never commanded a premium for its wines, the most meaningful change in the zone involves yields. It's a pocketbook issue. The more clusters per vine, the more bottles of wine. To prune for fewer clusters (and then do a "green harvest" where you remove clusters in mid-summer) is psychically and financially painful. Yet that's what the best Montepulciano d'Abruzzo growers are doing. And the wines are better for it—and, yes, more expensive. (*Somebody's* got to pay for such improvements.)

Of course, there are also the expected improvements in winemaking facilities such as temperature-controlled stainless steel tanks and the use of small oak barrels. Also there are ambitious proprietarily named blends, typically adding Merlot or Cabernet Sauvignon on to a foundation of Montepulciano. These are never sold under the name Montepulciano d'Abruzzo because the law allows only the use of Sangiovese and that to a 15 percent maximum.

The best Montepulciano d'Abruzzo wines are powerfully concentrated, rich and deceptively gentle. The inky color makes you brace for a backwash of tannins, yet that almost never occurs. (If the wine is tannic, with a harsh, astringent, puckering texture, you can bet it's from the wood tannins of the small oak barrels, not the grape.)

Worth noting is that, good as it drinks when young, the best, most structured Montepulciano d'Abruzzo wines can age for upwards of twenty years. They get smoother, rounder, and a little more floral while losing some of the palate-popping ripe fruitiness that makes them so appealing in their youth. So if you lose one in your cellar, no worries. You'll be pleasantly surprised.

Some labels now refer to a new legal district designation called Montepulciano d'Abruzzo Colline Teramane. The Teramo province is a lower-elevation zone closer to the Adriatic Sea, which is thought by the locals to be capable of creating a distinctively different wine. Time will tell. It's still a Montepulciano d'Abruzzo, however.

ABOUT CERASUOLO—The Montepulciano grape, because it is so fruity and contains so much color in its skin, also lends itself to an unusually good (and often a little darker than usual) rosé or *rosato* that's locally called Cerasuolo (cheh-rah-*swoh*-loh).

Although not renowned, Cerasuolo is one of the world's great rosés and deserves to be better known. Many of the best red wine producers (proudly) offer a Cerasuolo as well. It's surprisingly flavorful for a rosé—too often they're insipid—delivering a cherry scent and taste and a cherry-red hue, hence the name Cerasuolo, which refers to cherries. It's worth seeking out.

Noteworthy Producers (The Traditionalists / The Modernists): It's a rare statement but true: There are almost no bad Montepulciano d'Abruzzo wines. Oh, there are plenty of simple ones. They are made by big winegrowers' cooperatives. They're light, fresh, clean, and grapey. They're also cheap. Fair enough.

This kind of wine (and bargain) is sold under such widely distributed labels as Casal Thaulero and Citra, among many others. They are not to be dismissed, as they are well-made, clean, and straightforward.

More ambitious producers offer more striking or even profound wine. Sometimes even these aren't so expensive either, although at least two (Valentini and Emidio Pepe) are as expensive as other top Italian reds.

BARONE CORNACCHIA—A reliably good producer with 79 acres of vines with three versions of Montepulciano d'Abruzzo. The regular wine (85 to 90 percent Montepulciano with 10 to 15 percent Sangiovese) is a very good example of Montepulciano d'Abruzzo and is attractively priced. Sterner stuff is found in the 100 percent Montepuliciano single-vineyard Le Coste bottling, with the Poggio Varano bottling seeing time in small oak barrels.

COL DEL MONDO—A relatively new producer issuing excellent Montepulciano d'Abruzzo in a fresh, modern style with excellent depth. Better yet is a knockout Cerasuolo (rosé) with a scent of wild cherries and a whiff of minerals.

FARNESE—A large, ambitious producer with several different versions of Montepulciano d'Abruzzo on offer. The regular bottling, simply called Farnese, is reliably good. Better yet are the Casale Vecchio and Opis bottlings, both of which are more intense and sturdier, as well as discernibly oaky—a little too much so for this taster. Still, the quality is apparent.

ILLUMINATI—One of the top names in the zone. Illuminati delivers the real goods, with 150 acres of vines. Look for the Riparosso bottling, which is a dense, rich creature with the savor of berries, jam, and sage. It's capable of aging beautifully, too. Various other bottling, designated Illico, Pieluni, and Zanna, all see varying times in small oak barrels. All are rich, intense wines that reward extended aging. Oakiness varies with the wine and the vintage, but all emphasize a modern, clean style with dramatic depth and concentration. Look also for a very good Cerasuola rosé called Campirosa. To seek out.

MASCIARELLI—A producer that in recent years has gone from strength to strength. Masciarelli's widely distributed basic Montepulciano d'Abruzzo is consistently one of the most reliable "bargain reds" on the market today. Soft, fruity, and silky, it's ready to drink the day you bring it home. More serious and strongly oak-inflected—or is that oak-inflicted?—is the Villa Gemma bottling, which is powerful and elegant. Another line, named after Gianni Masciarelli's wife, Marina Cvetic, is striking in depth and concentration. Masciarelli, with 195 acres of vines, is now one of the powerhouses of the zone, both economically and aesthetically.

MONTI—Small producer with two Montepulicoano bottlings: a good, regular version that delivers all the right stuffing and a powerful, somewhat oaky single-vineyard bottling called Pignotto. Both are excellent examples of their respective breeds.

NICODEMI—Small family winery in the new (2003) Colline Teramane subzone. Good, solid wines. The regular Montepulciano d'Abruzzo is all it should be. The Notàri bottling is (inevitably) aged in small oak barrels. It's intense, rich, and noticeably oak-influenced, but very fine.

EMIDIO PEPE—Every great wine region needs its resident eccentric genius. The Abruzzo has two, one of whom is Emidio Pepe. (The other is Edoardo Valentini.) Emidio Pepe's wines are like no others anywhere in Italy, perhaps the world.

Since taking over the family winery in 1964, Pepe has had an unusual, and unswerving, winemaking approach. He uses no barrels or wood casks. His organically grown grapes are fermented and aged in glass-lined tanks for eighteen to twenty-four months.

Then they are transferred, unfined (a technique of clarifying a wine by electrostatic attraction of tiny particles held in suspension, usually by whisking egg whites in the wine, which settle and carry the particles to the bottom), and unfiltered. He adds no sulfur dioxide (SO_2) during the winemaking, which is risky unless scrupulous cleanliness is maintained. Otherwise, wines can go "off."

Pepe then ages his Montepulciano wines for years in glass bottles. Before releasing them for sale, the wines are decanted from the "storage" bottles and transferred to a new bottle. Effectively, Pepe's Montepulciano d'Abruzzo spends its entire life, from the first day of fermentation, in glass. They have uniquely little contact with oxygen, which makes them very "primary" in the fruit flavors for years, even decades.

This idiosyncratic winemaking approach is not to everyone's palate. Emidio Pepe's Montepulciano is powerful, intense, utterly pure, even savage, when young. It also needs considerable exposure to air when you decide to serve it, first by decanting it a few hours ahead of time and then in a good-size wine glass.

But the result is memorable. Pepe's Montepulciano d'Abruzzo is one of the world's great reds. You get a real understanding of the possibilities of the Montepulciano grape, as Pepe's wines—at least after, say, fifteen years of aging—deliver an intense, almost wild taste of licorice, wild cherries, and various herbs. Pepe's wine is, in a word, thrilling. But it must be approached respectfully, with the certain knowledge that this is a wine that needs both time *and* understanding.

TORRE DEI BEATI—Torre dei Beati is a new winery created by a young couple—both of whom are restaurant wine stewards—who were given a thirty-year-old vineyard as a wedding present by the father of the bride.

Their Montepulciano d'Abruzzo, both a regular bottling as well as the richer, denser single-vineyard bottling Vigneto Cocciapazza, are straightforward, honest wines with no apparent oak or winemaking razzmatazz. Lovely wines that reflect Abruzzo's frank rusticity, in the best sense of that word.

Torre dei Beati's Cerasuolo rosé is superb and made differently than most. It is a blend of two batches of Montepulciano juice. The first batch is from grapes selected for their higher acidity. This gives the rosé structure. The second batch is obtained from a *saignée* (literally, bleeding) taken from the juice intended for their red Montepulciano d'Abruzzo wine. This juice gives the rosé its fruitiness and intensifies the color. This blend is then fermented into wine at a cool temperature and quickly bottled.

Redolent of dark cherries with a lip-smacking earthiness, this is a quite dark-hued rosé of exceptional quality.

Uᴍᴀɴɪ Rᴏɴᴄʜɪ—The well-known Marche region producer reaches to neighboring Abruzzo to create a generous supply of quite good, straightforward Montepulciano d'Abruzzo. Good quality and good value.

Lᴀ Vᴀʟᴇɴᴛɪɴᴀ—An ambitious winery that has attracted quite a lot of attention for its modern winemaking and ambitious standards under the guidance of a well-known consulting enologist, Luca d'Attoma (who consults for more than two dozen wineries including the Lambrusco producer Villa di Corlo, see page 154).

La Valentina's basic Montepulciano d'Abruzzo is anything but: It is superb. Dense and beautifully delineated, it is a model of Montepulciano modernity. A much-acclaimed joint venture with Stefano Inama in Soave and La Valentina to create a distinctive Montepulciano created the proprietarily named Binomio (literally, two names). A very rich wine of higher-than-usual alcohol, it is (predictably) quite oaky and striking on first sip. It's the kind of wine that wows but does not seduce. Then again, it was created precisely to do the former and not the latter.

La Valentina is already a top Montepulciano producer, with surely yet more goodies to come.

Vᴀʟᴇɴᴛɪɴɪ—Like his equally idiosyncratic colleague Emidio Pepe, the wines of the late Edoardo Valentini are not for everyone. For starters, they are eye-poppingly expensive. Second, they take ages to fully come around. A typical Valentini Montepulciano d'Abruzzo really hits its stride only after fifteen years. Third, the style is perceived, especially by critics or tasters comparing various Montepulciano d'Abruzzo wines side by side in large numbers, as overly rustic, even crude.

Edoardo Valentini couldn't have cared less. Famously secretive, he told no one how he makes his wines. But it's clear from the wine itself that he was a traditionalist (no small French oak barrels in his winery). And that his vineyard yields are very low. He built his Montepulciano for the ages, and they're worth the wait. (Whether they're worth the money is an entirely separate question.)

Valentini is even more famous for his one-of-a-kind Trebbiano d'Abruzzo, which may well be Italy's single greatest dry white wine.

VALLE REALE—An up-and-comer with 147 acres of recently planted vines. Three different Montepulciano d'Abruzzo bottlings are offered: a basic version that's admirable; the Vigne Nuove (new vines), which sees no oak and delivers a pristine intensity; and San Calisto, which is noticeably oaky, thanks to fifteen months in small new French oak barrels. The Vigne Nuove is this taster's ticket. To watch.

CICCIO ZACCAGNINI—A good-sized producer (50,000) with an expansive line of wines. Multiple Montepulcianos are offered: a basic Montepulciano d'Abruzzo, Chronicon (one year in small oak barrels), and San Clemente (fourteen to eighteen months in small oak barrels). The differences are a function of oak aging and, in the case of San Clemente, a radically reduced vineyard yield. The San Clemente bottling comes from vines with only half the yield of the other two wines. It shows.

Two Cerasuolo rosés are offered as well, a basic Cerasuolo and another, rather deeply colored, which spends three months in oak casks, called Myosotis.

The overall standard at Ciccio Zaccagnini is impressively high. Look especially for the San Clemente bottling, at least for long-term aging. Its density and flavor profundity are impressive.

What Do The Locals Eat With This Wine? Abruzzo is a place with two culinary faces. One looks to the sea and offers the usual complement of straightforward fish dishes that Italians everywhere prefer: fish soups, sardines, anchovies, mussels, skate, and other seafoods, all presented simply.

Once you move to the mountainous interior (which is most of Abruzzo), the cuisine gets meaty and spicy. There's a lot of lamb and goat. And there's an almost ubiquitous use of hot peppers, which adds an elevating zest to what might otherwise be a pretty leaden daily diet of meat and pasta. The pasta, by the way, is characterized by a thick spaghetti called pasta alla chitarra, named for the garrotte-like wires stretched parallel to each other with which the pasta dough is cut. A tomato-based meat ragù is the inevitable saucing, with a touch of hot spiciness of course. It's a hearty, robust, honest cuisine that pairs perfectly with the hearty, robust, honest red wine of the area.

One Man's Taste—Whose Wine Would I Buy? Price no object, I'd reach for the Montepulcianos of Emidio Pepe and Edoardo Valentini. However, in the real world of wine buying, I reach for any of several, equally fine producers: Barone Cornacchia, Col del Mondo, Illuminati, Torre dei Beati, or Valle Reale. More than in most places, however, I feel freer in Montepulciano d'Abruzzo to willingly try an unknown name, secure in the near-fact that the wine will be fairly priced, at least tasty, and likely better than that.

Also, I really like the Cerasuolo rosés. They're all worth at least a try, as the Montepulciano grape performs beautifully with this style of wine. Keep an eye peeled.

Worth Searching For? Absolutely worth a search

Similar Wines From The Same Neighborhood: Numerous other wines also employ the Montepulciano grape variety in the neighboring regions of Marche (to the north) and Molise (to the south). Both of these regions create distinctive, worthwhile wines such as Marche's Rosso Cònero. Also there's a new (1996) appellation in Abruzzo called Controguerra, where the red wine must be at least 60 percent Montepulciano. Also, you find broadly defined zones such as Colline Pescaresi, which is a catchall name for the hills of the province of Pescara. Almost anything can (and is) blended and offered under this designation.

Morellino di Scansano

(more-eh-*leen*-oh dee scahn-*sah*-no)

RED

Region: Tuscany (north-central Italy)

Grapes: A minimum of 85 percent Sangiovese with the balance of those grape varieties authorized by the province of Grosseto, such as Mammolo, Canaiolo Nero, Alicante (which is the same as, or similar to, Grenache), Malvasia Nera, Nero Francese, Cabernet Sauvignon, Merlot, and Ciliegiolo, among others.

The Tradition: One of the latest "discoveries" in Tuscan reds, this long-overlooked zone creates terrific Sangiovese wines from a clone or strain locally called *morello*, a reference to the darkness of the resulting wine.

I recall visiting the area more than twenty years ago, after I stumbled across a terrific bottling, the front label of which was a couple of paragraphs of white-lettered verbiage on a black background. The label was gibberish to me (I didn't read Italian then), as well as graphically baffling. It read like a memo from the Bureau of Buildings, citing plot numbers and the like. But the wine was captivating: a fragrant scent and taste of wild black cherries with that dusty tannin taste you get from Sangiovese. (The producer was Sellari Franceschini, which hasn't been exported to America for years.)

Since that time, the once-obscure and still very small Morellino di Scansano district has become better known. Indeed, it boasts an international following among Italian wine *fashionisti*.

Originally, the wine was the product of the local strain of Sangiovese peculiar to the area, much like Montalcino has its strain (called Brunello) or Montepulciano (called Prugnolo Gentile). Just how different the Morello strain of Sangiovese really is I cannot say.

But the locals insist that it's different. The problem, however, is that as plantings increased, an indeterminate amount of the new Sangiovese planted is not necessarily this Morello strain.

How It's Changed: It's difficult to say today, with any assurance, precisely what Morellino di Scansano *should* taste like. The reason for this is that there are so many new plantings, and so much experimentation, that it's anybody's guess, or assertion, as to what *il vero* Morellino di Scansano really is.

Today, the wines are all over the taste map. You have Sangiovese blended with Cabernet Sauvignon called Morellino di Scansano. Or blended with Merlot. Or blended with both. Inevitably, there's the use of small oak barrels. In fairness, there was always a tradition of blending Sangiovese, typically with Malvasia Nera, Canaiolo Nero, or Mammolo, among other local varieties

Yet some producers are choosing a more traditional route, creating 100 percent Sangiovese versions or with small dollops of traditional grapes.

Perhaps the best way to understand these differences to see the Morellino di Scansano zone as really part of a much larger area of Tuscany that's undergoing major modernization, the area called the Maremma.

The Maremma is the name given to the southern, coastal part of Tuscany (see Bolgheri, page ___). At one time it was swampy and malarial. It was confined to grazing. Vast tracts of the Maremma were owned by aristocrats and nobles, some of whom built hunting lodges in the hills close to the sea. Today the Maremma has become so chic that French superchef Alain Ducasse has opened a thirty-three-room luxury inn and has plans to open his own winery.

Morellino di Scansano, at a dozen or so miles inland from the sea at the southern end of the Tuscan coast, is in the sphere of influence of the larger Maremma renaissance. Although technically not part of the Maremma (it's too far inland for that), the enormous interest in growing wine near the Tuscan coast has made Morellino di Scansano fashionable and an area of investment by other Tuscan producers such as

Brunello's Fattoria dei Barbi, Jacopo Biondi-Santi, and Caparzo; the Mazzei family of Castello di Fonterutoli in Chianti Classico; the big Tuscan house of Frescobaldi; Poliziano from Montepulciano, and others.

What will emerge in the next decade or so as the effervescence of fashion and experimentation dies down remains to be seen. Likely what's happening now is all to the good. But eventually, Morellino di Scansano will have to create a wine of distinction that is consistently and rewardingly different from other Tuscan Sangiovese-based wines, Otherwise, it will be swallowed up under a larger regional designation. And that would be a pity.

That said, for this taster, a good, typical Morellino di Scansano should be a rich, not especially tannic Sangiovese that combines black cherry/wild cherry fruit with a gentle, classically Sangiovese dustiness. It shouldn't be hard or oaky or necessarily long-lived, but rather inviting, contoured, and supple.

Noteworthy Producers (The Traditionalists/The Modernists): Only a handful of the fifty-plus producers in Morellino di Scansano are seen in America. However fashionable the area is in Tuscany today, demand is still slight on these shores. The producers to follow are all found in the United States with varying degrees of distribution.

TENUTA BELGUARDO—The Mazzei family of Castello di Fonterutoli is one of the deep-pocketed newcomers to Morellino di Scansano. The Mazzeis bought the 74-acre property in the mid-1990s and promptly began a replanting project to what they submit are better clones of Sangiovese as well as Cabernet Sauvignon and Merlot. The estate won't be fully producing until 2010.

Only one Morellino di Scansano is offered, a single-vineyard called Poggio Bronzone, which is admirably made 100 percent from Sangiovese. It is dense, rich, and very promising. Other wines from the estate are various blends of Sangiovese with Cabernet and/or Merlot, all labeled with the regional appellation Maremma Toscana. To watch closely.

ERIK BANTI—One of the leaders, and innovators, of Morellino di

Scansano, Erik Banti is a modernist who employs both international grapes such as Merlot and Cabernet Sauvignon for his Morellino di Scansano wines and uses new small oak barrels.

He is, however, quite deft in this, and Banti's wines are reliably appetizing, if not quite as characterful as one might wish. The basic Morellino di Scansano is 90 percent Sangiovese and 10 percent Cabernet Sauvignon. It's always a good buy and pleasant enough. Much more substantive is the single-vineyard Ciabatta bottling, which is a Morellino di Scansano Riserva made 100 percent from Sangiovese. This wine, although vanilla-scented from oak, does show just why Morellino di Scansano is different from other Tuscan versions of Sangiovese. It's lush, intense, and rounded yet still delivers Sangiovese's dusty firmness.

MORIS FARMS—One of the larger producers of the zone, the oddly named Moris Farms (the owner, Adolfo Parentini, is Italian) issues good, solid Morellino di Scansano that's pleasing to drink but not inspiring. Like others in the zone, Moris Farms issues other wines that are blended, such as Avvolture, a blend of 75 percent Sangiovese with 20 percent Cabernet and 5 percent Syrah that sees a lot of time in new French oak. It has garnered raves from critics who see this zone as better suited to growing such varieties as Cabernet, Merlot, and Syrah. In fairness, there does seem to be a vocation for that in the Scansano area, so there's reason for their enthusiasm, in addition to the siren persuasion of a world market that embraces such wines.

FATTORIA LE PUPILLE—Rather light, but elegant Morellino di Scansano from this longtime, reliably good producer. Look especially for the single-vineyard Poggio Valente bottling, which is significantly richer and denser than the regular bottling (90 percent Sangiovese and 10 percent Alicante). Worth noting is that owner Elisabetta Geppetti blends her Sangiovese only with Alicante and Malvasia Nera, rather than the more fashionable international varieties.

What Do The Locals Eat With This Wine? As elsewhere in Tuscany, Morellino di Scansano finds its place with local pastas, especially with a ragù di cinghiale or wild boar sauce. Braised meats are a good pairing and especially game birds such as quail and pheasant.

One Man's Taste—Whose Wine Would I Buy? Right now I'd be looking at Tenuta Belguardo, which strikes this taster as the up-and-comer of the zone, along with Fattoria Le Pupille's Poggio Valente bottling.

Worth Searching For? Only if you see it

Similar Wines From The Same Neighborhood: Any of a number of Sangiovese bottlings from one of the Chianti districts, or look for the broad regional appellation Maremma Toscana.

Moscato d'Asti

(moss-*caht*-toh *dah*-stee)
White

Region: Piedmont (northwest Italy)

Grapes: 100 percent Moscato Bianco (white)

The Tradition: The rarest wine I ever drank was filtered through a sock. It was a Moscato d'Asti. When you hear the story, you'll know all about the ancient tradition of this slightly sparkling—what Italians call *frizzante*, lightly bubbling—very low alcohol (5 percent) sweet white wine made entirely from the Moscato Bianco grape grown on the very steep, chalky-clay hillsides in northwest Italy's Piedmont region. Moscato d'Asti has a delicacy, an ethereal quality, that almost no other wine can rival.

While the world-famous Asti Spumante, which is produced in industrial quantities by big wineries, is also 100 percent Moscato Bianco, even the best Asti Spumante gives only a hint of what the far more artisanal Moscato d'Asti can achieve.

What's the difference? Essentially, it's that between a workhorse and a racehorse. Moscato d'Asti is the thoroughbred, thanks to the way it's made and its vineyard lineage. It's what the growers make for themselves. Production is small. A grower could make such a wine in his home cellar. A fully foaming (*spumante*) Moscato, however, requires expensive, special vats that only big wineries can afford.

Because it was so artisanal and localized, Moscato d'Asti was only rarely commercialized. A grower made it for himself, his family and friends, and a few private customers. It was, and is, the ideal conclusion to one of Piedmont's heroic dinners, which until very recently saw six successive plates of antipasti, two pasta courses, and then a meat course.

By the end of such a siege, you had no room left for anything but a refreshing glass of light Moscato.

Anyway, I mentioned to Barolo producer Aldo Conterno that I was a great fan of Moscato d'Asti. "Moscato?" said Aldo. "Why, you've never tasted the real Moscato. You have to taste Signora Gemma Chionetti's homemade Moscato. That's the real thing. She puts it through a sock."

When I heard that, I was quivering like a springer spaniel on the scent. I had read about how traditional Moscato was made by filtering the wine through a sock. But I never thought that even in Piedmont, a pretty hidebound place, anybody was still doing it.

You see, the way Moscato is made *frizzante*, or lightly bubbling, is by bottling the very young wine while it's still fermenting. But you don't want the yeasts to remain in the bottle, as the sealed bottle will then explode from the pressure of too much carbon dioxide. (When yeasts feed on the sugar in the grape juice, they create alcohol and carbon dioxide. Put this process in an airtight bottle or tank and, voilà!, you've got sparkling wine.)

So the old-timers used to filter the still-fermenting wine through a series of hemp tubes or socks. This would remove dead yeast cells as well as most of the living, still-engaged-in-fermenting ones. A rough filtration, it was performed multiple times until the wine emerged reasonably clear. Then it was bottled and corked up.

To say this was an inexact science hardly captures the rough-and-ready quality of the procedure. As a result, part—sometimes all—of a year's production would explode in the cellar. Too many live yeasts made it through the sock and continued fermenting inside the corked bottle, feasting on the sweet wine, in the process creating more pressure from carbon dioxide than the bottle could withstand.

A month or two later, you'd hear a shockingly loud explosion in the cellar and find a fragrant mess with glass shards everywhere. And heaven help you if you're in the cellar when a bottle explodes. You can be seriously injured. (In the old days, cellar workers in big wineries making sparkling wines wore stiff leather chest protectors and fencing masks.)

But things weren't always so predictable. Cellars would be so cold in the winter that yeasts went dormant. But once summer arrived, cellars warmed up and the dormant yeasts would resume feeding and multiplying inside the bottle. And then, boom! (Today, filtration is exact. You can remove every yeast cell.)

Now you know why I was so surprised and excited to hear that Signora Gemma Chionetti made a Moscato the old way. (Her husband, Quinto Chionetti, is famous for his red Dolcetto wine.) I pleaded with Aldo Conterno to ask Signora Chionetti to let me taste her filtered-through-a-sock Moscato. She assented.

"Oh, I make maybe 120 bottles a year for ourselves and our friends," she said when I visited her. By the time I got there, it was summer and she was down to her last dozen bottles. "At least I think that's how many I've got," she laughed. "I haven't been down to the cellar to see if anything has broken."

She returned with three bottles carefully held upright so as not to disturb the heavy sediment from the dead yeasts that had made the wine bubbly in the bottle. "You don't want to shake it too much." She was not smiling when she said that.

She pulled the cork, and the wine that emerged was glorious. It was similar to today's best Moscato d'Asti bottlings in its freshness, vibrancy, and incisive, delineated flavors.

But there was one big difference: texture. Her Moscato was thick on the tongue, denser than any other I'd tasted before or since. It was the most dramatic demonstration of the effects of filtering—or rather, nonfiltering—that I've experienced. The glycerin richness of that texture is absent in today's necessarily more finely filtered renditions.

She offered me two bottles to take home that evening. "How far away do you live?" she inquired. "Not far," I replied, "maybe thirty minutes away." "Then it's okay," she said. "The bottles should make it there safely. Because once they warm up, well, you never know. Anyway, you'd better drink them fast."

I made it home in record time and gingerly cradled the two bottles to the refrigerator as if they were gelignite. They didn't explode in the night. Figuring that such luck wouldn't hold forever, my wife and I greedily polished off both bottles the next day. It's the rarest wine I've ever drunk.

How It's Changed: The big change in Moscato d'Asti today is that commercial producers are, as they must be, far more attentive to the scientific elements of putting a *frizzante* Moscato in the bottle. Today they use temperature-controlled, stainless steel vats that hold unfermented Moscato juice at near-freezing temperatures. This ensures great freshness, which you want with Moscato, which has a rapturous perfume. Then, every few months during the year, they will create a secondary fermentation with added yeasts, filter every last one of those yeasts from the tank, and immediately bottle and ship the now-*frizzante* Moscato.

One thing is worth noting: There really aren't any bad Moscato d'Asti wines on the market. Unlike Asti Spumante, it's still an artisanal item and the market demand is not (yet) so great as to invite the wine industrialists into the picture. Of course, there are better and worse versions, but they're all pretty good.

Noteworthy Producers (The Traditionalists / The Modernists): Freshness is the key with Moscato d'Asti. You want the latest vintage. Serve it very cool but not refrigerator-cold to get the fullest effect of Moscato's fragrance and taste.

CERETTO—Although better known for Barolo, Barbaresco, and Arneis, the Ceretto brothers have long issued a very fine Moscato d'Asti in a dramatic tapering tower of a bottle. Good delicacy, although not as much depth of flavor as the absolute best. Still, it's very fine Moscato.

FORTETO DELLA LUJA—A small producer in an off-the-map village called Loazzolo. Forteto della Luja creates an unusually heavy and rich Moscato that's different from all others, thanks to the sourcing of the grapes. Where the best Moscatos marry amazing acidity and delicacy with penetrating fruit, Forteto della Luja's version is all about power and depth. It may not be classic, but it sure is delicious. Look also for this producer's extraordinary Moscato *passito* and, rarer yet, the Brachetto *passito* (a red grape).

ICARDI—Lovely, elegant lighter-style Moscato with superb delicacy.

ELIO PERRONE—A very serious producer of Moscato with two bottlings. One is the amusing-to-English-speakers Sourgal (properly pronounced soor-gahl), which is released in November every year. The other, richer and more "serious," is the single-vineyard Clarté, from a five-acre vineyard with 40-year-old vines. Both wines are superb, among the very best in Moscato d'Asti.

PAOLO SARACCO—The best producer of all, for this taster, is Paolo Saracco. Saracco's Moscato comes closer to what I tasted, in terms of textural density and high-wire delicacy, from Signora Chionetti than any other. Rich, dense, fresh, and pure. Saracco is the benchmark producer.

LA SPINETTA/RIVETTI—The great rival to Saracco is Giorgio Rivetti's La Spinetta. Although the Rivetti family has branched out in a major way into making red wines, their Moscato d'Asti remains a signature wine for them and is one of the finest of all. Where Saracco delivers depth and texture, Rivetti's version is like the purest soprano note. It has gossamer delicacy allied to superb fruit.

VIETTI—This Barolo producer has long issued a lovely Moscato d'Asti under the name La Cascinetta. Pure, rich, and rewarding.

What Do The Locals Eat With This Wine?: The Piedmontese are not big dessert eaters, which is not surprising given the scale of their traditional meals. Moscato d'Asti is typically served with the Piedmontese cornmeal cookies called krumiri or with butter cookies. Or often with a crème caramel-type of flan. And quite often it's served just on its own as dessert. And it's gorgeous with dark chocolate.

One Man's Taste—Whose Wine Would I Buy? I buy Saracco as our house Moscato d'Asti. But I'm delighted to drink La Spinetta-Rivetti,

Forteto della Luja, and Elio Perrone, among the others mentioned previously. Really, you can't go wrong.

Worth Searching For? Don't die without trying it

Similar Wines From The Same Neighborhood: Asti Spumante

Nebbiolo d'Alba

(neb-*yoh*-loh *dahl*-bah)
RED

Region: Piedmont (northwest Italy)

Grape: 100 percent Nebbiolo (red)

The Tradition: To the uninitiated, wine names seem to have no rhyme or reason. Why, for example, are the 100 percent Nebbiolo wines called Barbaresco and Barolo not called Nebbiolo di Barolo or Nebbiolo di Barbaresco? What makes them different than the 100 percent Nebbiolo wine called Nebbiolo d'Alba?

The answer, in a word, is "breed." Over centuries, growers in Piedmont's Langhe hills discovered that Nebbiolo grown in certain zones created a wine apart. The wines were so much better—richer, more dimensional, more long-lived, more layered—that simply to call them by the grape name didn't do justice.

Great wines really are liquid geography. Over time it became apparent that what was important about these wines was not that they were made from Nebbiolo, but that they came from particular areas. Maybe they did once say the mouthful "Nebbiolo di Barolo." But soon it became clear that the "Barolo" part was what mattered. "Nebbiolo" went by the linguistic wayside.

Over time, the boundaries of the Barolo zone and the Barbaresco zone became defined, mapped and—most importantly—locally accepted. Wine law everywhere is always a reflection of local usage and acceptability. The names we use today are reflections of deep local understandings.

So what happened is that Barolo and Barbaresco became the king and queen of Nebbiolo, legally able to cite their place names without any further explanation. It has to do with soils (a chalky clay called marl) and ideal, sun-rich exposures (which helps the late-ripening Nebbiolo achieve full ripeness). It's *assumed* that you know that they are both entirely Nebbiolo. Italian wine law does specify it, however.

Any wine made from Nebbiolo in the Langhe hills not grown within the boundaries of the Barolo or Barbaresco zones is entitled only to the legal catchall designation Nebbiolo d'Alba. There are boundaries to the Nebbiolo d'Alba appellation, but they are generously drawn.

Worth noting is that the Nebbiolo d'Alba appellation incorporates the subset districts of Barolo and Barbaresco. So if you're a grower in one of those districts and because of a bad vintage you don't want to issue your Nebbiolo wine as Barolo or Barbaresco (depending upon where you're located), you can "declassify" your wine to the broader, more generic—and less lucrative—Nebbiolo d'Alba designation. Actually, this happens more often than you might suspect, especially among the best producers, who are protective of their reputations.

How It's Changed: Nebbiolo d'Alba has changed in the same way that Barolo and Barbaresco have: The wines are fresher, cleaner, and more brightly flavorful. However, there's one big difference: There's less likelihood of oakiness in a Nebbiolo d'Alba bottling than in Barolo or Barbaresco.

Precisely because Nebbiolo d'Alba typically comes from lesser locations (sandy soils or a less-than-ideal exposure on a hillside) or from young vines (less character and depth), producers are less inclined to treat Nebbiolo d'Alba to expensive small oak barrels. And since Nebbiolo d'Alba always commands a modest price, there's no economic incentive to do so either.

A good Nebbiolo d'Alba should convey the same ethereal scents of berries, a whiff of tar, rose petals and herbs than the more *basso profondo* Barolo and Barbaresco do. The difference is a matter of weight, scale, layers of complexity, earlier maturation, and potential longevity.

Where a good-vintage Barolo is at its best a decade or more after the vintage date and a Barbaresco comes around only a few years soon-er than that (if at all), a good-vintage Nebbiolo d'Alba is swell drink-ing with only a few years' age. The best bottlings—top producers and a great vintage—can certainly reward as much as ten years of cellaring.

But that's not the idea of Nebbiolo d'Alba. Instead, this is the wine that Barolo and Barbaresco lovers buy and drink while waiting for their prized (and more expensive) "Killer Bs" to mature. Besides, they're special occasion wines, and Nebbiolo d'Alba is, if not an every-day tipple, then a once-a-week pour.

A good Nebbiolo d'Alba should be fragrant yet only medium-weight. It should have all the distinctiveness and flavor definition of its big-league, big-name brethren, but not as much stuffing. It shouldn't be too tannic, as it's meant for early consumption. And if there's any oak at all (some producers use older *barriques* or small oak barrels), it should be subtle, a wink rather than a distracting tic.

Worth noting is the new (1994) creation of a "generic" category of what are frequently Nebbiolo-based red wines simple designated as "Langhe." Many winemakers who previously offered a Nebbiolo d'Alba have shifted their allegiance to the new Langhe designation, sometimes labeling their wines "Nebbiolo Langhe." The reason is that the new Langhe DOC allows for much greater flexibility: The pro-ducer can blend in whatever he or she likes. Or the wine can be labeled Nebbiolo Langhe. This new category has siphoned some atten-tion from the older, more restrictive Nebbiolo d'Alba designation (see Langhe Rosso, page 156).

Noteworthy Producers (The Traditionalists / The Modernists): A simple and good rule of thumb for buying Nebbiolo d'Alba is also the most obvious one: The top producers of Barolo and Barbaresco usually deliver the best Nebbiolo d'Alba bottlings too.

The reasons are as simple as they are compelling. First, the best Barolo and Barbaresco producers are terrific winegrowers. They have rigorous standards that they apply to everything they do, including a "modest" Nebbiolo d'Alba. Also, their vineyard sites are in choice locations. The vines meant for Nebbiolo d'Alba will never get the best exposures (those would be reserved for Barolo or Barbaresco bottlings), but they'll still be plausible for the finicky Nebbiolo. And the yields will be reasonably low.

Also, these growers will often divert the grapes from young vines in their best exposures into their Nebbiolo d'Alba bottling, the better to ensure a rigorously high standard for their signature Barolo or Barbaresco bottling.

That acknowledged, there are good Nebbiolo d'Alba wines that come from outside of the choice precincts of Barolo and Barbaresco. This "golden rule" is not an absolute.

Many good Nebbiolo d'Albas come, in fact, from the Roero district. A zone of rolling hills, it's outside of the deeply plunging Langhe hills. The soil in Roero is sandier, which creates lighter-weight, more early-maturing but very perfumey and supple Nebbiolo. You often see the single-vineyard name Occhetti on various Nebbiolo d'Alba bottlings; it's a Roero wine. (Roero is more famous as the source of the white wine and grape called Arneis; see page 45.)

Among the consistently best producers of Nebbiolo d'Alba are:

BRUNO GIACOSA—A Roero-grown Nebbiolo from the Valmaggiore di Vezza d'Alba vineyard.

FRATELLI BROVIA—Roero-grown Nebbiolo from Valmaggiore di Vezza d'Alba.

ELIO GRASSO—From Barolo district vineyard Gavarini.

PRODUTTORI DEL BARBARESCO—Nebbiolo grown in the Barbaresco zone. Always an exceptional value.

PRUNOTTO—Nebbiolo from the Occhetti vineyard in Roero.

RENATO RATTI—Nebbiolo from the Occhetti vineyard in Roero.

What Do The Locals Eat With This Wine? Precisely because Nebbiolo d'Alba (and Nebbiolo Langhe) are seen as preludes to the more symphonic Barolo and Barbaresco, this wine is frequently served with antipasti or the *primo*, meaning pasta such as tajarìn (tagliatelle) or agnolotti (Piedmontese ravioli). A dish such as pasta with a meat sauce, braised meats, or ravioli is ideal.

One Man's Taste—Whose Wine Would I Buy? My first choice is the consistently good, rewarding, and non-oaky Nebbiolo d'Alba from Bruno Giacosa. He has always issued unusually good bottlings and is well distributed, too. The grower Renato Ratti makes superb Nebbiolo d'Alba from the Occhetti vineyard in Roero. Look also for another Occhetti vineyard bottling from the shipper Prunotto.

Worth Searching For? If you happen to see it

Similar Wines From The Same Neighborhood: Langhe Rosso, Nebbiolo Langhe, other lighter-style Nebbiolo-based wines from farther north in Piedmont such as Ghemme, Fara, Sizzano, Carema, and Lessona

Orvieto

(or-vee-*eh*-toh)
WHITE

Region: Umbria (central Italy). Orvieto is about 75 miles southwest of Perugia.

Grapes: Trebbiano Toscano (Procanico), 50 to 65 percent; Verdello 15 to 25 percent; Grechetto, Drupeggio, and/or Malvasia toscana, 20 to 30 percent (all white). Untraditional grapes such as Chardonnay, Pinot Bianco, and Sauvignon Blanc are often added to the preceding varieties as well.

The Tradition: Orvieto is another example of how the gods first make fashionable that which they would destroy. And fashionable Orvieto surely was, for centuries. Even by Italian standards Orvieto is an ancient winegrowing area. Located in a basin surrounded by slopes and side gullies from nearby rivers, the chalk-clay soil of the zone and the exposure afforded by the slopes were perfect for growing grapes. Indeed, the Orvieto zone can trace its winegrowing history back to the Etruscans, which puts things before the founding of ancient Rome.

Worth noting—because it helps explain Orvieto's renown and former glory—is the fact that this same valley sees autumn fogs. These fogs, along with otherwise moderate autumn temperatures and (usually) afternoon sunshine, encourage the creation of a grape skin fungus called *Botrytis cinerea.*

This fungus shrivels the grape and, although unappetizing in appearance, imparts a distinctly delicious flavor to wines made from botrytised grapes, a sort of spicy, cinnamon scent and taste. The wines are thicker-textured as well because much of the water from the grape has evaporated through the microscopic pores in the grape skin created by the fungus. (The French dessert wine Sauternes is a famous botrytised wine, as are the sweetest German Rieslings, among others.)

Until the 1960s or early '70s—as recently as that—Orvieto was always a sweet wine. It wasn't overly sweet. But it wasn't dry either. It was what the Italians call *abboccato* or *amabile* (ah-*mah*-bee-leh) and what in English we'd call off-dry. This was, for centuries, the preferred style of many, even most, Italian white wines until well after World War II. (France was no different. Most white Bordeaux, for example, were off-dry until very recently.)

Orvieto's great fame came from one important person: the Pope. Because of Orvieto's comparatively cool summer climate, when things got literally too hot in the Vatican in Rome, popes over the centuries retreated for the summer to the papal palace in Orvieto. No prizes for guessing what they drank. And they loved the slightly sweet Orvieto wine, so much so that one pope (Gregory XVI, 1831 to 1846) famously requested that his body be washed in Orvieto wine prior to his funeral.

How It's Changed: With Orvieto as one of Italy's most famous wines, it was inevitable that the wine would become industrialized. (The same happened with Soave.) Most Orvieto wines today are bland, dull, vacuous white wines of no redeeming character. This is both ironic and sad because the "real" Orvieto is surprisingly characterful, even memorable.

The big changes in Orvieto are two: the rise of the industrial item, sluiced from the winegrowers' cooperatives in the area and commercialized by big shippers, and, after World War II, the transformation of Orvieto from a slightly sweet white to a resolutely dry wine, following the popular (and universal) change in wine drinkers' tastes.

As always in Italy, there remain at least a few producers who seek to restore Orvieto to something more rewarding than the average bottling, both for the dry version as well as the traditional sweeter style. Such bottlings are very much worth pursuing, as they are almost shockingly good. However, given the zone's immense tourism, it is inevitable that the great majority of Orvieto wine offered for sale will continue to be banal.

A good dry Orvieto will display a slightly greenish tint and offer a faint scent of bitter almond along with minerals, melon, and various citrus fruits such as grapefruit and orange blossom. Richer/sweeter versions magnify these flavors, as well as provide a greater textural density. The sweetest versions will be noticeably marked by the presence of *botrytis cinerea* or noble rot (*muffa nobile*), giving the wines a thick texture and a rapturously spicy scent along with the other flavors previously described.

Noteworthy Producers: The best Orvieto wine, by universal agreement, comes from the Orvieto Classico zone, which label designation refers to the heart of a zone almost anywhere in Italy. It's certainly so in Orvieto, where the area entitled to called itself Classico is indeed the most ancient, and best, part of the larger Orvieto area.

Because Orvieto rings the changes from dry to sweet, Orvieto wine labels often specify *secco* (dry), *abboccato* (slightly sweet), *amabile* (medium sweet), and *dolce* (sweet; typically botrytised).

BARBERANI-VALLESANTA—This estate is easily and unquestionably the best in Orvieto Classico. Everything Barberani offers is estate grown (the 124-acre vineyard is called Vallesanta, hence the hyphenated name). Barberani, more than any other producer, delivers the goods across the entire range of Orvieto possibilities, from dry to sweet.

The Orvieto Classico *secco* is a benchmark bottling, redolent of melons and minerals. Better yet are the two Orvieto Classico *amabile* bottlings, both superb. One whiff and sip of this slightly sweet wine will tell you just why this most traditional of Orvietos was so acclaimed and sought after for all those centuries. You realize, after tasting this, that the *secco* or dry version is an aberration rather than a defining version (and vision) of Orvieto. Really, this is the way Orvieto actually should be. But modern tastes forbid its popularization.

The superior of the two Orvieto Classico *amabile* wines is the single-vineyard "Pulicchio," which is richer, denser, and sweeter than the regular *amabile*.

Sweeter and more impressive yet, for it is blessed with botrytis, is the *dolce* Orvieto called Orvieto Classico "Calcaia" Muffa Nobile. Here, Orvieto becomes a true dessert wine: liquorous, extravagantly scented, and truly memorable.

LA CARRAIA—A promising new Orvieto Classico made by one of Italy's most famous consulting enologists (winemakers), Riccardo Cotarella. Although more famous for his luscious, brightly modern red wines, Cotarella's dab hand extends to dry whites as well. This very good, peach- and orange blossom–scented dry Orvieto, superior to most in the zone, sees some time in small oak barrels.

CASTELLO DELLA SALA—This is the Orvieto-area estate of the famous Tuscan wine shipper Antinori, which has long had a connection to the Orvieto zone. Antinori's Orvieto wines should be the very greatest of the zone, even a rallying cry to a return to greatness. They are merely very good. The Orvieto Classico secco is certainly one of the best of the area. Better yet is the Orvieto Classico *secco* called Campogrande and an *amabile* version called Casasole.

The best bottling is, in fact, the only Orvieto Classico that's entirely estate-grown called Castello della Sala Orvieto Classico Superiore. The "Superiore" designation dictates a lower yield than for regular Orvieto Classico, as well as a later harvest date to ensure greater ripeness. The rigor shows: This is the best Orvieto Classico offered by Antinori.

TENUTA LE VELETTE—Two versions of Orvieto Classico are offered by this admirable estate, an oak-aged version that includes Chardonnay in the blend called "Velico" and a more traditional—and much superior—Orvieto Classico Superiore that sees no oak and no internationalization called "Lunato."

What Do The Locals Eat With This Wine? Umbrian food everywhere, including the Orvieto zone, is hearty and unpretentious. They are great lovers of sausages, beans, lentils (the best in Italy), and the like. Because of its rich qualities, the *abboccato* and *amabile* Orvieto wines are ideal with liver, especially liver pâté or foie gras. Orvieto *secco* serves best where most dry whites work, namely, with shellfish, seafood, and cheeses such as chevre. The *dolce* Orvieto is best on its own or with a simple dessert such as pound cake or a custard.

One Man's Taste—Whose Wine Would I Buy? The easy favorite is Barberani. There's no need to look further, really. Antinori's Castello della Sala Orvieto Classico Superiore is a good second choice if you can't find Barberani.

Worth Searching For? Only if you see it

Similar Wines From The Same Neighborhood: The Orvieto zone also issues many proprietarily named wines from nontraditional grapes such as Chardonnay, Sauvignon Blanc, and numerous blends both dry and sweet. It sometimes seems as if more energy is spent inventing new wines than in trying to uphold (or re-create) the original glory that was Orvieto wine itself.

Recioto della Valpolicella

(reh-chee-*oh*-toh dell-ah vahl-pole-ee-*chell*-lah)

RED

Region: Veneto (northeast Italy, about ten miles northwest of Verona)

Grapes: Corvina Veronese, 40 to 70 percent; Rondinella 20 to 40 percent; Molinara 5 to 25 percent; Negrara/Trentina/Rossignola/Barbera/Sangiovese up to 15 percent (all red)

The Tradition: As the name suggests, Recioto della Valpolicella is a version of the table wine called Valpolicella (see page 245). It's from the same district, called Valpolicella. And it's the same blend of red grapes, the blend being mostly Corvina Veronese and Rondinella, typically about 70 percent Corvina and 30 percent Rondinella, with one or another of the other permitted grapes nibbling 5 percent or so from the two mainstay varieties.

The most significant element of this wine's name is "recioto," most likely derived from the dialect word *recie* (in Italian *orrechie*) or ears. This refers to the original practice of selecting the "ears" or the wings or shoulders of the cluster to dry them before making the wine. The "ears" of the cluster are always the ripest, most flavor-mature part of the cluster thanks to their greater exposure to the sun.

The recioto process is ancient and by no means confined to the Valpolicella district. It's just more famous in Valpolicella than anywhere else. The process is simple enough. Centuries ago and still today, growers would take their best clusters (either the "ears" or, more commonly today, their best whole clusters) and place them only one cluster deep in straw racks. (Plastic racks are increasingly used.)

These racks are placed in well-ventilated structures (barns in the old days), where the grape clusters are allowed to raisin or partially dehydrate. You'll now see eight or ten wide racks, with ample space between each rack, stacked up in temperature- and humidity-controlled rooms supplied with a constant current of air from multiple small fans.

Anywhere from three to five months after the harvest, the grapes are semi-dry. They're not totally raisined, by the way, as the grower wants some juice left in the grapes. But that juice is greatly concentrated. These semi-dry grapes are then lightly crushed to release the juice and a conventional fermentation proceeds, the yeasts feasting on the sugar-rich juice.

This process has been used in Valpolicella for literally thousands of years, since ancient Roman times. Originally it was a way of concentrating the sugars in the grapes to create a wine of higher alcohol that would be more stable and not go "off." In the old days, that was vital. Also, the same sugar-rich juice allowed for the creation of a sweet wine, which was much admired and preferred in all those centuries when sugar was a rare and expensive commodity. Sweetness in winter was a rare treat.

This desire for a sweet wine explains why until relatively recently, if you said "Recioto della Valpolicella," it was expected that what you got was a strong red wine of higher-than-usual alcohol and noticeable sweetness. Indeed, to this day, if the label says only "Recioto della Valpolicella" without any further qualification (notably "Amarone"), then the wine is the *classico* version, which means some level of sweetness.

Then came a qualifier: *amarone*, from *amaro* or bitter. Today, we most frequently see the full phrase "Recioto della Valpolicella Amarone." It would seem to be ancient. But it's not. That "Amarone" tacked on at the end is relatively new. Nobody knows quite when an "Amarone" version of a recioto wine in Valpolicella first appeared. Probably it always existed, as some years the juice surely fermented to complete dryness. But specifying it on the label is recent.

What is known, however, is that a dry or Amarone recioto was not the preferred version until the mid-twentieth century. Where today the most common type of Recioto della Valpolicella is, by far, the

Amarone version, prior to the 1960s it was the sweet (*dolce*) version that was preferred. Both types are still made today, although you have to look hard to find Recioto della Valpolicella *dolce* in America. Some does get imported, though.

How It's Changed: Apart from the obvious change from sweet to dry in the preferred version of Recioto della Valpolicella today, the biggest changes have admirably involved allying modern winemaking techniques to traditional standards of quality. Inevitably, there are better and worse bottlings, but a surprising number are at least pretty good. A handful are flat-out great.

To begin with, Recioto della Valpolicella, in either version, is high in alcohol, typically between 14 to 16 percent. That's a big wine by anybody's palate. It's always an inky black color. And it certainly benefits from extended cellaring, upwards of two decades.

Recioto della Valpolicella *dolce* is the easier of the two to appreciate immediately, as well as when it's younger. The *dolce* version is lush and purplish-black. It tastes like, well, the world's most wonderful and complex cough syrup. It's not *that* sweet, but it is awfully smooth and rich-tasting, with scents and tastes of black cherry, plums, cinnamon, and an uplifting note of sweetness that makes the wine glide down the gullet—so much so that it might be described as a "wine of greed." You want more. It's terrific with strong cheeses, roasted chestnuts (my favorite), or blue cheeses such as Gorgonzola or Roquefort.

Recioto della Valpolicella Amarone is a more formidable creature. A classic example of what the Italians call a *vino da meditazione* or a wine to meditate over, Amarone (a shorthand contraction used by everyone) is serious stuff. It, too, is a powerful wine with alcohol levels between 15 and 17 percent. It's usually higher in alcohol than the dolce version because the residual sugar found in the *dolce* version has, in the Amarone, been converted into alcohol.

More than the *dolce* rendition, an Amarone rewards lengthy cellaring. In a good vintage, it won't fully reveal itself for several years after the vintage date. And then it will continue to become more layered and dimensional for at least another decade after that. All but the richest Amarones are at their best somewhere between six and fifteen years of age.

Is it worth the wait? You bet. A good Amarone is like no other red wine in the world. You get scents and tastes of preserved cherries, various black fruits, whiffs of licorice and tar, along with a swirl of spices. It's an austere wine. It demands—and rewards—attention.

Collectively, the wines have changed only for the better in the past two decades. Numerous producers are increasingly offering single-vineyard bottlings, which shows an attention to the peculiar needs of the *recioto* process, as only the cleanest, best grapes can withstand the drying process successfully.

Inevitably, there's the usual divide between those who employ new small French oak barrels for their vanilla scent and "sweet" tannins and traditionalists who prefer using the time-honored *botte* or large casks.

Sometimes it's easy to land on one side or the other of this divide. But for once, there's no clear choice. Amarone does respond admirably to the flavor and textural effect of small oak barrels. After all, it's a big boy and can handle itself. On the other hand, it's so intensively flavorful that it doesn't *need* any help. Still, you can't go wrong either way.

Noteworthy Producers (The Traditionalists / The Modernists)

SERÈGO ALIGHIERI—A single-vineyard traditional Amarone called Vaio Armaron and a stunning *dolce* bottling called Casal dei Ronchi Recioto Classico. They are made in conjunction with the much larger producer Masi.

ALLEGRINI—A top *recioto* producer in the modern, small new oak style. Both a very fine Amarone and an updated version of a dolce called Recioto Giovanni Allegrini.

BERTANI—Long a standard-bearer for traditionally made Amarone, this otherwise rather commercial producer continues to issue top-drawer Amarones with an unbeatable track record for aging for decades.

BOLLA—A famously commercial producer whose Amarone is . . .

not bad. Hardly a benchmark, it's still the real thing.

ROMANO DAL FORNO—A cult producer who, along with Quintarelli, is by far the most expensive and sought after producer of Amarone. Huge, powerful, intense Amarone. Romano dal Forno came out with his own label only in 1983. His yields are exceptionally low, and he likes using new small French oak barrels. The quality is certainly there, but so is a lot of winemaking flourish. Two recioto bottlings are made: an Amarone of massive intensity and a superb *amabile* (not as sweet as a true *dolce*) recioto simply called Recioto della Valpolicella with no further qualifier.

GUERRIERI-RIZZARDI—A very fine producer of two bottlings of Amarone, both excellent. There's a regular bottling and a superior single-vineyard version from an especially stony site called Calcarole.

MASI—Very likely the greatest recioto specialist issuing no fewer than eight different recioto wines, including two from the Serègo Alighieri vineyards (see above). In addition to an excellent regular Amarone, look especially for the single vineyard bottlings of Costasera, Campolongo di Torbe, and—the best of all—Mazzano vineyards. They are benchmarks. In addition, there is an *amabile* bottling, also single-vineyard, called Mezzannella Amandorlato Recioto, which is neither an Amarone nor a *dolce*. Unlike the other Amarone bottlings, this one spends nearly two years in small new oak barrels, where the others are aged in traditional casks. All are superb.

GIUSEPPE QUINTARELLI—If there's a greater version of Recioto della Valpolicella Amarone than Giuseppe Quintarelli's, I haven't tasted it. Quintarelli's wines—all of them really, including a terrific regular Valpolicella, an Amarone, and a *dolce*—are pinnacles of what can be done in the zone.

Quintarelli is also a great traditionalist, so much so in fact that sometimes his wines can (regrettably) vary from one bottle to the next. Nevertheless, there are no other Amarones quite like Quintarelli's in their depth, dimension, or complexity. Others may be bigger scale (Romano dal Forno's for example), but for substance allied to finesse,

Giuseppe Quintarelli is the master. Not surprisingly, his wines are expensive and available only in small quantities. But they are imported to America, where they have an ardent following. Both the Amarone and the Recioto della Valpolicella (*dolce*) are equally without rival.

Quintarelli also offers another wine that is, effectively, an Amarone. But he doesn't call it that. For whatever reasons, the exacting Quintarelli sometimes decides that a certain Amarone wine is worthy of being sold as that. So he "declassifies" the wine, selling it as Rosso del Bepi. ("Bepi" or "Beppe" are common diminutives of Giuseppe.) It's far from cheap, but it's a kind of secret Quintarelli Amarone at roughly half the price.

LUIGI RIGHETTI—A small, traditional producer creating a slightly soft but delectable style of Amarone. Very appealing and age worthy.

SPERI—Two single vineyard recioto wines, one an Amarone and the other toward the dolce end of the spectrum. Vigneto Sant'Urbano is the Amarone, aged in large oak casks, while the La Roggia bottling spends two years in new small French oak barrels, which is thought to emphasize and enhance its residual sweetness. Both are very well made and strongly marked by their respective cellaring differences.

FRATELLI TEDESCHI—A traditional producer offering three recioto bottlings, a regular Amarone and two single-vineyard bottlings, one Amarone and the other *dolce*. The regular Amarone is admirable but overshadowed by the single-vineyard Capitel Monte Olmi. It's a classic Amarone that rewards extended aging. The dolce bottling is called Capitel Monte Fontana and it too is a classic of its kind.

TOMMASI—A serious producer offering several recioto bottlings. Tommasi's regular Amarone is very fine, but better is the single-vineyard Ca' Florian, which sees a little time (six months) in small new oak barrels. The excellent *dolce* version is another single-vineyard bottling call Fiorato. It emphasizes a greater freshness than some other versions, spending six months in stainless steel and six months in small oak barrels.

What Do The Locals Eat With This Wine? Despite its flavor intensity and elevated alcohol, it would be a mistake not to recognize that Recioto della Valpolicella is meant to accompany food. In the region, it's often served simply with chunks of room temperature Parmigiano-Reggiano cheese. And that is, certainly, a heavenly pairing. A dark-meated game bird such as a guinea hen, wild duck, goose, or even a pheasant with sausage stuffing goes with an Amarone with at least some age on it.

Still, the liquorous texture of Recioto della Valpolicella does lend itself best to an after-dinner *meditazione*. Roasted chestnuts, a jagged shard of Parmigiano-Reggiano, or a nice bite of bittersweet chocolate are all elevated by a good Recioto—and vice-versa.

One Man's Taste—Whose Wine Would I Buy? Price no object, I would reach for Quintarelli every time. But price usually *is* an object. So I would always look first for one of Masi's bottlings, especially the Mazzano and Campolongo di Torbe, as well as the two wines sourced from Serègo Alighieri vineyards. Also, I'm a big fan of Tedeschi and Luigi Righetti, both of whose wines are very reasonably priced for their (high) quality. And what about Romano dal Forno? Wonderful wine, no doubt about it. But praise has pushed the prices to the painfully prohibitive. However, if someone else is paying . . .

Worth Searching For? Don't die without trying it

Similar Wines From The Same Neighborhood: Ripasso-style Valpolicella, Valpolicella Classico, Recioto di Soave (white)

Ribolla Gialla

(ree-*bow*-lah *jah*-lah)
WHITE

Region: Friuli (northeast Italy)

Grapes: 100 percent Ribolla Gialla (white)

The Tradition: One of the two really distinctive indigenous white varieties of Friuli (the other is Tocai Friulano), Ribolla Gialla creates an unusually lush, golden-hued dry white wine like no other in the world. A specialty of the easternmost section of Friuli, where the districts called Collio, Colli Orientali del Friuli, Isonzo, and Carso are located, it's grown almost nowhere else in the world.

Like all of the other whites of those districts, the old tradition was for bulk wines that often were oxidized and rather flat. Like everything else in Friuli—all of Italy, really—that's changed with ferocious speed.

How It's Changed: The big change with Ribolla Gialla is that for other Friulian whites as well: temperature-controlled fermentations in stainless steel tanks, lowered vineyard yields, and pursuit of depth and definition in the wine itself.

Ribolla Gialla is worth mentioning because of its unusually lush, rich quality. No, it's not one of the world's great whites, something capable of rivaling famous white Burgundies. But it is one of Italy's most distinctive dry white wines: texturally dense and highly aromatic, with notes of bitter honey, almonds, and spices such as a hint of clove.

The other element of Ribolla Gialla that makes it stand out is that it's a vehicle for some of the most fascinating winemaking experimentalism occurring anywhere in the world. Friulian producers such as Josko Gravner, Stanislao Radikon, and Damijan Podversic employ

Ribolla Gialla in their treat-the-white-grape-as-if-it-were-red approach. They ferment Ribolla Gialla with its skins, like a red wine. This flies in the face of today's winemaking convention where the skins are whisked away immediately. With the skins, the resulting wine emerges looking vaguely like apple cider. Yet the flavors are intense, rich and—if you close your eyes—you'd believe you were drinking a red, so meaty and rich are the flavors and scents.

More conventionally made Ribolla Giallas are brilliantly clear, light straw gold with the fresh, beautiful fragrances previously noted. They are lovely dry white wines in their own (mainstream) right.

Noteworthy Producers (The Traditionalists / The Modernists): Nearly all of the top producers in Collio, Colli Orientali del Friuli, Isonzo, and Carso make a Ribolla Gialla (see page 199 for discussions of these producers).

But it's worth emphasizing what might be called the "radical Ribollas" of Radikon, Gravner, and Podversic. They may not change your mind about your taste preferences for dry white wines, but they will make you think. And Ribolla Gialla, with its rich lushness, is an ideal medium for their radical white-as-red approach.

What Do The Locals Eat With This Wine? Because of its lush qualities, Ribolla Gialla is often served with soups in the area, especially during their nippy winters. Indeed, it is an ideal choice for cream soups. Also, it's an excellent white wine for many cheeses. Richer-tasting fish dishes are perfect for Ribolla Gialla as well. The locals tend to choose it when a softer, gentler white wine is called for (a pork dish, for example) rather than, say, the sharper-edged Sauvignon Blanc.

One Man's Taste—Whose Wine Would I Buy? Among the "radical" Ribolla Giallas, my first choice would be Josko Gravner. More conventionally, I'd reach for Jermann's bottling called Vinnae (see page 124).

Worth Searching For? Absolutely worth trying

Similar Wines From The Same Neighborhood: Any of the many other dry white wines from Friuli, especially the other fascinating indigenous white, Tocai Friulano

Sagrantino di Montefalco

(sah-grahn-*tee*-noh dee mawn teh-*fahl*-koh)
RED

Region: Umbria (central Italy, about 25 miles southeast of Perugia)

Grape: Sagrantino (red)

The Tradition: Should you ever need proof that there is, in fact, something new under the ancient Italian sun, you need point only to Sagrantino di Montefalco. As little as twenty years ago, it barely existed. Even today, there's little more than 250 acres of Sagrantino grown in Montefalco, although there surely will be more to come as Sagrantino gains attention.

Of course, there was always red wine grown in the little town of Montefalco. This is Italy, after all. But it was mostly plain old *rosso*, offered in demijohns, mostly made from the ubiquitous (in Umbria and neighboring Tuscany anyway) Sangiovese. A local grape called Sagrantino (possible brought in by Spanish Franciscan monks, as Montefalco has an ancient monastery) was intermixed in the vineyards with Sangiovese.

Despite assertions about its origins (it came from the Saracens centuries ago, or from Piedmont, or from Catalan-speaking Spain via Franciscan monks), the fact is that written references to Sagrantino date only to the 1800s. By Italian standards—which measure time in millennia—something datable only to the nineteenth century is a newcomer. Likely it existed long before that, but there's no indisputable proof.

No matter. What's significant is that, until very recently, Sagrantino was traditionally intermixed with Sangiovese in the local wine. And only in the late twentieth century did it step out for a solo performance—to great applause, surprise, and acclaim.

How It's Changed: The first change was having Sagrantino as a solo act at all. That done—the first dry or non-sweet Sagrantino appeared only with the 1979 vintage—the usual modernizing improvements concerning controlled fermentations and small oak barrels quickly ensued.

The challenge of Sagrantino is that it's a strong, tannic red grape capable of creating equally strong, tannic red wine. The trick is taming it into something more refined. Because of this, it requires longer-than-usual aging in barrel or cask as well as bottle. Indeed, the law requires that Sagrantino not be released until two and one-half years after the harvest.

Also, there's the question of whether to make a conventional, fairly high-in-alcohol (typically 14 percent) dry Sagrantino or to employ the *passito* (literally, dried) process, where the clusters are allowed to raisin, losing much of their water, and are then made into a (much stronger) wine that's also sweet (see Recioto della Valpolicella, page 245).

A third alternative is to revert to tradition and combine Sagrantino with Sangiovese to create a differently labeled wine called Montefalco Rosso. This is an admirable use for Sagrantino, as it's pretty strong (wine) medicine in its own right and using it to add backbone, depth, and dark color to Sangiovese makes a lot of sense.

Montefalco's dozen or so producers each takes one or all three of these routes. Most make at least a Montefalco Rosso, which usually is a dark-hued red wine with some of Sangiovese's attractive "dustiness" allied with the more jammy berryishness of Sagrantino. Usually there's some Cabernet Sauvignon or Merlot added also. A typical Montefalco Rosso is 65 to 70 percent Sangiovese and only 10 to 15 percent Sagrantino, with the balance being Cabernet or Merlot. It's ideal with a good sausage, a plate of pasta with a meat ragù, or a good hamburger, for that matter.

More ambitious is a proper Sagrantino di Montefalco, which must, by law, be 100 percent Sagrantino. Here you're getting a very strong, intense, jammy (blackberries) red wine with a certain dried-berry intensity, along with a good dose of tannins. (One is reminded of

California Zinfandel, which has that same jamminess.)

Finally, there's Sagrantino di Montefalco Passito, made from semi-dried grapes. The alcohol, as with Recioto della Valpolicella, soars to 15 percent or higher. But in a way, the *passito* process plays to Sagrantino's (literal) strength. It's already a rather jammy, blackberryish, high-alcohol red. Why not go for broke?

The *passito* version is almost black in color, rich, intense, powerful, tannic, and somehow thrilling. It's not a wine you wish to drink unremittingly, but it's also not a wine quite like any other, even among Italy's many other *passito* reds.

Noteworthy Producers (The Traditionalists/The Modernists): With only a dozen or so producers, the choices for Sagrantino di Montefalco are easily narrowed. Happily, all of the best producers can be found on these shores. Three stand out.

FILIPPO ANTONELLI—Antonelli's Sagrantino di Montefalco is rich, intense, and almost luscious. His Montefalco Rosso, by the way, is one of the best. He also offers a rarely seen Riserva version that is allowed, by law, to incorporate a little more Sagrantino in the blend than the legally mandated limit of just 15 percent Sagrantino.

PAOLO BEA—Now in his mid-seventies, Paolo Bea (pronounced bay-ah) is the cult wine producer in Montefalco. Although his sons now do the grunt work, the father continues to set the tone. Bea's Sagrantino di Montefalco is as intense and concentrated as any, but less polished and, paradoxically, more persuasive as a result.

Where Arnaldo Caprai polishes Sagrantino to a high buff, Bea allows Sagrantino's intrinsic rusticity to show, but only just enough to add dimension, rather than coarsen the wine. He is a very great producer with the sort of individuality that sets apart the finest artisans. The great (American) writer about Italian wines, Burton Anderson, once called Paolo Bea's *passito* Sagrantino "titanic." I can do no better.

ARNALDO CAPRAI—The biggest name in Montefalco is Arnaldo Caprai. The Caprai family is Montefalco's version of Montalcino's

Biondi-Santi clan (see page 96). More than anyone else, the Caprai family pioneered Sagrantino (the father, Arnaldo) while his son (Marco) amplified and improved upon his father's pioneering efforts by lowering yields and modernizing the winemaking.

Today, Caprai's Sagrantino di Montefalco is the benchmark, a wine of great concentration, depth, and power delivering gusts of tar, licorice, spices, and jammy fruit. Less often seen, and equally desirable, is Caprai's *passito* Sagrantino, which is sold only in half-bottles, so potent is it.

Other good names—certainly worth buying if you spot them—are Adanti and Rocca di Fabbri.

What Do The Locals Eat With This Wine? Because Sagrantino di Montefalco is such a thunderous red, it works only with equally big mouthfuls of flavor. The locals fork into *cinghiale* or wild boar, which abound in both Umbria and Tuscany. You also see pasta with a wild boar meat sauce. Anything gamey and strong-flavored is the ticket. Or a hard strong cheese such as aged Pecorino.

Sagrantino passito, like its northern compatriot Recioto della Valpolicella *dolce*, is delicious indeed with a chunk of Parmigiano-Reggiano, some roasted chestnuts, or bittersweet chocolate. It's a true *vino da meditazione*, a wine to meditate over.

One Man's Taste—Whose Wine Would I Buy? My first choice is Paolo Bea, whose production is very small and is consequently not easy to locate. But his wines do reach America. A close second is Arnaldo Caprai, whose wines are magnificent in their own right.

Worth Searching For? Absolutely worth an effort

Similar Wines From The Same Neighborhood: Montefalco Rosso, Arquata Rosso dell'Umbria from Adanti (a blend of Sangiovese, Sagrantino, and Merlot)

Salice Salentino

(*sah*-lee-cheh sahl-en-*teen*-oh)
RED AND WHITE

Region: Apulia/Puglia (southern Italy; the toe of the boot)

Grapes: For red and rosé (*rosato*): Negroamaro with the allowable addition of up to 20 percent Malvasia Nera. White wines are also offered using Chardonnay, Pinot Bianco, Sauvignon Blanc, and local indigenous varieties. Sweet wines are made most from Aleatico, a red-skinned strain of Muscat.

The Tradition: Apulia, like everywhere else in southern Italy, was once devoted (or confined) to producing floods of cheap red wines that wound up in big shippers' bulk bottlings or were surreptitiously added to more famous Italian wines. The locals knew and liked what they made. And above all, the Salicesi knew that in their great indigenous red variety, Negroamaro (literally black bitter), they had something special.

But poverty, lack of ambition, opportunity, and capital, along with northern Italy's own condescension of all things connected to the South conspired to keep Apulian wines from fulfilling their promise. Winemaking until recently was rustic and crude. Facilities were limited, and winemaking was strictly traditional, resulting in wines that were oxidized, overly tannic, and unrevealing of Negroamaro's potential.

This story is hardly unique to Apulia. It could be said of virtually all areas of Italy south of Rome until as recently as the 1980s.

How It's Changed: Few areas of Italy have seen such a dramatic transformation—and such quick international acceptance—as Salice Salentino. When it first appeared on the American market in the 1980s, few wine drinkers (myself included) had ever heard of Salice Salentino.

And fewer still knew how to pronounce it correctly, either, as the accent is in the first syllable: *sah*-lee-cheh. (Many southern Italian words have an accented first syllable rather than one of the middle syllables, as is common in northern and central Italian pronunciation. It derives from southern Italian dialects, which more frequently accent the first syllable of a word.)

When these wines first arrived in the United States in quantity, wine lovers everywhere were astonished by the low price and the sheer accessible goodness of these Negroamaro-based wines. They were (and are) dark, rich, and intense, with spicy, gamey, and even vaguely port-like qualities. They were (and are) soft, lush, and gulpable. You thought pizza, spaghetti, and hamburgers. Above all, you wondered how anyone could offer a wine that good and that cheap (it was $5.95 a bottle).

Far from being offended, the producers of Salice Salentino were delighted. They had broken out of the box. They actually made money selling wines that, even after importers', wholesalers', and retailers' markups, could still cost so little. Think of what a pittance the producers must have gotten. Yet they made money. And above all, they put Salice Salentino on the wine map.

To their credit, the Salicesi reinvested the profits into creating better wineries, lowering yields to offer better wines (or at least more expensive ones), and playing with the use of previously unaffordable small oak barrels. It was a liberation of sorts, as well as a welcome confirmation of what they knew for generations: Negroamaro makes a helluva nice red wine.

Today, the number of producers has increased. And the most established growers have increased their vineyards and modernized extensively. Yet prices remain modest. Of course there are the usual *bella figura* bottlings with too much oak and too high a price for the result. But that was inevitable. And besides, it's worth a try. Who knows what an expense-no-object Negroamaro can taste like?

Salice Salentino does issue wines other than its signature red. But the white wines are, so far, nothing special, although the sweet dessert wines made from Aleatico are enjoyable. Still, to say Salice Salentino today is synonymous with saying "red."

A good Salice Salentino rosso should be inky black, lush, soft, and rich-tasting with notes of spices, leather, a certain gamy note, and a definite, mouthwatering edge of bitterness in the final taste. (They call the grape variety "black bitter" for a reason.)

Noteworthy Producers (The Traditionalists/The Modernists): Everyone in Salice Salentino today is a modernist, if only because everyone agrees that the tradition, so-called, was well worth discarding. Who needs or wants rustic, coarse, oxidized red wines? We don't, and neither do they. So there's no conflict in Salice Salentino today on that account. Everyone is on the "up" escalator for both style and quality.

As a general rule—and this is something the Salicesi don't want to hear—their best wines are the less expensive ones in a producer's line-up. The more expensive wines are invariably very oaky, sometimes too tannic (from excessive wood tannins), and just not worth the often considerable price differential. It's best to stick with the *normale* offerings where you'll never go wrong for the money.

CANDIDO—A good, solid producer of straight-down-the-middle Salice Salentino made from 85 percent Negroamaro and 15 percent Malvasia Nera. Production is sizable as the estate has 385 acres of vineyards, in addition to which the Candido brothers have access to an additional 650 acres owned by close relatives and neighbors.

LEONE DE CASTRIS—A very large and ambitious producer, which, along with the Taurino family, is a leader in the region. Leone di Castris issues more than a dozen different wines, red and white, sweet and dry. Indeed, if you want to taste the scope and ambition of Salice Salentino today, you can do no better than to work your way through the Leone di Castris portfolio.

The best bet for this producer is its least "ambitious" wine, namely their Salice Salentino Riserva. Actually, there's plenty of ambition with this wine, as it's one of the best of its type made in Salice Salentino today. But unlike the much more expensive "Donna Lisa" bottling, it sees no time in expensive small oak barrels. And unlike the "Messere Andrea" Rosso Salento bottling (a blend of Negroamara and Cabernet Sauvignon) or "Illemos" Rosso Salento (a blend of Negroamaro with Primitivo and Merlot), the regular Saluice Salentino has no international varieties modifying its intrinsically fine flavors.

Leone di Castris is a great producer whose experiements are driving Salice Salentino and all of Apulia forward. They are always worth watching and tasting.

TAURINO—It was the wines of the late Cosimo Taurino that first enlightened Americans to the possibilities of Salice Salentino. Indeed, for a while there it seemed that Taurino was the *only* producer in Salice Salentino. It took a while for others to realize what a chunk of the American market the Taurino family had wolfed down.

Some observers suggest that the quality of Taurino's wines declined as market success surged. More likely, others, especially Leone di Castris, provided both competition and context. Nevertheless, Taurino remains one of the leaders in Salice Salentino, and their Salice Salentino Rosso Riserva is one of the benchmark bottlings of the zone.

Taurino's more ambitious wines, both aged in small oak barrels, called Notarpanaro and Patriglione, are quite oaky but filled with dramatic intensity. They are very good wines of their sort. But the basic Salice Salentino Rosso remains the deal. Worth noting is that the Taurino family has had its head turned by international varieties. This is a house that remains devoted to Apulia's traditional grape varieties. Their wines—and their focus—are the better for it. After all these years, Taurino still is the benchmark.

What Do The Locals Eat With This Wine? The Salento peninsula that makes up most of Apulia is the second largest "flat spot" in Italy after the vast Po Valley in the north. And, of course, compared to northern Italy's Po Valley, it's much warmer in Apulia for most of the year.

Consequently, there's an unusually large production of field crops such as fava beans, artichokes, chicory, and various greens including rucola (rocket), eggplant, peppers, and cauliflower, among other vegetables.

Worth noting is Apulia's huge olive and olive oil production from the largest olive trees I've ever seen. Apulia produces fully half of all Italian olive oil. Seemingly everything that stands still long enough in Apulia gets deep-fried in olive oil. (What's not to like?) The most famous Apulian pasta is the now ubiquitous (and very fashionable in northern Italy today) orecchiette pasta, which is a disc-shaped, chewy cuplike item.

Salice Salentino Rosso is typically served with Apulia's meats of choice, which are lamb or kid. Or with orecchiette with a meat ragù. In America, it's an ideal red for all sorts of barbecue (it stands up well to marinades and spicy rubs).

One Man's Taste—Whose Wine Would I Buy? The easy winners here are the basic Salice Salentino reds from Leone di Castris and Taurino. You can't go wrong with either.

Worth Searching For? Absolutely worth an effort.

Similar Wines From The Same Neighborhood: Apulia is now offering ever-better reds from the Primitivo grape variety, which was long thought to be identical to California's Zinfandel grape. (For the record, the University of California at Davis, using DNA profiling, has established that Zinfandel's parent is really the Croatian variety called Crljenak Kasteljanski and that Primitivo is, in fact, not Zinfandel's parent but its sibling, as it too derives from Crljenak Kasteljanski.)

Anyway, Apulia is now issuing reds called Primitivo that are appealing and—dare I say it?—Zinfandel-like.

Sardinia

Sardegna
(sahr-*den*-yah)
RED AND WHITE

Region: Island off of Italy's west coast in the Mediterranean Ocean

Grapes: Numerous varieties are grown, both indigenous and international. In addition to the usual Chardonnay, Sauvignon Blanc, Cabernet Sauvignon, and Merlot are such indigenous—or at least long-established—varieties as:

Red: Cannonau (a Sardinian strain of Grenache), Bovale Sardo, Carignano del Sulcis, Girò, Monica, Pascale, and Sangiovese

White: Malvasia, Moscato, Nasco, Nuragus, Torbato, Trebbiano, Vermentino, and Vernaccia

The Tradition: The oddity of Sardinia, at least for wine lovers living on the "mainland" (the Sardinians say the *continente*), is how few Sardinian wines anybody sees compared to the surprising amount of wine grown on this small island. It's tempting to compare Sardinia to Sicily because they are similar in size. (Sicily is 9,926 square miles compared to Sardinia's 9,194 square miles.)

Both islands enjoy strong self-identification, with distinctive local dialects, strong influences from both North Africa and Spain, highly individual (and wonderful) cuisines, and an array of indigenous or long-established grape varieties.

But when it comes to wine, Sardinia has recently taken a different path from Sicily. Until the past few decades, Sardinia played the same role as Sicily, namely as a supplier of cheap bulk wines used for blending by big mainland Italy producers.

A comparison between the two islands—Sardinia has always had fewer vineyard acres than Sicily as it's is more mountainous and has less arable land—tells the story succinctly:

Sardinia has 107,000 acres of vines. (Sicily has 341,000 acres.)

Sardinia produces 28 million gallons of wine. (Sicily produces 185 million gallons.)

Sixteen percent of Sardinia's vineyards are in controlled appellations, e.g. DOC or DOCG. (Sicily has little more than 6 percent of its vines under controlled appellation.)

How It's Changed: Starting in the late 1970s, Sardinia (unlike Sicily) began to reduce its vineyard acreage significantly, seeking to replace quantity with quality. This effort was assisted by subsidies from the European Union, which would very much like to drain Europe's overflowing "wine lake," a good portion of which is composed of cheap wines made by politically powerful winegrowers' cooperatives. These wines eventually get distilled into industrial alcohol at great cost to the EU.

But Sardinia also was spurred by the demands of its unusually high-end tourist clientele, many of whom are wealthy, expense-account sorts who expect (and demand) better-quality wines. One look at the number of huge yachts and private jets that arrive in Sardinia in winter and summer will tell you that these are no ordinary tourists. And although they're interested in local wines, they expect them to be more than ordinary.

The elevation of Sardinian wines from rustic to refined is still ongoing. And much of what gets made will probably never leave Sardinia to duke it out in competitive, hard-to-penetrate foreign markets such as the United States. Consequently, the reality is that Americans see only a handful of large, sophisticated Sardinian producers that make refined wines in large enough quantities to make exporting and marketing feasible, as well as price-competitive.

Noteworthy Producers: It's a bit embarrassing to write about Sardinian wines because of the paucity of offerings in America. Effectively, we see just two major entrants: Argiolas and Sella e Mosca.

If you see any Sardinian wines at all, those are the wineries you'll see.

It would be a mistake to conclude, however, that Sardinia doesn't have other good growers. Or that its wines aren't worthy of attention and discussion. Perhaps more than any other major Italian wine region, Sardinia is underrepresented in the American market. Look at the considerable increase in new offerings from Campania, Basilicata, and Sicily in the American market. Sardinia has not yet seen a similar degree of interest. Given the growing number, and sophistication, of American lovers of Italian wines, one trusts that Sardinia's day will soon arrive.

In the meantime, you will find these two major players on many wine shelves across the nation:

ARGIOLAS—Like so many of Italy's high-achieving wineries, Argiolas is the result of one man's unrelenting vision and ambition. Antonio Argiolas, who is in his late nineties at this writing, inherited a tiny operation from his father, Francesco, who founded the winery in 1918.

Antonio Argiolas' commitment to wine was tested by the carrot dangled by the European Union in the late 1970s: "We'll pay you to get out of the wine business and uproot or at least reduce the size of your vineyards." Many Sardinian growers, working uneconomic vines, gladly took up the EU bureaucrats on their offer.

But Argiolas did the opposite, deciding to buy more (and better) vineyards and become larger. Given that the demand for Sardinian wines at the time was hardly intense or remunerative, it was a dramatically confident commitment to a presumed better future. He was right, although surely his neighbors thought him foolhardy at the time.

Still, it was a tough slog. It was only in 1990 that Argiolas sold more of its wines in bottle than in bulk. Today, everything is bottled and the majority of Argiolas' 200,000-plus cases of wine, from more than six hundred acres of vines, are exported outside of Italy. Even by modern Italian standards of high-flying wine achievement (there are hundreds of such marketing successes), it's a pretty good rags-to-riches saga given Sardinia's low wine profile compared to, say, Piedmont or Tuscany.

The array of wines offered is sizable, and not all of it, understandably, reaches America, although nearly a dozen offerings do. Among Argiolas' best wines are:

Costera—A single-vineyard red (90 percent Cannonau, 5 percent Carignano, and 5 percent Bovale Sardo) that sees six to eight months of aging in small oak barrels. It's earthy, spicy, redolent of black currants, and lip-smackingly smooth.

Perdera—A single-vineyard red (90 percent Monica, 5 percent Carignano, and 5 percent Bovale Sardo) that's rather rustic and vibrantly fruity with whiffs of cherry and black pepper.

Turriga—A single-vineyard red (85 percent Cannonau and 15 percent Malvasia Nera, Carignano, and Bovale Sardo) of exceptional intensity and refinement, with strong gusts of wild cherries, black currant, and noticeable oakiness. This is Argiolas' best red wine.

Vermentino Costamolino di Sardegna—A dry white wine made 100 percent from Vermentino, delivering a tangy mix of citrus fruits with some thickness on the palate. It's a fine example of one of Sardinia's signature white grapes.

Selegas Nuragus di Cagliari—A white made 100 percent from Sicily's indigenous Nuragus grape, which creates a sort of appley white wine with hints of peaches and herbs. It, too, has palate density.

As previously mentioned, Argiolas has yet other offerings. Considering that prices remain exceedingly reasonable for the quality, this is a producer that you buy with the confidence that whatever you get will at minimum be worth the money and at maximum is a deal.

SELLA E MOSCA—The biggest private winery in Sardinia, Sella e Mosca was founded in 1899 by Erminio Sella, an engineer, and Edgardo Mosca, a lawyer. They originally saw Sardinia simply as a good place to hunt. Wine, ironically, was not their intent. Yet today, the winery, which is now owned by the Campari liquor company, has what the company says is the second largest contiguous vineyard (1,200 acres) in Italy. It's a big, sophisticated winery by anybody's standards, issuing more than a half-million cases of wine annually.

As might be expected from so large an operation, Sella e Mosca's wine offerings are numerous. Although the wines are well made, they tend to be rather commercial, rarely exhibiting the kind of depth that one might like to see. Prices are reasonable, but the quality is merely "correct."

What Do The Locals Eat With This Wine? Sardinia's cuisine is one of Italy's most distinctive. It's also strongly delineated between coastal and inland, with the coastal areas naturally emphasizing seafood and the inland cooking concentrating on mushrooms, game, and, especially, meats cooked on a spit. Lamb and pork are Sardinian favorites.

As might be imagined, the wines pair off accordingly, with Sardinia's dry whites such as Vermentino marrying perfectly with seafood and the rustic, earthy, rich reds such as Cannonau and Monica, among others, the perfect foil for the likes of roast lamb or suckling pig. They are ideal barbecue reds, by the way, capable of holding their own against spicy marinades and rubs.

One Man's Taste—Whose Wine Would I Buy? Clearly, it's Argiolas. You can't go wrong with its wines and, frankly, the overall standard of Argiolas is superior to that of Sella e Mosca.

Worth Searching For? Only if you see it

Similar Wines From The Same Neighborhood: Sardinia, and its wines, are a world of their own.

Sicily

Sicilia

(see-*cheel*-yah)

RED AND WHITE

Region: Southern Italy

Grapes: Ten native varieties—Cataratto, Frappato, Grecanico, Grillo, Inzolia, Nerello Mascalese, Nero D'Avola, Nerello Cappuccio, Perricone, and Zibibbo—account for 80 percent of all of the vines grown in Sicily today. But at least another twenty-eight other indigenous varieties have been identified. Also such international varieties as Chardonnay, Cabernet Sauvignon, Merlot, Syrah, and others.

The Tradition: Sicily's wine tradition is really all about size. A few numbers put it quickly into perspective: In 2003 (the latest available year for official statistics), Sicily had 341,000 acres of vines and produced 185 million gallons of wine.

This puts Sicily third in wines and vines after such giants as California (513,000 acres of vines and 444 million gallons in 2004) and Australia (398,000 acres of vines and 370 million gallons of wine in 2004).

That's an awful lot of wine for an island that's just 6 percent of the size of California and a microscopic three-one-thousandths the size of Australia.

What these numbers, dry as they are, tell us is that Sicily is—and always has been—awash in wine. And much of it, traditionally and to this day, is utterly forgettable. Sicily has long been the bulk wine capital of Italy. Only recently (2001) did Sicily reach the tipping point where it exported more wines in bottle than in bulk.

This preponderance of cheap no-account wines is reflected in how few of Sicily's vineyards have achieved some kind of controlled appellation status (IGT, DOC, or DOCG). The total production of all of the wines entitled to these designations—a bare minimum for many other areas of Italy—is little more than 5 percent of Sicily's entire wine output.

Change in Sicily's wine, and its attitude about wine, dates only to the 1980s. It's as recent as that. Before then, the overwhelming majority of Sicilian wines were pleasant, simple reds along with a vast sea of sweetish whites, and a dwindling but still sizable amount of sweet Marsala wine, which is still Sicily's most famous single wine.

How It's Changed: Sicily's long, troubled political saga hardly needs retelling. But it's no coincidence that the new interest in creating finer, more expensive Sicilian wines parallels the island's lurching but increasingly successful struggle against organized crime and equally organized (or at least institutionalized) corruption.

But believers—both local and mainland Italian—in a better Sicilian future have rallied and are making themselves felt. As in Tuscany, some of Sicily's best wines are today made by "outsiders" who, in turn, have inspired previously complacent locals to improve their own vineyards and wines.

Much of the change, not surprisingly given what's occurred elsewhere in Italy, involve the installation of international grapes such as Chardonnay, Syrah, Merlot, and Cabernet Sauvignon along with the (inevitable) use of small new oak barrels. Whether any or all of these are necessary is beside the point: It's how progress is made today. It's a first, important, step.

Precisely because this occurred so recently, almost simultaneously came a renewed interest in indigenous local varieties. This interest in Italy's unrivaled indigenous grape patrimony was occurring in already "modernized" wine regions such as Tuscany, Friuli, and Umbria.

Sicily is a trove of indigenous varieties with possibly more highly localized grape varieties than almost anywhere else in Italy. And if it doesn't hold that crown, it's certainly a contender, with indigenous varieties numbering in the dozens. Its claim to antiquity is unrivaled.

Sicily was one of ancient Greece's earliest conquests, dating to at least the eighth century BC. So many of the grapes that later migrated to the Italian mainland first arrived in Sicily via the Greeks or the innumerable traders from the Mediterranean basin for whom Sicily was a major destination for business or military conquest. For example, the white grape called Inzolia in Sicily was later transported to seacoast Tuscany, where it became known as Ansonica. The grape is still grown in both places.

The reality of Sicilian wine today is that it is shape-shifting to a degree extreme even for Italy. You've got a vast sea of insipidity. (Four-fifths of Sicily's wines are made by state-subsidized winegrowers' cooperatives.)

At the opposite extreme, you've got a growing smattering of *bella figura* bottlings of oaky, often very expensive wines made from international grapes offered by producers intent on demonstrating Sicily's determined new modernity. Sometimes these wines are blends of indigenous red grapes, such as Sicily's best red variety, Nero d'Avola, abetted by Cabernet Sauvignon or Merlot (or both), along with a shiny gloss of new oak.

Are these wines desirable? It's a matter of taste, of course. Often they are pleasing and familiar tasting. But rarely are they deeply gratifying, if only because you don't quite get that soul-satisfaction of tasting something *really* original.

For that, you need to seek out the increasing number of Sicilian wines made exclusively from Sicily's native grapes such as Cataratto, Frappato, Grecanico, Grillo, Inzolia, Nerello Mascalese, Nero D'Avola, Nerello Cappuccio, Perricone, and Zibibbo. Mind you, just because native grapes are employed doesn't automatically mean the resulting wines are worthwhile. Too many Sicilian wines, even from well-intentioned growers, are still lackluster.

The biggest change in Sicily's grapegrowing is the relocation of vineyards from baking-hot valley floors to higher-elevation (read cooler) vineyard sites. In such locations, where nighttime temperatures can drop considerably—thus allowing the grape to retain needed and desirable acidity—these same indigenous varieties emerge with greater flavor definition, brighter flavors, and more character than when grown on valley floors.

If all of this sounds like a confusingly mixed bag, it is. That's Sicily today: a mixed bag of the banal, the superficial, the sincere, and the increasingly accomplished. Given the newness of the ambition, and the difficulties of making yourself felt in an ever more competitive international wine world, how could it be anything else?

Noteworthy Producers (The Traditionalists / The Modernists):

ABBAZIA SANT'ANASTASIA—A former Benedictine monastery at a high elevation on Sicily's northern coast. Its owner originally intended to develop the twelfth-century complex as a resort but became enthralled by wine instead. Today there are about 250 acres of vines, many of them international varieties such as Cabernet Sauvignon, Syrah, and Merlot. Two of Italy's most famous consulting enologists (Riccardo Cotarella and Giacomo Tachis) were brought in to advise on winemaking and grapegrowing.

The wines offered today are highly internationalized, including a pure Cabernet Sauvignon called Litra Rosso and blends such as Montanero Rosso (Nero d'Avola, Cabernet Sauvignon, and Merlot). High quality in a glossy, chic fashion.

BENANTI—Arguably the finest of all the "nativist" wine producers in Sicily. Located on the slopes of Mount Etna, owner Giuseppe Benanti revitalized his family's old vineyard in 1988 with a focused passion for native Sicilian varieties. The results are magnificent. When you taste Benanti's carefully crafted wines, you can understand almost instantly why Sicily has a future in truly fine wine that's more than a knockoff of what others elsewhere—California, Australia, France—have already done.

Look for Il Monovitigno Nerello Mascalese to understand the mouthwatering appeal of this native red grape, with its wild cherry and citrus notes. Or the unusual variant of the same grape labeled Il Monovitigno Nerello Cappuccio, which has more pigments in its skin than its lighter and more tannic cousin Nerello Mascalese. Not least is a benchmark Nero d'Avola, with its deep, almost opaque blackish-garnet hue and cherry/plum/black pepper scent and taste.

These wines, among others (there's a delicious dry white called Pietramarina made entirely from Carricante that's a delicious combination of minerals and citrus notes), are some of Sicily's finest wines. Considering that Benanti's "resurrection" began only in 1988, it's safe to predict greater achievements yet.

COTTANERA—Another fine producer on the slopes of Mount Etna that Solomonically divides the wine baby between 100 percent bottlings of several non-Sicilian grape varieties (Merlot, Syrah, Cabernet Sauvignon, and Mondeuse, a.k.a. Refosco) as well as Sicilian grapes such as Nero d'Avola, Nerello Mascalese, and Inzolia.

Given the modern-mindedness, it's no surprise to discover a good amount of oakiness in the wines, especially with the international varieties.

That noted, this is a very promising producer across the board. Look especially for Barbazzale Bianco, a floral and peachy dry white with no oak made entirely from the indigenous Inzolia variety. Barbazzale Rosso, for its part, is 90 percent Nerello Mascalese and 10 percent Nero d'Avola, and is a superb example of the rich, intense, black cherry virtues of these wines.

Worth noting is the inspired planting of Mondeuse or Refosco grape, which is the sole variety in a wine called L'Ardenza Rosso. Here, perhaps more than with Merlot or Cabernet Sauvignon, the possibilities of allying Sicily's volcanic soil and hot, dry climate to a non-native grape makes (taste) sense. This is lovely wine, displaying Refosco's inherent rusticity with an unusually rich depth of fruit.

All told, Cottanera is a serious producer to be watched closely.

CUSUMANO—A large producer with numerous vineyards in various locations around Sicily. Pleasing wines in a fruit-forward, drink-now style. Best bets include a lovely white Inzolia, all peaches, citrus, and almond, and a very good, soft but gulpable Nero d'Avola.

DE BARTOLI—The master of Marsala. Created by the English two centuries ago, Marsala, a city in western Sicily, became a substitute for rum in the British navy. Unlike rum, which is a distilled liquor, Marsala is a wine aged in wood for years (which explains its deep orange hue) that is fortified with a touch of brandy, the better to help it survive long sea voyages. (The British also "invented" a red wine from Portugal along the same brandy-fortified line now famous today as port.)

Several different sorts of Marsala are made, the golden- or amber-hued Marsalas made from native white grapes such as Grillo, Cataratto, Inzolia, and Damaschino for golden and amber Marsala. The less often seen red Marsala is made from such red varieties as Pignatello, Calabrese, Nerello Mascalese, and Nero d'Avola.

Marsala is made very much like another British-beloved wine, sherry. What the Spanish called a "solera" is a system where a "pyramid" of old wines are used as a base to blend with younger, newer wines. The idea is to keep cycling the old with the new to create not just a consistent product but also one infused with the aged qualities achieved by the "grandfather" barrels. Such a solera can last for a century or more, with at least a molecular amount of the original hundred-year-old barrel coursing through the veins of the newest-vintage generation.

Marsala was for centuries Sicily's most famous and lucrative wine. Indeed, it was Sicily's sole contribution to the larger wine world. Once it was much appreciated. Today it is almost synonymous with cooking wine. Think veal in Marsala or chicken Marsala or, famously, the warm egg yolk and sugar custard called zabaglione, in which Marsala is the informing flavor.

Marco de Bartoli single-handedly revived Marsala as a serious wine deserving equally serious attention. No one makes better, more artisanal Marsala than de Bartoli, along with an absolutely stunning Moscato di Pantelleria Passito called Bukkuram, grown on the tiny island of Pantelleria, which is closer to the African coast of Tunisia (23 miles) than it is to Sicily (29 miles).

Among de Bartoli's several Marsalas, look especially for Vecchio Samperi 20 Anni, one of its most aged versions. It is surprisingly delicate yet intense, a deep amber color, dry, and almost kaleidoscopic in its dizzying array of scents and flavors including white chocolate, raisins, almonds, and lemon and orange zest. Less elaborated, if you will, is the amber Marsala Superiore, which is surprisingly dry and redolent of lemon rind, nuts, herbs, and bitter almond.

These wines are ideal as an after-dinner sip or as an accompaniment to a delicate custard or flan or pound cake. When you taste de Bartoli's Marsalas or his Bukkuram Moscato di Pantelleria, you will be happily transported to the taste of another time—and wonder how and why we ever let it slip past us.

DONNAFUGATA—A famous name in Sicilian wine (and literature), and rightly so. The name is resonant because in Giuseppe Tomasi di Lampedusa's landmark novel *Il Gattopardo* (*The Leopard*), it was to the town and palace of Donnafugata that the Prince traveled to escape Palermo's oppressive summer heat. Actually, the palace described in the novel is not the impressive pile in Donnafugata itself, but an even more impressive one in San Margherita di Belice in the province of Agrigento.

Making matters more confusing yet is that the winery called Donnafugata is neither in the town of Donnafugata nor in San Margherita di Belice. Indeed, it has nothing to do with either place. The winery called Donnafugata is in the province of Trapani at the westernmost tip of Sicily; the town (and palace) of Donnafugata is in the province of Ragusa, at the opposite end of the island.

Nevertheless, the winery plays up the name to the utmost. Still, it's the wines of Donnafugata that matter and they are lovely. Indeed they are exemplars of forward thinking, with an extensive lineup of both reds and whites. The labels, by the way, are among the most charming you'll see anywhere, with most thematically linked by images of women, usually with long, floating tresses.

The white wines are well made and usually mercifully free of oak. Look for Anthilia, a fifty-fifty blend of Ansonica and Cataratto; Lighea (40 percent Zibibbo, 30 percent Ansonica, and 30 percent Cataratto); and Vigna di Gabri (100 percent Ansonica), among others.

The reds are more impressive yet. A 100 percent Nero d'Avola is called Sèdara, a reference to the family name of one of the characters in *The Leopard* (Angelica, who married the Prince's nephew). It's a good, true Nero d'Avola. A fifty-fifty blend of Nero d'Avola and Merlot called Angheli is less persuasive, but still attractive.

More persuasive is the seventy-thirty blend of Nero d'Avola and Cabernet Sauvignon called Tancredi (who was the Prince's nephew who married the beauteous Angelica). A bit oaky, it nevertheless has depth and muscle, as well as some formidable tannins.

The most impressive wine is fancifully called Mille e Una Notte (A Thousand and One Nights), which is 90 percent Nero d'Avola rounded out with other native red varieties. This is simply gorgeous red wine: intense, rich, polished, and yet absolutely original tasting. It is arguably the finest Nero d'Avola in Sicily—at least it's the finest that this taster has come upon so far. "Luxurious" might be the best descriptor. (The palace shown on the artistically drawn label is, in fact, the Donnafugata of *The Leopard*, the one in Santa Margherita di Belice.)

Donnafugata is easily one of the stars of Sicilian wine. And if the wines inspire you to read *The Leopard*, all the better, as it's a star of Italian literature in its own right.

FEUDO MONTONI—Not yet especially well known, Feudo Montoni issues terrific Nero d'Avola from vines ranging from ten to fifty years old. Grown at elevations between 1,300 and 2,230 feet, the high elevation prevents this red variety from baking in valley-floor heat. Two versions of Nero d'Avola are offered: a regular bottling of impressive depth and definition and a more dramatic, lush, intense bottling called Nero d'Avola Selezione Speciale Vrucara. Yields are low and lower, respectively. Both wines show noticeable oak, but you can't fault the density and luxuriance of the wines. They are standouts.

FEUDO PRINCIPI DI BUTERA—Owned by the giant northern Italian wine producer Zonin, this producer continues to improve with every vintage. Look for good Nero d'Avola, a rather brutish Cabernet Sauvignon, and a pleasant white Inzolia, among others.

GULFI—In 1996, owner Vito Catania decided to make wine from

the grapes he previously sold to others. With the advice of winemaker Salvo Foti, the talented winemaker of Benanti, he sought vineyard sites in southeastern Sicily, eventually acquiring 225 acres, some of which were previously planted to vines. Other sections were newly planted by Catania. Significantly, these new vines were planted to a high density for the express purpose of low yields.

Gulfi is unquestionably one of the greatest producers of Nero d'Avola in Sicily, with a dazzling array of bottlings including three extraordinary single-vineyard bottlings. Nearly all of them sport tongue-twisting names.

The most easygoing of them is Rosso Ibleo, a light, guzzle-able picnic red meant to be served cool. More serious and intense is Neroibleo, made entirely from Nero d'Avola, all black fruits and black pepper. Yet another bottling, another step up in intensity, depth and dimension is Nerobufaleffi, which has a surprising minerality absent in many other Nero d'Avola bottlings.

Most dramatic and impressive of all are the intense and minerally single-vineyard Nero d'Avola bottlings: Neromaccarj, Nerobarronj, and Nerosanlorenzj. All three come from the Val di Noto, the valley between the cities of Pachino and Noto in the southeastern tip of Sicily. Based on these extraordinary wines, it's safe to say that the Val di Noto is a potential *grand cru* for growing Nero d'Avola. Gulfi is a great producer destined for more fame than it currently enjoys.

CARLO HAUNER—I remember the first time I tasted the near-legendary Malvasia delle Lipari. It must have been twenty years ago, at least. I was at a dinner with Burton Anderson, the great American authority on Italian wines who lives in Tuscany. He chose this dessert wine, which I had never heard of. "I think you'll like this," he said rather neutrally. After two sips, I was boggled. Infatuated. Astonished. It was, and is, not so simply one of the greatest sweet wines in the world, a wine that can be invoked in the same scented breath as France's Chateau d'Yquem, Germany's great late-picked Rieslings, or Hungary's Tokaj Aszù.

Subsequently I met Carlo Hauner several times at the big Vinitaly trade fair in Verona and eventually made my way to his vineyard and winery on the tiny island of Salina (662 acres), which is one of the fabled Aeolian Islands off of Sicily's northern coast. (Lipari is the largest of the seven volcanic islands and five islets that comprise the Aeolians. Wine labeled Malvasia delle Lipari can come from any of the islands, although Salina and Lipari are pretty much the two sources.)

I was, and still am, captivated by Hauner's Malvasia della Lipari wine, especially the intense, liquorous *passito* (partially dried grape) version. In addition to Malvasia's classic scents and tastes of apricots, figs, and almonds, the passito version delivers an almost shockingly intense scent of wild herbs.

When I met Hauner (an artist of German background from Brescia in northern Italy who first came to Salina, for the light, in 1963), I commented admiringly about this captivating herbal quality to his Malvasia *passito*. I had the temerity—or rudeness—to ask him if he added anything to the wine to achieve this unique taste, as no other Malvasia delle Lipari that I, at least, had tasted had anything quite like it. Hauner took this rather bold, potentially offensive question with courteous grace. He said he understood how one could wonder such a thing, but that, no, nothing was added. It came from the sheer intensity and rigor of the desertlike growing conditions of his vineyards on Salina.

Those conditions—soil, sun, and grudging rainfall—create as extreme a vineyard site as any I've seen anywhere in the world. Part of Hauner's vineyards are planted in almost pure pumice (there's an old pumice quarry on Salina). You could literally drive your fist into the soil, so called, and go down as far as your armpit with little resistance. I'm not making this up.

Hauner died in 1996. By then, he and his Malvasia wine were famous. Hauner had single-handedly revived the stature and fame of the traditional Malvasia delle Lipari. Today, the winery is run by his son Carlo Jr.

Hauner Malvasia delle Lipari, both the almost gulpable *naturale* and the sippable *passito*, are extraordinary sweet white wines, filled with exotic fruit flavors and possessed of surprisingly refreshing acidity. There's also a Riserva bottling that's vintage-dated. Look also for two very good table wines, a Salina Bianco made from Inzolia and Cataratto and a Salina Rosso employing Nerello Mascalese and Nero d'Avola. Both dry wines are well made and characterful. (Hauner also offers very good sun-dried capers preserved in salt, a specialty of Salina.)

But it is the Malvasia delle Lipari wines that linger on the palate and in the mind. It is definitively in the "Don't die without trying it" pantheon of Italy's most compelling wines.

MORGANTE—A good, solid producer of Nero d'Avola. The wines are smooth and easy to like, but not in Sicily's top rank. Two versions are offered, an affable regular Nero d'Avola and a much more concentrated and intense bottling called Don Antonio.

PLANETA—Sicily's most acclaimed winery, Planeta is the island's exemplar of *bella figura*. A vocal advocate for international varieties such as Chardonnay, Merlot, Cabernet Sauvignon and Syrah, as well as—you guessed it—small new oak barrels, Planeta is the darling of wine critics eager to proclaim the arrival of sophisticated Sicilian wine, albeit a night-club sort of "sophistication." For this taster, Planeta's wines are predictable and certainly pleasant. They are well made and most pleasing to people who seek tastes already familiar to them. They are Dolce and Gabbana opulent, with a you-can't-miss-it accessibility. Although Planeta may be Sicily's most celebrated winery today, it's far from Sicily's best producer for this taster.

CASA VINICOLA DUCA DI SALAPARUTA (CORVO)—Corvo (crow) used to be Sicily's best-distributed red wine in America, and it may still be. But it's very far from the best, or even the best-value, wine Sicily sends to America today. Made primarily from Nero d'Avola, Corvo is soft, pleasantly fruity, cheap, and utterly forgettable.

Casa Vinicola Duca di Salaparuta is a vast operation that was owned by the regional government of Sicily since 1961. It was sold in 2000 to the owners of the big Marsala house Florio. (The new owner, Illva Saranno S.p.A., created a new holding company called Case Vinicole di Sicilia.) The best, if overpriced, bottling is the oaky Nero d'Avola called Duca Enrico.

TASCA D'AMERITA/REGALEALI—Tasca d'Amerita is the family name of the aristocratic Marchesi Tasca d'Amerita. But it is far better known by its winery name, Regaleali (reh-gah-leh-*ah*-lee). No Sicilian producer is better known. It's an old estate with a taste for modernity, as well as a high profile in the food world thanks to Marchesa Anna Tasca Lanza, who runs a famous cooking school showcasing Sicilian food on the property and written several well-received cookbooks. (Her brother, Lucio, runs the winery.)

Both reds and whites are consistently good at this property. And not to be forgotten is a stellar rosé or *rosato*, a blend of Nerello Masacalese and Nero d'Avola. It's one of the world's great rosés.

The most famous red wine from Regaleali is the Rosso del Conte Contea di Sclafani, a blend of 90 percent Nero d'Avola and 10 percent Perricone, one of Sicily's rarer indigenous grapes. Deeply colored and very oaky, it offers Nero d'Avola's signature scents and tastes of black cherry, leather, and black pepper, all heavily perfumed by the vanilla of small new oak barrels. It would be a more appealing wine if some of the sluttish oak makeup were removed. Ironically, the regular Nero d'Avola bottling, also with 10 percent Perricone, is a more appealing wine, if not quite as dense.

Look also for an attractive dry white called Leone d'Almerita Bianco, which is a blend of 70 percent Inzolia and 30 percent Chardonnay. With whiffs of herbs and lemon zest, it's an attractive dry white that sees no oak and doesn't need any.

The Regaleali portfolio also includes a good but hardly stellar Cabernet Sauvignon, as well as an oaky Nero d'Avola and Cabernet Sauvignon blend called Cygnus, among other wines.

What Do The Locals Eat With This Wine? Sicilian cuisine is famously rich, complicated cooking that reflects its ancient crossroads existence between mainland Italy and the Arabic influence (sweet flavors, nuts, raisins, dates, pistachios) from nearby North Africa. It is difficult to generalize, and hardly necessarily, to specify what goes with what with Sicilian food and wine. Suffice it to say that any good Nero d'Avola red is ideal for anything from a good hamburger to a great loin of lamb or prime rib. Roast pig sounds good, too. It's a lusty red wine that rewards equally lusty, hearty, rib-sticking meat dishes.

The dry whites of Sicily, notably Inzolia, are meant for fish served pure and pristine, which even the Sicilians, who like to add a confetti of thin strips of red and yellow peppers and maybe some slivers of black olives and garlic, ultimately prefer. They're great lovers of tuna and swordfish, and the flavors, even with some classic Sicilian condiment accessories, still manage to come out very pure-tasting.

One Man's Taste—Whose Wine Would I Buy? I much prefer the indigenous grapes of Sicily to the "Look-Ma-what-I-can-do" fanfare of the international varieties. But by now you already knew that. I'd reach for such producers as Benanti and Gulfi for almost anything they offer, Regaleali for rosé, Carlo Hauner for haunting Malvasia delle Lipari, and de Bartoli for equally memorable Marsala.

Worth saying is that Sicily is changing perhaps more rapidly than any other major Italian wine region. So an open mind, as much as a willing palate, is more important than anything else. If the price is right, you should give almost any new or unknown-to-you producer a try, especially if the wine promises the originality of Sicily's indigenous grape varieties.

Worth Searching For? Absolutely worth an effort

Similar Wines From The Same Neighborhood: None. The island of Sicily truly is a world—wine and otherwise—unto itself.

Soave

(s'*wah*-veh)
WHITE

Region: Veneto (northeast Italy). Soave is thirteen miles west of Verona.

Grapes: Garganega (gar-*gah*-neh-gah) is the key grape. Also allowed: Trebbiano di Soave and Trebbiano Toscano up to 30 percent. Chardonnay is used as well.

The Tradition: For centuries, Soave was a local white wine that was sluiced into nearby Verona. Italian white wines, until very recently, had no reputation worth mentioning. Indeed, to this day, if you play a word association game with an Italian and say "wine" he or she will likely say "red." They simply (and wrongly) do not take white wines seriously.

However, even Italians recognized that Soave was something special—at least for a white wine. This was mostly because of its unusual grape variety, garganega. When grown with low yields, garganega delivers a crisp, dry white wine with a Chablis-like mineraliness or stoniness. Such compelling Soaves were (and are) grown in the choicest hillsides east and north of the town of Soave, the area that is now legally delimited as Soave Classico.

How It's Changed: After World War II, tourists to Italy—especially Americans and Brits—decided that *they* liked the light, crisp, flinty dry white wine called Soave. Probably, they also liked saying it, too. To order Soave seemed, well, *molto soave*—very suave. From this emerged a massive local wine industry. And that, in turn, transformed Soave from a delicious local white wine with a whiff of almonds and minerals to a bland and dreary white wine with an inviting name and little else. Soave is now issued in industrial quantities, upward of 5 million cases a year. Vineyards have expanded from the desirable hillsides to the Po Valley floor, where high yields rule.

More rewarding is a revived tradition of creating sweet, dessert-style Soave from partially raisined grapes. Called Recioto di Soave, good versions are rich, luscious, voluptuous sweet white wines that marry beautifully with fruit tarts such as pear and apple (see also Recioto della Valpolicella, page 192).

Noteworthy Producers (The Traditionalists / The Modernists): Concepts of "traditional" and "modern" are turned on their heads in Soave. Today the "tradition" in Soave is now regrettably the vast flood of industrial Soave issued by wine giants such as Bolla and the Cantina Sociale di Soave or the Soave growers' cooperative. Their efforts near-ly—but not quite—washed away all memory of how distinctive a true artisanal Soave could be.

The "modernists" in Soave are actually the real traditionalists. They insist on low yields in their vineyards and offer single-vineyard desig-nated bottlings from the best hillsides.

At the same time, some of these same "traditionalists" are also indis-putably modernist in their use of small French oak barrels and "inter-national" grape varieties such as Chardonnay. These were never part of Soave's traditional taste. Many of the best producers swing both ways.

Anselmi—Roberto Anselmi became so fed up with the Soave DOC regulations, which allowed (read encouraged) local growers to pursue ever-higher yields, that he very publicly quit using the name for his "Soave" wines altogether. Instead he uses single-vineyard or proprietary names. Anselmi rings all the changes: Some wines see small French oak barrels (Capitel Croce, I Capitelli) while others are fer-mented only in stainless steel (Capitel Foscarino). Yet others are rather radically blended with Chardonnay (San Vincenzo).

Gini—New Wave producer creating intense wines. His Soave Classico bottle sees no oak and is pure Garganega; single-vineyards La Froscà and Salvarenza have both oak and Chardonnay. High quality, but with a strong winemaking signature.

INAMA—Like others, a variety of good-quality Soave bottlings, all 100 percent Garganega. Single vineyards Vigneto Foscarino and Vigneto du Lot are barrel-fermented with the lees (sediment) stirred, Burgundy-style. A bit too New Wave for real quality, as there are a lot of stylistic flourishes here.

PIEROPAN—One of Soave's finest artisan traditionalists. No oak; no Chardonnay. The real thing. Two single-vineyard bottlings, Calvarino (70 percent Garganega and 30 percent Trebbiano) and La Rocca (100 percent Garganega), are the best wines; Soave Classico is a benchmark regular bottling. Also superb Recioto di Soave.

PRÀ—Brothers Sergio and Graziano Prà create what is arguably the finest traditional artisanal Soave, especially their unoaked Soave Classico and single-vineyard Monte Grande, the latter being one of Soave's greatest renditions. More New Wave is their oaky Sant'Antonio bottling.

What Do The Locals Eat With This Wine? For the locals, Soave is an all-purpose white for any antipasti and fish. The best Soaves are ideal for tortelloni with radicchio and ricotta, as well as local smoked trout from nearby Lake Garda. The classic accompaniment to sweet Recioto di Soave is apple strudel. (Austria annexed northeast Italy from 1814 to 1866. The locals hated their rulers, but they did acquire a liking for strudel.)

One Man's Taste—Whose Wine Would I Buy? My first choice would be Prà Soave Classico and Prà's single vineyard Monte Grande. This is closely followed by Pieropan, especially its single-vineyard La Rocca bottling. Prà and Pieropan wines improve with age, by the way, for at least five years after the vintage. Anselmi is my other pick, especially Capitel Foscarino. All of these producers' regular Soave Classico bottlings are sure things.

Worth Searching For? The top producers are absolutely worth an effort. The others aren't worth your bother.

Similar Wines From The Same Neighborhood: Bianco di Custoza (near Lake Garda). Look also for excellent white, sweet *recioto* wines with proprietary names from the Valpolicella zone that are similar to Recioto di Soave.

Taurasi

(t'ow-*rah*-see)
RED

Region: Campania (southern Italy)

Grapes: Minimum of 85 percent Aglianico (ahl-*yahn*-ee-koh) with the possible addition of other "non-aromatic red varieties recommended or authorized by the province of Avellino," e.g., Piedirosso, up to 15 percent. Most Taurasi wines, however, tend to be 100 percent Aglianico or nearly so.

The Tradition: No red wine south of Tuscany has stirred such interest and assertions of greatness as Campania's Taurasi district, a good-size zone encompassing an array of slopes (but not valley floors) in the same growing area where you find such whites as Greco di Tufo, Falanghina, and Fiano di Avellino.

Until the late 1960s, however, there was no such wine as Taurasi, not sold as such, at least I've never seen any. The Aglianico wine that has grown there for centuries was called, like other Aglianico wines of Campania to this day, Irpinia Aglianico. (Other local versions are Aglianico del Taburno and Sannio Aglianico.)

But the aptly named *maestri* of the zone, the Mastroberardino family, insisted that the upper slopes of the Irpinia area were something special for Aglianico and introduced to the world a bottling called Taurasi, which is the name of a local commune or district in the zone. Whether Mastroberardino's wine was the first ever so named I cannot say. But it surely was the first wine called Taurasi that pretty much everyone outside of the area had ever seen. And people were knocked for a loop. Longtime Italian wine cognoscenti are *still* talking about the now-fabled 1968 Taurasi from Mastroberardino.

What's the Taurasi zone got that other Aglianico growing areas lack? Good public relations, certainly. And the locomotive force of such producers as Mastroberardino, Feudi di San Gregorio, and Terredora di Paolo. But good PR can get you only so far. You've got to deliver the goods. And the best Taurasi bottlings surely do.

When asked about the source of Taurasi's distinction, the local producers point to Taurasi's required-by-law higher elevations, which, in turn, require a long "hang time" of the grapes on the vine before harvesting. Never mind the popular vision of the hot, sunny South. Aglianico from the Taurasi area typically isn't fully ripe until late October or early November. That's a long, cool growing season by anybody's standards.

Taurasi is very likely the most reliably good, and often great, source of Aglianico anywhere in southern Italy. But it would be a mistake to assume that this distinction is exclusive. Southern Italy's Aglianico renaissance has only just begun and, given the widespread planting of this ancient variety, there surely are other zones that can and will rival Taurasi.

But Taurasi has one profound advantage: ambitious and well-funded producers. This is no small thing. Such producers set a standard that others seek to match or exceed. It's an upward spiral of competition and pride that begets ever-finer wines. Zealously competitive producers lower their yields, make winery investments, and prospect for more advantageous vineyard sites. This is why great wine areas spiral upwards (one thinks immediately of Napa Valley), while potentially good zones often never fulfill their possibilities

A good Taurasi is not a subtle wine. Instead it is, or should be, an inky, almost opaque red wine with substantial tannins and a depth and dimension that go well beyond being merely "hearty." There's a genuine elegance to Taurasi, but more in the sense of a powerful linebacker of uncommon grace and surefootedness than, say, the slim, lithe, delicate qualities of Fred Astaire. Aglianico anywhere, and especially from the Taurasi zone, is a wine of burly goodness as well as nuance.

You should find loads of black fruits, such as black raspberry, blackberry, and plums, along with clear notes of coffee, leather, tobacco, and black pepper. You would have to be a single-minded vegetarian indeed not to think of meat when deciding what to serve with this powerful, potent red. Taurasi is a wine seemingly designed by God himself (or herself) for happy carnivores everywhere.

How It's Changed: The changes in Taurasi have been surprisingly few, if only because the area is relatively new on the world's markets and its best producers were already forward thinking. You will not be surprised to learn that we're seeing more Taurasi aged in new small oak barrels than there were twenty years ago. No matter. This is red wine that can stand up to such treatment and not lose its soul or character in the process.

Producers such as Feudi di San Gregorio have shifted the aesthetic slightly—and perhaps for the better—by emphasizing a more glossy fruit in keeping with modern tastes. Older Taurasi bottlings could sometimes seem a little dusty-tasting, derived from hard tannins that are today avoided by lower yields, more nuanced decisions about when to pick, and more deft winemaking techniques.

Noteworthy Producers (The Traditionalists/The Modernists): Taurasi so far seems a surprisingly exclusive zone with only a relative handful of producers (fewer than twenty) supplied by a much larger number (upwards of 150) growers. Indeed, only a half-dozen or so producers reach the American market, or any others for that matter, in any quantity.

CAGGIANO—Antonio Caggiano is a newcomer to Taurasi, but his wines, aged in small oak barrels, have already created a considerable stir. Indeed, they are excellent, in a modern style with very rich, deep, bright fruit from a single vineyard called Macchia dei Goti. Worth seeking out.

FEUDI DI SAN GREGORIO—The powerhouse producer in Campania today, Feudi di San Gregorio seems to have an unerring touch with almost everything it makes, including Taurasi. Aged for eighteen months in small oak barrels, Feudi di San Gregorio's "Piano di Monte Vergine" Taurasi Riserva is decidedly oaky. But the depth of fruit is not short of massive. Yet there's still grace, as well as a mineral note. It's one of the great modern Taurasi wines. There's also a regular, less oaky "basic" Taurasi that's an excellent value, if not quite as striking as the "Piano di Monte Vergine" bottling.

MASTROBERARDINO—The flagship producer of the zone, Mastroberardino is no unthinking traditionalist. Its Taurasi Radici (the Radici or roots designation is applied to several other wines in the portfolio, signaling wines from what Mastroberardino considers exceptional sites) spends twenty-four months in oak, divided between small barrels (225 liters or 60 gallons) and larger oak casks (40 hectoliters or 1,057 gallons). Less intrusively oaky than its rival Feudi di San Gregorio, the Taurasi of Mastroberardino is as intense yet more layered and nuanced. A regular and Riserva bottling is offered.

Worth noting in passing, if only because it's a Taurasi in all but name, is Mastroberardino's Irpinia IGT "Naturalis Historia," which is 85 to 90 percent Aglianico with the balance composed of the indigenous red grape Piedirosso. Legally, it could be called Taurasi because the regulations permit the addition of up to 15 percent Piedirosso to Aglianico, but Mastroberardino feels that having two Taurasi wines is confusing. The Piedirosso makes for a nice addition, though, adding deeper color as well as a bit of soft fleshiness.

MOLETTIERI—Salvatore Molettieri is another relative newcomer to Taurasi, issuing his first wine only in 1995. Molettieri is a small producer, and his single-vineyard Taurasi from the "Cinque Querce" (five oaks) plot is superb Taurasi. Look also for Molettieri's "Aglianico Irpinia," which is really a "baby Taurasi" and a bargain red of uncommon goodness.

STRUZZIERO—Less well known than the "big boys," Struzziero issues two fine Taurasi bottlings: "Campoceraso" and "Villa Fosca." Both are rich, deep intense wines devoid of oakiness (no small oak barrels are used) and delivering the cherry/leather/spice qualities of Aglianico with uncommon grace. Struzziero deserves to be better known.

TERREDORA DI PAOLO—The "other" Mastroberardino, which broke away from the original family winery in 1994. Of course, its Taurasi quickly became the equal of the other contenders in the zone. How could it not given the resources and deep-rooted family talent inherent in this "new" producer? Noticeably oaky, Terredora's Taurasi "Fatica Contadina" is a modern Taurasi with all of the trimmings, as well as the depth expected of contemporary Taurasi. Look also for Terredora's Aglianico Irpinia bottling, which has some of the same goodness, but less aging and a lower price.

What Do The Locals Eat With This Wine? The robust food of Campania, dominated by pastas such as ziti, perciatelli, spaghetti, and fusilli sauced with the local San Marzano variety tomatoes, is almost narcotically good. But when Taurasi is brought to the table, the locals think meat: wild boar, goat, wild hare, and various kinds of salami. Taurasi is made for meat and any kind of steak or braised beef is ideal. But consider also braised duck with olives, a roast goose, or any cut of lamb.

One Man's Taste—Whose Wine Would I Buy? It's a pleasure to say that, really, there are no bad Taurasi wines. I certainly would reach for Feudi di San Gregorio and, if I spied it, Struzziero. Mastroberardino is swell too, as is Terredora di Paolo. You're bound to land on something worthwhile no matter which of these producers you choose.

Worth Searching For? Absolutely worth an effort

Similar Wines From The Same Neighborhood: Any Aglianico wine is comparable to Taurasi. Look especially for anything labeled Irpinia Aglianico, as it's the same (if more generously defined) zone or Sannio Aglianico (another geographical name). Look also for Aglianico del Taburno, especially from the producer Ocone. It rivals Taurasi itself.

Teroldego

(teh-*rawl*-deh-go)
RED

Region: Trentino (northeast Italy); in the Campo Rotaliano plain about twenty miles north of the city of Trento.

Grape: 100 percent Teroldego (red)

The Tradition: Teroldego reveals just why, and how, Italy has so many grape varieties. Like Moses washed up in the bulrushes, Teroldego is found only in one spot: a large, flat, very gravelly river bottom plain near the Adige River in northern Italy called Campo Rotaliano

The question, *à la* Moses, is: How did Teroldego get there? You see, Teroldego is distinctively different from any other red wine grape, yet it does taste like some similar, known-to-be-indigenous varieties such as Lagrein. Genetic research reveals that Teroldego is indeed related to Lagrein (grown to the north, along the Adige River), as well as Marzemino (grown south around Lake Garda) and Syrah (who knows?). All of these, and probably yet other varieties, combined to create a wholly new grape that came to be christened Teroldego.

Even the origins of Teroldego's name are open to dispute. Some say it derives from the German *teer* or tar, which flavor the wine (appetizingly) evokes. Others submit that it comes from its traditional trellising technique, involving wires or *tirelle*. Nobody really knows.

What *is* known is this: Teroldego likes low yields. This is a key fact because when Teroldego is pruned for low yields (fewer clusters per vine), what results is a memorable, lush, intense red wine with few tannins and a real come-hither quality with scents of berries, tar, black and wild cherries along with whiffs of herbs allied to a lush, dense texture. But when it is not low yielding, Teroldego is just another enjoyable

Italian red of indeterminate quality.

Regrettably, few Teroldegos meet their heavenly tasting reward on Earth. The lesser ones are easily identified: They're lighter, more dilute-tasting, and indistinct.

How It's Changed: For too long, Teroldego supplied a local market content to quaff a pleasingly soft red wine. Such Teroldegos were certainly better than other red wines in the zone, hence the historical local acclaim. But when you taste such specimens you know in a sniff and a sip why they were "local." (Not every wine, however appealingly quirky or unique, justifies a world audience.)

Then along came the strong-willed, high-minded, ambitious Elisabetta Foradori. While still in her twenties, she single-handedly transformed her family winery, now called Azienda Agricola Elisabetta Foradori, not just into the best producer in the district but into a world ambassador for the previously unrecognized—unrealized, really—greatness of Teroldego.

Noteworthy Producers (The Traditionalists/The Modernists): Relatively few Teroldegos are exported to America, in part because there isn't that much produced: about 375,000 cases from fewer than a thousand acres of vines. That's the production of just one good-size Napa Valley winery.

Reasonably good Teroldego can be had from Zeni. A good part of the area's production gets sluiced into the local winegrowers' cooperative, Cantina Rotaliano. The results are ho-hum. Diego Bolognani, a small producer, offers a good one.

But really, only one Teroldego producer matters: Elisabetta Foradori. Happily, her wines are amply distributed. Foradori's regular Teroldego is always a good buy. It's pure, dense, and oak-free, an exemplar of the variety. Foradori's signature wine is called Granato. It's richer, lusher, more intense, and sees some time in small oak barrels. It also rewards as much as ten years worth of cellaring, where the regular bottling is good to go upon release. Granato is, natch, more expensive—but worth it.

What Do The Locals Eat With This Wine? Trentino cuisine is a mixture of Venetian, Lombard, and Hapsburg (Austrian) tastes. One sees, surprisingly to the unprepared, a lot of strudels, as well as dumplings. Mushrooms abound as well. Not least is polenta (cornmeal mush), which is a staple. With a wine like Teroldego, the locals would certainly choose game such as pheasant or venison, or a stuffed chicken, or more luxuriously, a capon. Teroldego is a perfect foil for steak, turkey, braised meats of any kind, or just a good, simple pork chop.

One Man's Taste—Whose Wine Would I Buy? Obviously it's Foradori. There's really no competition. And if your interest (and wallet) is sufficient, do seek out Foradori's signature wine called Granato.

Worth Searching For? Absolutely worth an effort

Similar Wines From The Same Neighborhood: Lagrein from farther north in the Alto Adige region (see page 147)

Tocai Friulano

(toe-kai free-oo-*lah*-noh)

WHITE

Region: Friuli (northeast Italy, north of Venice)

Grapes: 100 percent Tocai Friulano; after 2007, the name will change to "Friulano" (white)

The Tradition: The Friuli region in northeast Italy is a trove of grape varieties, both red and white. It's famous for its white wines, however. The best of them, arguably, is an indigenous variety long called Tocai Friulano. It's also the most widely planted variety in Friuli, accounting for about 20 percent of all of the vines planted. The name itself, clearly reminiscent of Hungary's famous sweet wine Tokaj (which the Hungarians pronounce toe-*koy*, by the way), became the focus of a heated international legal dispute.

The short version is that the European Union seeks to eliminate competing trademarks and the like. In Europe, only the Greeks can now call their cheese feta, for example. All other feta makers (France, Denmark) must use another name.

Hungary, recently admitted into the European Union, objected to Italy's use of Tocai Friulano on wine labels, saying it impinged on their famous and even more demonstrably ancient Tokaj wine, which is made from the Furmint grape variety. Italy objected. They lost. So too did France's Alsace region, which has long made a wine called Tokay, made entirely from Pinot Gris. (This ubiquity of "Tocai/Tokay" shows, if nothing else, how famous the original Hungarian Tokaj wine once was. And that brand-name knock-offs are nothing new.)

Anyway, starting in 2007, the grape formerly known as Tocai

Friulano will simply be called Friulano.

What matters, of course, is the wine itself. And here Friulano (we may as well get used to saying it that way) shines. It creates a dry white wine that is a light yellow gold in color and unusually dense and thick-textured with scents of wildflowers, citrus blossom, almonds, and apples. "Herbal" often pops up in my notes. Also, there's typically a slight, invigorating bitterness in the aftertaste or finish. The best versions offer a mineral note as well.

Oddly, this same grape variety is not viewed favorably in France. It turns out that Friulano is, genetically anyway, the same grape as one called Sauvigonasse or Sauvignon Vert in France—never mind that Friulano doesn't taste anything like the sharp-scented Sauvignon Blanc, which it was apparently thought to resemble. France's most famous ampelographer (researcher of grape origins), Professor Pierre Galet, dismisses Sauvignonasse as "not a variety for premium wine vineyards."

Maybe so for France, but for Friuli the apparently same grape has adapted and thrived, in every sense. It's a terrific dry white wine in Friuli. Very likely, what's grown in Friuli today has, over the centuries, mutated into something quite different. That happens all the time in grapegrowing.

How It's Changed: As everywhere in Italian white wine production, the changes in Friuli center around the now-universal use of temperature-controlled stainless steel tanks, slow, cool fermentations, and the discreet (if any at all) use of oak.

Above all, the best Friuli whites, including Friulano, come from well-sited vineyards with lower-than-usual yields. Excessive yields are the bane of Friulian winegrowing. So the producer matters mightily, as the lesser wines are always too thin and dilute. The best ones, across the board, always benefit from rigorous grapegrowing in addition to the (now expected) competent winemaking.

Noteworthy Producers: It's not a coincidence that the best producers of

Friulano (and most of Friuli's other grapes as well) are all located in the Collio district of Friuli, which is hard by the border of Slovenia. The Collio is a range of hills in the northern part of the province of Gorizia. They run from east to west, which allows for a large number of (ideal) south-facing areas. The soil is typically a mix of marl (chalky clay) and sandstone.

These producers are among the very best. Any of them are worth pursuing: Bastianich, Branko, Doro Princic, Livio Felluga, Gradnik, Ronco del Gelso, Villa Russiz, Schiopetto, Venica e Venica, and Volpe Pasini (see Collio for more discussion about these producers, page 117).

What Do The Locals Eat With This Wine? The cooking of Friuli in general, and Collio in particular, is like no other in Italy as it's strongly influenced by Austria to the north, Venice to the south, and, not least, Slovenia to the east. Mostly it's hardy country fare, with lots of ham (Friuli's famous San Daniele variety), pork, beans, potato and cheese omelets called *frico,* and various strudels. Pasta includes the tortellini-like *cjalson*, which is filled with potatoes, sugar, butter, mint, nutmeg, and cinnamon, and served with melted butter and grated smoked ricotta cheese.

Locals will serve Friulano with almost any dish among the antipasti and, of course, with fish. It's certainly a white wine that pairs surprisingly well with pork and herbed roasted chicken, as well as many cheeses. Friulano is an exceptionally versatile dry white wine in part because of its dense texture compared to many other Italian whites.

One Man's Taste—Whose Wine Would I Buy? Any producer in the preceding list is really fine. My top pick, which is gratifyingly well distributed, is Livio Felluga. Its Friulano is always a benchmark. Ditto for Schiopetto. And if you can find Branko, which is very small, that's a treat.

Worth Searching For? Absolutely worth an effort

Similar Wines From The Same Neighborhood: Any of Friuli's other dry white wines, notably Pinot Bianco, Chardonnay, Sauvignon Blanc, and above all, the endearing indigenous white grape, Ribolla Gialla (see page 199). Look for these wines from any of the producers recommended for Friulano and you won't go wrong.

Valpolicella

(vahl-pohl-ee-*cheh*-lah)

RED

Region: Veneto (northeast Italy, about 10 miles northwest of Verona)

Grapes: Corvina Veronese 40 to 70 percent; Rondinella 20 to 40 percent; Molinara 5 to 25 percent; Negrara/Trentina/Rossignola/Barbera/Sangiovese up to 15 percent (all red)

The Tradition: Like so many others in Italy, Valpolicella (named after a valley of the same name in the heart of the production zone) is ancient. They've been growing grapes since ancient Rome, if not earlier. Over the centuries, the locals developed a liking for a light red wine that you could practically quaff. Indeed, it went well with the local cuisine, and besides, they were the only ones drinking it.

By the time the late twentieth century rolled around, Valpolicella was practically in a stupor of complacency. If all you're doing is making a light red wine for early (and local) consumption, then you certainly don't need low yields in your vineyards, do you? So the grapegrowers happily pruned their vines for high yields. Besides, prices were derisory, what choice did they have?

In the meantime, the tastes of outsiders changed. Foreign clients—Germans, British, Americans, Swiss—wanted stronger, richer, more flavor-intensive wines than the ordinary Valpolicella bottlings offered.

The wine laws reflected this difference. You've got Valpolicella Classico, where the maximum permitted vineyard yield is 5.5 tons of grapes per acre.

However, the category of Valpolicella Classico Superiore, requires that the wine be aged in wood (casks or barrels) for a minimum of one year and is one degree higher in alcohol than mere Classico: 12 percent minimum rather than 11 percent. To do that, you need lower yields. Most "Superiore" wines come from vines bearing 3.1 tons per acre, which is much more reasonable.

(See also Recioto della Valpolicella, page 192. The yield for a Recioto wine, *before* they are dried, is lower yet: 1.8 tons per acre.)

How It's Changed: Valpolicella, like neighboring Soave, exists in two disproportionate realms. The larger realm is that of large commercial bottlings. Regrettably, this is the most commonly available Valpolicella, and it's thin stuff indeed. Too often, these commercial Valpolicellas are most people's introduction to this wine, and the adage about how first impressions count surely applies here. I'd guess that many never try the wine again.

The second, much smaller realm is composed of serious Valpolicella producers who really deliver the goods. This means a red wine of a definite delicacy allied to a surprisingly powerful (for its apparent weight) fragrance and taste. A really good Valpolicella, to use a boxing phrase, punches above its weight, delivering a powerful floral scent with underlying hints of tar and spices and a pleasing red-berry flavor with notes of strawberries and cherries. It's mouth-watering.

Of course, to do that, you need lower vineyard yields. And a seriousness of purpose, which, sadly, too many producers simply lack. It's too easy to sluice everyday, ordinary Valpolicella to the never-ending stream of tourists in nearby Verona or the many hotels and restaurants around close-by Lake Garda.

Many serious producers have, inevitably, chosen to employ small oak barrels. Too often the weight of even the best Valpolicella Classico Superiore cannot stand up to the penetrating vanilla scent of new oak. It smells like a teenager on a first date doused in dime-store cologne. However, as the vogue for experiment with small oak barrels has matured into something more nuanced and practiced—which means not every small oak barrel in the winery is new—the influence of small barrels is becoming less noticeable, although it's still prominent in some unfortunate cases. (Only new oak offers the human catnip of vanilla.

Older oak barrels, say after three years' use, are nearly flavor-neutral.)

ABOUT RIPASSO—Starting in the 1964 vintage, the admirable Valpolicella producer Masi revived an ancient technique of fortifying the flavors of a regular, already fully fermented Valpolicella wine by fermenting it yet again on the skins and lees (sediment) of the powerful Recioto della Valpolicella, made from highly concentrated semidried grapes of the exact same varieties used for regular Valpolicella.

The resulting wine emerges much darker and more powerfully, even pungently flavorful, than a conventional Valpolicella. Masi christened this practice "ripasso," meaning, "passed through again." It was a sensation, creating a wholly new modern Valpolicella that answered the growing demand for a stronger, richer, more dark-hued wine. (Masi calls their *ripasso* wine Campofiorin.)

As the technique began to be copied by other producers, many of whom described their version as a Valpolicella ripasso, Masi eventually decided to trademark the term. This caused some ill will. So Masi made the use of the word available to producers willing to adhere to what Masi believes is the proper way to create a "ripasso" Valpolicella. Some producers accepted the imposed requirements, while others declined. Some producers have taken to using the term *ripassa*, rather than *ripasso*, which apparently somehow slips the legal noose of Masi's trademark.

Consumers, however, are under no such obligations, and the term *ripasso* has become a generic. It means a Valpolicella refermented on the skins and lees of a Recioto wine. Some producers, such as Masi, add whole clusters of Recioto grapes as well, the better to add more flavor dimension and softer tannins.

A *ripasso* Valpolicella is always a powerful, rich, fully dry wine with a higher alcohol content than regular Valpolicella, thanks to the second fermentation. But it's nowhere near as potent as a full-blown Recioto della Valpolicella Amarone, although it shares the dark, brooding look and licorice-inflected qualities of its step-parent. It's best reserved for foods such as braised meats, game, and strong cheeses where the *ripasso* wine's intensive flavors are congruent rather than bullying.

Noteworthy Producers (The Traditionalists/The Modernists): A good Valpolicella should not (the *ripasso/ripassa* wines excepted) be a heavy, dense, imposing red wine. It should have a certain delicacy, which is not, it should be noted, the same thing as thinness. A good Valpolicella should have density allied to deftness.

Worth noting is that a non-*ripasso* Valpolicella is a wine best drunk young and fresh. While good ones can age, they rarely improve much because of it. Ripasso Valpolicellas, like the Amarones they descend from, do reward additional aging, upward of ten years. But again, it's not essential.

ALLEGRINI—A modernistic producer creating sleek, rich wines. Very good Valpolicella, rich, beautifully balanced, and fresh tasting. Allegrini's *ripasso* Valpolicella is called Palazzo della Torre. It's a stand-out bottling and exceptionally smooth and concentrated. Yet another *ripasso* version is called La Grola. It's oakier than Palazzo della Torre, not to any advantage for this taster.

A third wine called La Poja is fascinating, as it's 100 percent Corvina Veronese. Technically it's not a Valpolicella, but it nevertheless reveals just how good this grape variety can be. La Poja does see some oak, but it's impressively dense and rich, with notes of chocolate, raspberries, and black cherries.

BERTANI—An old-line standard-bearer in Valpolicella. The regular Valpolicella is pretty commercial. The "Superiore" version *is* noticeably better. There's also a ripasso Valpolicella called Secco-Bertani that's quite good.

BRIGALDARA—Very good Valpolicella Classico, with solid flavors and good stuffing.

BUSSOLA—Tommaso Bussola is a traditionalist producer (influenced by the master, Giuseppe Quintarelli) who is going from strength to strength in recent years. Pleasing, delicate Valpolicella Classico that is easily overshadowed by a more substantial, dimensional Valpolicella Superiore. Bussola's labels semaphore a quality difference: The "standard" wines are designated "BG" (Bussola Giuseppe, who was

Tommaso Bussola's uncle); the more select bottlings are designated "TB" (for, of course, Tommaso Bussola). Both are exceptional for their respective classes. If Bussola makes a *ripasso* wine, I haven't seen it.

MASI—The powerhouse producer in Valpolicella (along with Allegrini), Masi offers a solid, attractive basic Valpolicella. But Masi's real specialty is the *ripasso* wine it pioneered called Campofiorin. That wine, in turn, has been bested by a kind of super-Campofiorin, the recently offered *ripasso* wine called Brolo di Campofiorin. It's a special selection bottling. Both wines are impressive in their richness and, especially, suaveness. Where other *ripasso* wines can sometimes be heavy-handed, Masi's versions always are well mannered, in the best sense.

Two other, very unusual reds that are not technically Valpolicella deserve mention. Both are proprietarily named: Toar (meaning basalt) and Osar. Toar is a blend of Corvina and a very rare local grape called Oseleta. Osar, for its part, is 100 percent Oseleta. It's exceptionally dense, strong, and noticeably tannic. All of Masi's wines are worthy of pursuit, as they are exceptional and always fascinating.

QUINTARELLI—Giuseppe Quintarelli is the *maestro,* and it's no surprise that his Valpolicella bottlings are hugely characterful and impressive. The prices, alas, are similarly striking. Nevertheless, Quintarelli's wines are a benchmark. Look for the single-vineyard Valpolicella called Ca' del Merlo (a *merlo* is a blackbird). Quintarelli's *ripasso* wine is called Monte Ca' Palleta. Given the raw materials at hand, it will come as no surprise that this is a supremely powerful, intensive *ripasso* wine closer, frankly, to other producers' Amarones.

LUIGI RIGHETTI—A small producer offering consistently good quality. Lovely basic Valpolicella and a strikingly good *ripasso* called Campolieti ("happy field"), which shows a touch of oak, but just barely. To seek out.

SPERI—A fine traditionalist producer offering a good basic Valpolicella and a (much better) Superiore. The Superiore is a lovely rendition of Valpolicella at its delicate, classical best. Also an excellent *ripasso* called Sant'Urbano that sees some time in French oak barrels.

FRATELLI TEDESCHI—A traditionalist producer delivering the real goods. Excellent Valpolicella classico. A sizable step up is an even better Valpolicella Superiore, which is, in turn, exceeded by the richer, denser, more dimensional single-vineyard bottling called Capitel delle Lucchinne. Also, an excellent *ripasso* called Capitel San Nicolaó, which does see a bit of oak, but not intrusively so. Tedeschi is an always-reliable producer whose prices, thankfully, are as sane as their wines are honest and substantial.

ZENATO—A large commercial producer, Zenato issues a pretty good Valpolicella Superiore. Of all of the well-distributed, larger-quantity versions of Valpolicella on the market, Zenato's is one of the best. A rather oaky ripasso Valpolicella is also offered. Again, given the quantity involved, Zenato does a good job. If this producer's wines were everybody's introduction to Valpolicella, then the area's reputation would be considerably more lustrous than it is today. Credit where credit is due.

What Do The Locals Eat With This Wine? Regular Valpolicella is washed down in cities like Verona and at lakeside restaurants in nearby Lake Garda almost as freely (maybe more so) as bottled water. It's a "trattoria wine" with all that phrase implies: pasta dishes, veal, chicken. The ripasso wines are employed for heavier, often wintertime foods such as game and braised meats.

One Man's Taste—Whose Wine Would I Buy? Price no object, I'd certainly reach for Quintarelli. But the wines of Bussola and Masi are top-rate. Luigi Righetti is an old favorite as well. Many drinkers love Allegrini, with reason. They're a bit "modern" for my personal taste, but there's no denying their goodness, depth, and quality.

Worth Searching For? The top producers are absolutely worth an effort. Otherwise, only if you see it.

Similar Wines From The Same Neighborhood: Bardolino, Teroldego, Lagrein

Vermentino

(vair-men-*teen*-oh)
WHITE

Region: Several locations, notably Sardinia, Liguria, and Tuscany

Grapes: 100 percent Vermentino (white)

The Tradition: Like so many Italian white wines, Vermentino used to be a strictly local, and often oxidized, tipple. It was rarely, if ever, exported until late in the twentieth century. One of those many Italian wines that, when you went to Italy, was served to you by the carafe in restaurants. You got the latest (anonymous) vintage, and it tasted swell with your fish. For many Italians, then and now, that is the role of a dry white wine. It should deferentially partner with a nice piece of fish and stay out of the way, like a well-behaved child.

In fairness, Vermentino is not one of the great whites of the world. But it's tasty, rarely expensive, and deserves more and better than to be served as an anonymous carafe white. Although Vermentino varies in taste somewhat based on where it's grown, it's usually redolent of wild herbs, bitter almonds, and a whiff of hay. That's a pretty nice combination for a so-called simple dry white wine.

Not much Vermentino is exported to America. The largest quantity comes from Sardinia, especially from that island's very good and ambitious producer Argiolas, as well as its main competitor, Sella and Mosca. Both issue good, textbook Vermentinos.

But more refined, dimensional Vermentinos are found in Liguria, that sliver of land better known as the Italian Riviera. If you drive from Nice in France along the Mediterranean and cross the border into Italy, you've arrived in Liguria. Remember all those 1950s movies where the suave Italian man takes the beautiful woman on a thrilling ride in his convertible Alfa-Romeo on a twisting road high above the sea? *That's* the Ligurian Riviera.

The appellation is a bit of a mouthful: Riviera Ligure di Ponente. The first part is easy, as Riviera Ligure means the coastline of Liguria. "Ponente" is more obscure. It means "the spot on the horizon where the sun sets." (You can't beat the Italians for poetry.)

There's another zone, which straddles Liguria and Tuscany, which makes good Vermentino with the equally poetic appellation name Colli di Luni. A good Vermentino from this zone can be intensely flavorful with an extravagant, pungent herbal scent (sage, mint) and a definite note of bitter almonds.

Farther south along the same coastline into Tuscany, you find Vermentino grown all along Tuscany's Mediterranean coast.

How It's Changed: All of these previously mentioned districts have one thing in common: They're warm. More than many other white wine grapes, Vermentino likes mild weather and sunshine.

The challenge in growing warm-climate white grapes is preserving freshness and acidity. It's too easy for the flavor distinction of Vermentino to "bake out" from excessive heat or too-late picking. This is one reason why, until very recently, Vermentino was so localized and little-respected. The technical white-winemaking skills were absent. Today, such skills are abundant, and Vermentino, especially, is enjoying a kind of a renaissance, especially in coastal Tuscany.

Well into the 1970s, many Italian white wines were fermented with their skins, which can impart bitter flavors and a dark color. Fermentation temperatures were uncontrolled, creating oxidation from excessive heat. Today, temperature-controlled stainless steel tanks ensure a low, slow, nonoxidizing fermentation. And skins are whisked away immediately (although there's a small, cutting-edge trend returning to the old practice of leaving the skins with the juice).

Modern Vermentino is all about a bright, zingy freshness. You almost never, thankfully, find any oak in Vermentino. The good ones are beautifully balanced with distinctive, well-delineated flavors. Worth noting is Vermentino does not benefit from bottle aging. You're always best off drinking the latest vintage, the better to enjoy the fragrant freshness of the variety.

Noteworthy Producers (The Traditionalists / The Modernists): Nearly all of the good Vermentino producers make their wines in a modern fashion, using temperature-controlled stainless steel tanks, no grape skins, and slow, careful fermentations. In Liguria, some of the better names include Azienda Agricola Durin di Antonio Basso, Tenuta Giuncheo, Ottaviano Lambruschi (in the Colli di Luna appellation), and Colle dei Bardellini. These are just a few and all are small.

In Sardinia, the two big names are Argiolas and Sella & Mosca. Both are well distributed in America and certainly worth pursuing. Look also for the smaller Cantina Sandati, if you spot it.

In Tuscany, one major exporter of Vermentino is the famous Chianti wine house Antinori, from its property in Bolgheri (see page 88) called Tenuta Guado al Tasso. The big wine shipper Villa Banfi also makes a coastal Tuscany Vermentino called Litorale.

But surely Tuscany's—really, all of Italy's—most original Vermentino comes from the small family winery called Massa Vecchia. Located in the hills of southern Tuscany not far from the coast, owner-winemaker Fabrizio Niccolaini ferments his Vermentino in 264-gallon (ten hectoliters) open-topped chestnut casks. And he includes the skins as well.

Massa Vecchia calls this wine Ariento. And it's like no other Vermentino, a true original. At first it's a bit shocking, if only because of its light amber hue (from the skins, not oxidation). But the scent and taste are memorable, with notes of quince, lemons, and hazelnuts. It's a complete—and very successful—rethinking of what Vermentino might be and can be. Happily, Massa Vecchia is imported into the United States in small quantities.

What Do The Locals Eat With This Wine? Fish is the order for

Vermentino. In Liguria, the locals reach for what they call, in dialect, *ciuppin*. In San Francisco, this same fish stew is famous as cioppino. A clam chowder would be ideal. And of course any simply prepared fish shines with Vermentino. That's typically how the Tuscans and Sardinians enjoy their Vermentinos.

One Man's Taste—Whose Wine Would I Buy? If I saw (or sought out) Massa Vecchia's "Ariento," I would call it my first choice. But it's an idiosyncratic dry white wine and won't be for everybody. That wine aside, I'd look first for anything from Liguria's Riviera Ligure di Ponente. Producers are invariably small, so you take what you can find. Chances are the Vermentino will be very good. Also, if you happen to spy it, the Vermentino from Ottaviano Lambruschi in Colli di Luni is exceptional.

Worth Searching For? If you happen to see it

Similar Wines From The Same Neighborhood: In Liguria, the white grape called Pigato as well as the white wine blend called Cinque Terre bianco (from Bosco and Albarola grapes). In Tuscany, there's the famous Vernaccia di San Gimignano (see page 255) as well as various Trebbiano-based whites.

Vernaccia di San Gimignano

(vair-*nah*-cha dee sahn gee-meen-*yah*-noh)
WHITE

Region: Tuscany (north-central Italy)

Grapes: Vernaccia di San Gimignano (white)

The Tradition: Although white wines have never been Italy's hallmark, the indigenous Vernaccia grown in the town of San Gimignano (other strains of the Vernaccia grape are found elsewhere in Italy as well) on Tuscany's southern coast has had centuries of praise. This is unusual anywhere in Italy.

So the traditions of Vernaccia di San Gimignano stretch further back than most, aided surely by the unusual wealth of this equally unusual town. Indeed, the wine is famous today more because of the town than from any intrinsic greatness of the wine itself.

Today, San Gimignano is one of Tuscany's biggest tourist attractions. Famous for its narrow medieval stone towers (thirteen remain today, down from a fourteenth-century high of seventy-two towers), it was a medieval-era Manhattan. Busloads of tourists arrive daily to walk its narrow streets.

You get no prize for guessing what wine is served to these visitors at San Gimignano's numerous restaurants. Tourism led, probably inevitably, to mediocrity. After all, if you could sluice vast quantities of overcropped, dilute bland white wine to never-to-return tourists, why would you subject yourself to the expensive discipline of making really good white wine? (Venice and its food have slid down a similarly slippery slope.)

How It's Changed: Until very recently, really the last decade at best, Vernaccia di San Gimignano was synonymous with the dull, dilute, lackluster white wine flogged to starry-eyed tourists described above.

But—and here's the surprising twist—success bred self-contempt. Starting in 1993, the producers in the area took it upon themselves to impose more rigorous regulations requiring lower yields, among other features. This has made some difference, to be sure. But the fact remains that, with only a few exceptions, Vernaccia di San Gimignano is *still* more of a tourist item than a taste sensation. You still have to be choosy with Vernaccia di San Gimignano.

A good Vernaccia di San Gimignano should have a fleshy density, faint almond scent, and slightly bitter, invigorating aftertaste. The bad ones are thin, watery, and fruitless. Steer clear of the Riserva bottlings. Almost always they are unnecessarily oaky, as well as (unnecessarily) more expensive.

Noteworthy Producers (The Traditionalists/The Modernists)

FONTALEONI—A pleasing bottling with all of the characteristics of a good Vernaccia.

MONTENIDOLI—One of the leaders of what might be called the "good Vernaccia" movement, Montenidoli makes one of the best wines of the zone, a real benchmark.

MORMORAIA—This is quite possibly the best producer of Vernaccia di San Gimignano on the American market today. A small grower with low yields that you can really taste, the regular bottling of Mormoraia's Vernaccia di San Gimignano reminds you of why this wine acquired fame in the first place. The wine typically has a dense texture and a bell-clear note of bitter almond. The Riserva bottling, alas, is predictably and unnecessarily oaky, to no good effect.

PARADISO—A good, solid producer issuing benchmark Vernaccia di San Gimignano redolent of peaches, minerals, and herbs. A more expensive bottling called Biscondola adds 20 percent Chardonnay to the Vernaccia and ages in small oak barrels, neither of which additions adds much that's worthwhile.

SAN QUIRICO—A straightforward but good Vernaccia di San

Gimignano with characteristic spicy/bitter almond notes. The Riserva bottling is very oaky.

Teruzzi & Puthod—Bought by the Campari liquor group in December 2005, Teruzzi & Puthod is one of the leading producers of high-quality Vernaccia di San Gimignano, as well as a large producer. (Which explains why it was worth an estimated 12 million Euros to Campari.) The basic Vernaccia wine is very good and typical, in the best sense. Better yet is the Vigna Rondolino bottling, a single-vineyard Vernaccia that shows real distinction.

Terre di Tufi is an unusually good (and commercially successful) blend of Vernaccia, Chardonnay, Malvasia, and Vermentino. It's an impressively seamless blend that, for once, is a wine greater than the sum of its parts, with a minerally, floral quality that fairly begs for seafood. Less successful is another blend (of Chardonnay and Trebbiano) called Sarpinello.

What Do The Locals Eat With This Wine? There's no question in the minds of the locals, or anyone else, that Vernaccia di San Gimignano is a wine destined for fish and shellfish. The best bottlings do pair well with some cheeses, as long as they are not strongly flavored or especially well aged.

One Man's Taste—Whose Wine Would I Buy? My first pick would be Mormoraia, followed by Montenidoli and Teruzzi & Puthod.

Worth Searching For? Only if you see it

Similar Wines From The Same Neighborhood: Probably the closest competitor to Vernaccia is a relatively new category of white wine from the Chianti zone called Galestro. Taking its name from the rocky soil type common in Chianti, the idea behind Galestro was to create a vehicle for the unused white grapes (Trebbiano and Malvasia mostly) planted in Chianti vineyards that were being abandoned in the traditional red

Chianti blend under the new, more permissive appellation regulations.

It proved an attractive name, so much so that there's now red and rosé Galestro wines too. Quality in white Galestro is all over the map, so let the reputation of the producer be your guide.

Vin Santo

(veen *sahn*-toh)
WHITE

Region: Central Italy. Vin Santo is most closely associated with Tuscany.

Grapes: White grapes: Malvasia Toscana, Trebbiano Toscana, and Grechetto; red grapes: Sangiovese, sometimes called Prugnolo Gentile or Occhio di Pernice (eye of the partridge)

The Tradition: Everything about Vin Santo—at least everything about artisanal Vin Santo, as opposed to the soulless and unpleasant commercial versions—is about tradition. To this day, artisanal Vin Santo production more resembles winemaking from several centuries ago than today's modern winemaking. Even the name is antique, so much so that no one really knows its origin. This, inevitably, gives rise to several theories.

One theory says that Vin Santo (literally, saint wine) is so named because the winemaking process typically began on All Saints Day at the beginning of November. Yet others submit the liturgical opposite: It was called Vin Santo because it was bottled during Holy Week, the week before Easter. Yet others say that it was simply a type of *passito* or dried-grape wine preferred by priests for the sacrament, because it kept well.

The version I most like is also the most convoluted (which therefore makes it extremely unlikely). In 1439, during the Council of Florence, the patriarch of the Eastern Orthodox Church used the word *xantos* ("yellow" in Greek) in mentioning the wine. The Florentines mistakenly thought he had said *santo* or saint. Supposedly the wine, up to that linguistic turning point, was locally called (in Tuscan dialect) *vin pretto* or "pure wine." The Florentines liked the idea of *"vin santo"* better.

Obviously nobody really knows how this wine got its name. But it's revered today, and not even the most secular Italian would consider changing it.

Vin Santo is actually not that unusual a wine, at least at first glance. It's a *passito* wine, made from the juice of carefully selected bunches of dried grapes, most commonly the local white varieties such as Malvasia Toscana, Trebbiano Toscana, and Grechetto. You can find *passito* wines almost everywhere in Italy, most famously today for Recioto della Valpolicella (see page 192). It was a way of making both a sweet wine—as the grapes lost much of their water, thus concentrating the sugar—as well as a high-alcohol wine that could last far longer in barrels than conventional table wine.

So far, so ordinary. But Vin Santo takes a different turn in its cellaring. Most *passito* wines were and are stored like regular wines, which is to say in cool cellars. But Vin Santo, unusually, is aged in small barrels in the attics of wineries or growers' houses, subjected to the (oxidizing) heat of the summer as well as the cold of winter. And it remains there in tightly sealed barrels for years, sometimes even decades.

In this, Vin Santo more resembles *aceto balsamico* (balsamic vinegar), which is also barrel-aged in tiny barrels stored in attics. It, too, is made from the Trebbiano grape, although the production zone is exclusively in the northern province of Emilia-Romagna. And like Vin Santo, *aceto balsamico* has been industrialized to such a degree that the true artisanal version is very different from the mass distributed, commercialized item. Ditto for Vin Santo.

The similarity extends further yet, to a common use of what both the Vin Santo producers and vinegar makers called the "mother." Vin Santo is not vinegar—far from it. But both use a gelatinous, sludge-like mass to achieve their respective results. A vinegar "mother" is a dense film of bacteria and yeast that produces acetic acid, transforming wine into vinegar.

Vin Santo, for its part, has a "mother" of highly specialized yeast cells capable of very slowly fermenting the very high sugar content of the small amount of juice pressed from the dried grapes. This "mother" is dense and gelatinous.

The importance of these specialized yeasts cannot be overemphasized, because without this "mother," Vin Santo wouldn't be possible. A yeast cell is 65 percent water. When it is put into a solution with a higher density than its own, such as extremely sugar-rich grape juice, osmosis acts as a pressure, forcing the less-dense contents inside of the yeast cell to pass through the yeast's semipermeable cell wall to the other side in an attempt to equalize the differing densities. Osmosis sucks it dry, rendering the yeast inactive.

But yeasts adapt, evolving into different strains with greater tolerance to alcohol, temperature, carbon dioxide (useful for making sparkling wine), or even, as in the case of the yeasts that make up the Vin Santo "mother," a greater resistance to the pressure of osmosis.

To make Vin Santo, the grower picks ripe and undamaged grape clusters and places them on straw mats. Alternatively, the clusters are hung from rafters, which isn't done much today because it's less space-efficient than using straw (or plastic) mats stacked one on top of the other with a generous air space in between. The grapes are allowed to dry on the straw mats for several months, shriveling into near-raisins. (France had a similar winemaking tradition called *vin de paille* or straw wine, as did Germany for their *strohwein*.)

Because there was so little juice when the near-raisins got pressed, the containers used for Vin Santo, then and now, are commensurately small. These small oak barrels, called *caratelli*, hold just fifty liters or thirteen gallons. (The conventional small oak barrel or *barrique* used by wineries everywhere holds sixty gallons.)

These *caratelli* are filled only nine-tenths full with the juice, along with some of the yeast-rich "mother." The headspace is essential: It provides air for the fermenting yeasts as well as room for the carbon dioxide created by the fermentation. (When yeasts feed on sugar, they create alcohol and carbon dioxide.) If the small barrel was filled to the brim, it would explode from the accumulated carbon dioxide.

The barrel is immediately sealed with a bung wrapped in a cloth, which is hammered tightly into the bunghole and is, in turn, sometimes covered with a thick glob of wax to ensure a better seal yet.

The filled barrels are hauled up to the attic and they remain, absolutely untouched, for at least three years by law (four years if labeled Riserva). But the better producers will leave them untouched for twice as long.

Finally, like opening a time capsule—which, in a way, it is—the bung is prised from the barrel and the winemaker finally gets to taste the Vin Santo. This is an apprehensive moment, as there's no guarantee that the wine will be good. A bacterial infection could have occurred, making it undrinkable. Or the fermentation may never have completed. (It's pretty slow anyway, taking the better part of three years because of the sluggishness of the yeasts in such sugar-rich juice.) Or it just may not be as swell as one hoped, maybe because the original grapes from that vintage weren't good enough.

In an age where near-absolute control now extends to every part of the winemaking process, such literally hands-off winemaking is a true act of faith. To do so calls for a sincere reverence for the wisdom of one's forebears, along with an extravagance of time uncommon today.

If all went well, what emerges is an amber-hued wine with a definitely oxidized, i.e. sherry-like, scent. But Vin Santo is very different from sherry, even if it does share a commonality of oxidation from long barrel-aging. A good Vin Santo will deliver scents of nuts, apples, raisins, caramel or toffee, and honey and a salty/mineral note. It can be completely dry or retain an edge of sweetness. (If the clusters were very ripe before being dried, the sugar content of the juice will be so high that the yeasts can't transform it all into alcohol, leaving some residual sugar.) The texture can be like table wine, or it can be almost viscous. In short, there's no one, definitive Vin Santo.

But what is easy to establish, effortlessly, is a *bad* Vin Santo. It will be thin, fruitless, and somehow lifeless. You won't have a peacock's tail of flavor shadings. It will be dull, and you'll wonder why anybody bothered. Good question.

How It's Changed: Actually (and amazingly), artisanal Vin Santo really *hasn't* changed. Leaving aside industrial Vin Santo—its existence *is* new—artisanal Vin Santo is a relic of another winemaking time, almost a living fossil. So little has changed in its time-tested technique that it's scarcely worth mentioning, such as using modern pneumatic wine presses instead of the old squeeze-'em-dry screw press. Some producers like to use a bit of new oak to acquire a vanilla scent, which is decidedly untraditional. But that's about it. The whole point of artisanal Vin Santo is precisely to retain centuries-old goodness.

Noteworthy Producers: Not every top Tuscan wine producer makes a good Vin Santo or even bothers to make one at all. For some producers, Vin Santo simply isn't to their taste. Or they cannot wrap their minds around the antiquarian demands of the hands-off methodology and lavish time-indulgence of traditional Vin Santo.

Vin Santo is usually vintage-dated. And vintage does seem to matter. A good rule of thumb is that a good vintage for the red wines of Tuscany means a richer, more dimensional Vin Santo as well. That acknowledged, Vin Santo isn't quite as transparent to vintage differences, thanks to its unusual methodology and extended aging.

What's more, although a Vin Santo can—and does—transform in the bottle, unlike a regular table wine, most of its essential character and nature is created in the barrel. So there's no real need for cellaring Vin Santo for further transformation. On the other hand, if you lose a bottle in your cellar, no worries. Vin Santo is seemingly eternal. Maybe *that's* why it's called the "saint wine."

More than with many wines, high price often does correlate to higher quality with Vin Santo. It's an expensive wine to produce, and the best producers will give the wine far more barrel age than the minimum three or four years required by law. So, this once, you very likely will get (qualitatively) what you pay (a lot) for.

AVIGNONESI—Rarely is it possible to declare one winery to be the hands-down champion. Wine, after all, isn't a heavyweight prizefight. But in the case of Vin Santo, the greatest producer, the undisputed winner, is Avignonesi. Their Vin Santo is the richest, densest, most dimensional, and flat-out greatest version made. And, not surprisingly, it's also the most expensive.

Unusually, Avignonesi makes two Vin Santo wines: one made entirely from white grapes and another, much rarer, made from the red Sangiovese grape. That bottling is called Vin Santo Occhio del Pernice (eye of the partridge). Both are stellar: rich, dense, slightly sweet, and opulent. These are, easily, the reference standard Vin Santos. If you try only one Vin Santo, Avignonesi is the one to pursue, never mind the very high price asked. They're worth it.

ALTESINO—The Brunello di Montalcino producer issues a lovely, lemon zest-inflected Vin Santo with the characteristic dried-nut quality.

CASTELLARE—A top Chianti Classico producer offering a rather modern (there's a touch of vanilla from new oak) Vin Santo. A bit light, there's real quality here.

FATTORIA DI FELSINA—A great, rich Vin Santo from this great Chianti Classico producer. You get apricots, raisins, honey—a real mouthful.

FONTODI—Another top Chianti Classico producer issuing superb Vin Santo. Slightly sweet, rich, and very refined.

ISOLA E OLENA—A refined Vin Santo in a modernistic style (some vanilla is present). Dried figs, raisins, bitter almonds. Very pretty.

MASSA VECCHIA—This small Tuscan winery issues an exceptional Vin Santo made from Sangiovese (most Vin Santo is made from white grapes such as Malvasia Toscana, Trebbiano Toscana, and Grechetto). Because it's made from Sangiovese, it sports the designation Occhio del Pernice—eye of the partridge. Rich, intense, and succulent, Massa Vecchia's Vin Santo rivals Avignonesi's Occhio del Pernice Vin Santo—which is praise indeed.

What Do The Locals Eat With This Wine? The classic food combination with Vin Santo is biscotti, the very dry, dense cookies that Tuscans dote on. They will often dip the biscotti into the Vin Santo, which makes a lot of sense because true Tuscan biscotti are real jawbreakers. Personally, I prefer softened vanilla ice cream with Vin Santo. Or pound cake. Or both.

One Man's Taste—Whose Wine Would I Buy? A no-brainer: It's Avignonesi or Massa Vecchia. You will never forget Avignonesi's Vin Santo once you taste them. Like Chateau d'Yquem or Carlo Hauner Malvasia delle Lipari Passito, they are unique.

Worth Searching For? Absolutely worth an effort

Similar Wines From The Same Neighborhood: Other regions of Italy make wines similar to Vin Santo, but everyone agrees that the best versions hail from Tuscany.

Vino Nobile di Montepulciano

(vee-noh *noh*-bee-leh dee mohn-teh-pool-*chah*-noh)

RED

Region: Tuscany (north-central Italy)

Grapes: A minimum of 70 percent Sangiovese (known as Prugnolo Gentile in Montepulciano, which is the same strain of Sangiovese as that called Brunello in Montalcino) to which may be added a maximum of 20 percent Canaiolo Nero and up to a maximum of 20 percent of other varieties authorized by the province of Siena, such as Mammolo

The Tradition: The name is the giveaway: the noble wine of Montepulciano. The town of Montepulciano has for centuries prided itself on the historical luster of its Sangiovese-based wine. (There's always confusion between the Montepulciano grape variety, which is the signature grape in the regions of Abruzzo and Marche, and the town of Montepulciano in Tuscany. They have nothing to do with each other.)

Few Tuscan wines have recorded more historical accolades than Vino Nobile di Montepulciano. The locals are forever trotting out this or that plaudit starting from the Renaissance. And the unusual number of extensive underground cellars in the zone testifies to the demand for Montepulciano's Sangiovese-based wine.

That's the (charitably brief) story. Today's saga is less noble. Of all of the famous wines in Tuscany, none has lagged in quality quite like Vino Nobile di Montepulciano. To this observer, it's a textbook case of forever looking in the rear-view mirror. Surely they once made memorable wine. But until very recently, just the last ten years really, the only thing *nobile* about Montepulciano was the posturing of its producers, who believed their own label language.

How It's Changed: The opinions expressed above are not unique to this critic. Others have expressed similarly sour sentiments, with some harsher yet. The producers in Montepulciano have taken notice. Competition, especially from neighboring Chianti Classico and Brunello di Montalcino—which is seen as an upstart to the history-proud Montepulcinese—have prodded producers into recognizing that past luster does not shine in today's competitive, opportunistic wine market. Most wine drinkers simply don't *care* what someone said centuries ago.

So starting in the 1980s, but really taking grip only in the 1990s, the producers of Vino Nobile di Montepulciano began to seek improvements. Yields were lowered; winemaking was modernized. A more resolute focus became the watchword.

To their credit, the producers in Montepulciano have rejected the inclusion of international varieties for their Vino Nobile bottlings, although grapes such as Cabernet Sauvignon, Merlot, and Syrah are grown in the zone for use in other, proprietarily named bottlings. Resisting the siren call of these grapes—which modernist critics have lauded when used in other Tuscan wines—takes backbone. It deserves respect.

The challenge today is to demonstrate that there really is something different, and superior, about Vino Nobile di Montepulciano from other top-quality Sangiovese wines in Tuscany. This has not been easy and is still a work in progress. Producers are fiddling with just the right amount of small new oak barrels and fine-tuning the percentages of their blends of Canaiolo Nero (for lush softness and fruitiness) and Mammolo (for fragrance and color).

All of this takes time, and it seems that only now are the efforts beginning to see the results. What cannot be said so far is that there's any consistency to Vino Nobile di Montepulciano wines. Some are opulent, vanilla-scent fruit bombs, while others are tightly knit and restrained. As in neighboring Brunello di Montalcino, there's also a Rosso di Montepulciano, which sees less time in barrel and bottle and can come from higher yields. The grape varieties and the district boundaries are the same as for the parental Vino Nobile wine.

Comparison with Brunello di Montalcino is inevitable. At its best, Vino Nobile should be, and is, a more substantial, sturdy, and long-lived Sangiovese than most Chianti Classicos. Indeed, it should compare more to Brunello in that regard. However, a good Vino Nobile should have more finesse and violet-and-mineral-scented elegance than Brunello. Ideally, Vino Nobile is a conciliation of the attributes of *both* Chianti Classico and Brunello di Montalcino, with the finesse of the former and the power, structure, and longevity of the latter.

A vision of what Montepulciano's twenty-first-century *nobilità* should taste like has yet to achieve consensus. Maybe it never will. But one senses that the unusually cohesive (for Italy) growers in Montepulciano stand a better chance than most at arriving at a collective vision of their signature wine. Time will tell.

Noteworthy Producers (The Traditionalists / The Modernists)

AVIGNONESI—Arguably the most famous producer in Montepulciano (and certainly the best-distributed in America), Avignonesi is slowly groping its way to a secure identity with its flagship wine. This seems to have proved difficult if only because the family's collective head has been turned by various international grapes (Cabernet Sauvignon, Merlot, Chardonnay) that have banalized their other offerings. A great Vino Nobile requires a liking of, and respect for, more austerity and restraint than Avignonesi's other table wines demonstrate. (Avignonesi's otherworldly Vin Santo is excepted here. There simply is none better, and the Vin Santo, and its makers, cannot be praised enough.)

This caveat duly noted, the latest Vino Nobile bottlings from Avignonesi show real promise. A great vintage such as 2001 shows the distinction that can set apart Vino Nobile di Montepulciano from other Tuscan Sangiovese wines, namely, a violet scent allied to a backbone of dense, dusty fruit that clearly lets the taster know that more time is needed. A Riserva bottling called Grandi Annate is issued in top vintages. It sees two years aging in bottle before being released compared to the six months in bottle given to the regular Vino Nobile.

At its best, Avignonesi represents a benchmark in Montepulciano. But one still senses a work in progress, albeit one clearly heading in the right direction.

BINDELLA—Pleasant, noticeably oaky wines. As with others in the zone, the wines vary considerably with the vintage. To watch.

BOSCARELLI—The creator of some very elegant wines over the years, Boscarelli is still something of a mixed bag. Like others in the zone, vintage seems to matter mightily. In the great years (1997, 2001), Boscarelli can be counted on to turn in a top performance. Look especially for the single-vineyard Vigna del Nocio bottling, which is easily one of Vino Nobile's best wines.

FATTORIA DI CERRO—Creating quite rich wines, Cerro is a mainstay producer in the zone. The wine to look for is the single-vineyard Vigneto Antica Chiusina bottling, which is among the very best wines made in the zone.

DEI—An up-and-comer in the zone, Dei shows some of the burly, Brunello-like distinction that Montepulciano can deliver. Reliably good, rich, sturdy wines that are unusually consistent and made in a (good) modernistic style. Look especially for the Riserva bottling designated "Mandorli."

POLIZIANO—A large producer pursuing a frankly modern, almost flagrantly fruity style of Vino Nobile with lots of flashy oak and very ripe-tasting, jammy fruit. The wines make a striking first impression, but one senses that they could have come from any number of other Tuscan zones. They certainly are pleasant to drink, no doubt about it, but not much "you-are-there" distinction to them.

RUFFINO—This large Tuscan wine shipper delivers a solid, fundamentally good Vino Nobile designated Lodola Nuova. (A *lodola* is a lark.) This is an estate, purchased in 1994 by the Folonari family, which owns the Ruffino brand that has seen replanting. A work in progress heading in the right direction.

VALDIPIATTA—A notable producer creating fairly rich, intense wines devoid of stylistic flourishes. Reliably good, the best bet is the single-vineyard Vigna d'Alfiero bottling, which is 100 percent Sangiovese. Worth seeking out.

What Do The Locals Eat With This Wine? As elsewhere in Tuscany, Vino Nobile di Montepulciano is a wine typically reserved for meats, especially game such as the wild boar (*cinghiale*) that abound in the area. Or with the big steaks that Tuscans, alone in Italy, love like Texans. This is a wine that pairs best with meats—whether in the form of sausages, salami, or in various cuts of beef or lamb.

One Man's Taste—Whose Wine Would I Buy? Frankly, I would buy Vino Nobile only in the best vintages. And in such vintages, I would seek Avignonesi and Boscarelli. There are numerous producers in the zone, and surely in the best vintages many, if not most, will turn in a worthy performance. But buying Vino Nobile is something best left to Italian wine adventurers as the prices are often hefty and the assurance of goodness still tentative.

Worth Searching For? Only if you see it

Similar Wines From The Same Neighborhood: Any number of Sangiovese wines such as Chianti Classico, Chianti Colli Senesi, Brunello di Montalcino, and Rosso di Montalcino, among others.

Endnote

"One of the secrets of a happy life is continuous small treats."
—IRIS MURDOCH, *The Sea, the Sea*

The joy of Italian wine is Italy's bone-deep understanding
of Iris Murdoch's concise revelation. More than any other
nation's, Italian wines are really all about quotidian happiness.
Not for the Italians is the sonorous drum roll that inevitably
accompanies the most "important" French wines. Nor does Italy
fetishize wine the way Americans or Brits do, obsessing over
points or endlessly comparing this vintage with that.

Instead, they are a seemingly endless series of small yet
substantial wine treats that you incorporate into your daily
life without a lot of hullabaloo—but with a real and sustaining
pleasure. I hope that *Making Sense of Italian Wine* conveys
that happy spirit. We need it, don't you think?

Index